The Korean War at Sixty

Korea used to be the 'forgotten war.' Now, however, experts widely view it as a pivotal moment in the history of the Cold War, while its legacy still scars contemporary East Asian politics.

The sixtieth anniversary of the Korean War is a fitting time both to assess the current state of historiography on the conflict and to showcase new research on its different dimensions. This book contains six essays by leading experts in the field. These essays explore all aspects of the war, from collective security and alliance relations, to home front politics and historical memory. They are also international in scope, focusing not just on the familiar Western belligerents but also on the actions of the two Koreas, China and the Soviet Union.

These stimulating essays shed new light on various aspects of the Korean War experience, as well as examining why the war remains so important to the politics of the region.

This book was originally published as a special issue of *Journal of Strategic Studies.*

Steven Casey is Reader in International History at the LSE. He is author of *Cautious Crusade: Franklin D. Roosevelt, American Public Opinion, and the War against Nazi Germany* (2001), and *Selling the Korean War: Propaganda, Politics, and Public Opinion* (2008), which won the Truman Book Award.

The Korean War at Sixty
New Approaches to the Study of the Korean War

Edited by
Steven Casey

LONDON AND NEW YORK

First published 2012
by Routledge
2 Park Square, Milton Park, Abingdon, Oxon, OX14 4RN

Simultaneously published in the USA and Canada
by Routledge
711 Third Avenue, New York, NY 10017

Routledge is an imprint of the Taylor & Francis Group, an informa business

© 2012 Taylor & Francis

This book is a reproduction of *Journal of Strategic Studies*, Volume 33, Issue 2. The Publisher requests to those authors who may be citing this book to state, also, the bibliographical details of the special issue on which the book was based.

All rights reserved. No part of this book may be reprinted or reproduced or utilised in any form or by any electronic, mechanical, or other means, now known or hereafter invented, including photocopying and recording, or in any information storage or retrieval system, without permission in writing from the publishers.

Trademark notice: Product or corporate names may be trademarks or registered trademarks, and are used only for identification and explanation without intent to infringe.

British Library Cataloguing in Publication Data
A catalogue record for this book is available from the British Library

ISBN13: 978-0-415-69996-9

Typeset in Times New Roman
by Taylor & Francis Books

Publisher's Note
The publisher would like to make readers aware that the chapters in this book may be referred to as articles as they are identical to the articles published in the special issue. The publisher accepts responsibility for any inconsistencies that may have arisen in the course of preparing this volume for print.

Contents

About the Contributors   vii

Introduction
Robert Barnes   1

1. 'An Alliance Forged in Blood': The American Occupation of Korea, the Korean War, and the US–South Korean Alliance
William Stueck and Boram Yi   15

2. China and the Dispatch of the Soviet Air Force: The Formation of the Chinese–Soviet–Korean Alliance in the Early Stage of the Korean War
Zhihua Shen   49

3. Branding an Aggressor: The Commonwealth, the United Nations and Chinese Intervention in the Korean War, November 1950–January 1951
Robert Barnes   69

4. Lost Chance or Lost Horizon? Strategic Opportunity and Escalation Risk in the Korean War, April July 1951
Colin F. Jackson   93

5. Casualty Reporting and Domestic Support for War: The US Experience during the Korean War
Steven Casey   129

6. POWs: The Hidden Reason for Forgetting Korea
Charles S. Young   155

Index   171

About the Contributors

William Stueck is distinguished research professor at the University of Georgia, USA, and has written extensively on the Korean War, including *The Road to Confrontation: American Policy Toward China and Korea, 1947–1950* (Chapel Hill: Univ. of North Carolina Press 1981), *The Korean War: An International History* (Princeton UP 1995) and *Rethinking the Korean War: A New Diplomatic and Strategic History* (Princeton UP 2002).

Boram Yi received her PhD in history at the University of Georgia, USA in 2007 and is now a lecturer in history at the University of Baltimore. She is currently working with William Stueck on two books, a history of the negotiation of the first status-of-forces agreement between the United States and Korea (concluded in 1966), and a topical history of US–Korean relations.

Zhihua Shen is professor of history and director of Center for Cold War International History Studies at East China Normal University. A leading authority on Cold War studies in China, he has published widely on the history of Sino-Soviet relations and the Korean War, including more than 80 academic articles and 10 books in Chinese, English, Russian and many other languages. His representative works include: *Sulian zhuanjia zai Zhongguo* [Soviet Experts in China] (2009, 2002); *Shikao yu xuanze: Cong zhishi fengzi huiyi dao fan youpai yundong* [Contemplation and Choice: From a Conference on Intellectuals to Anti-rightist Movement] (2008); *ZhongSu guanxi shigang, 1917–1991* [An Outline of the History of Sino-Soviet Relations, 1917–1991] (2007); *Mao Zedong, Sidalin yu Chaoxian zhanzheng* [Mao Zedong, Stalin and the Korean War] (2003). He is editor of several important document collections: *Meiguo dui Hua qingbao jiemi dang'an, 1948–1976* [US Intelligence Estimates on China] (2009); *Chaoxian zhanzheng: Eguo dang'anguan de jiemi wenjian* [The Korean War: Declassified Documents from the Russian Archives], 3 vols. (2003); *Sulian lishi dang'an xuanbian* [Collection of Selected Soviet Historical Documents], 34 vols. (2002).

Robert Barnes is a final year PhD student in the International History Department at the London School of Economics and Political Science, UK. His PhD thesis is entitled *The UN(Equal) Alliance: US–Commonwealth Relations, the United Nations and the Korean War, 1950–1953*.

ABOUT THE CONTRIBUTORS

Colin F. Jackson is an assistant professor of strategy at the US Naval War College in Newport, Rhode Island. Professor Jackson is a graduate of the Massachusetts Institute of Technology (PhD, Political Science), the University of Pennsylvania's Wharton School (MBA, Finance), Johns Hopkins' School of Advanced International Studies (MA, International Economics and Strategic Studies), Princeton University's Woodrow Wilson School (BA, Public and International Affairs). Professor Jackson's current research includes work on counterinsurgency, military operations in urban terrain, public and private sector risk management, organizational learning, and intelligence operations. His most recent publications include two chapters on US Army and Special Forces transformation in the 1990s in Harvey Sapolsky, Brendan Green, Benjamin Friedman's edited volume, *Creation without Destruction: US Military Innovation Since the Cold War*. Prior to entering academia, Professor Jackson worked for several years in the corporate sector in financial trading, telecommunications, transportation markets, and power development. He also served four years on active duty with the US Army in Germany as an armor and cavalry officer.

Steven Casey is senior lecturer in international history at the London School of Economics and Political Science, UK. He is author of *Cautious Crusade: Franklin D. Roosevelt, American Public Opinion, and the War against Nazi Germany* (New York: OUP 2001), and *Selling the Korean War: Propaganda, Politics, and Public Opinion* (New York: OUP 2008), which won the Neustadt Prize in American Politics and was runner-up for the Mott Award in Journalism and Communications Research. Dr Casey has written numerous articles on World War II, the early Cold War, and the Korean War. He was also the recipient of the Harry Truman Scholar's Award in 2005.

Charles S. Young (Rutgers, New Jersey 2003) is an assistant professor of history at Southern Arkansas University in Magnolia, USA. He has a book forthcoming from Oxford, *Name, Rank, and Serial Number: Korean War POWs and the Politics of Limited War*. In 2008 he delivered the paper 'Tattoo you: Controlling Korean War POWs on Koje-do, 1950–1954', to the Southwestern Historical Association. He also published 'Missing Action: POW Films, Brainwashing and the Korean War, 1954–1968', in *The Historical Journal of Film, Radio and Television* 18/1 (1998).

Introduction

ROBERT BARNES

The sixtieth anniversary of the outbreak of the Korean War is an ideal time to re-explore its complex history. To be sure, the conflict is no longer 'forgotten', as the well-worn cliché would have it.[1] On the contrary, we have the traditional, Western-centred accounts of the 1950s and 1960s that saw the war as a product of Soviet-inspired communist aggression. We have the Western-focused histories of the 1970s and 1980s that used declassified official documents to uncover the actions and motives of the United States and its allies. And in the last two decades, we have numerous studies based on Russian and Chinese documents that provide a much clearer picture of what was occurring behind the Iron Curtain.[2]

Nonetheless, as this volume shows, these earlier historiographical schools by no means uncovered every aspect of the Korean War. Much remains to be said about alliance diplomacy, military strategy, public opinion and historical memory. Each of the following essays explores one of these dimensions of the war. Their geographical vantage points differ: William Stueck and Boram Yi focus on the United States and South Korea; Zhihua Shen on the three Communist states involved, the USSR, China and North Korea; Robert Barnes on the British Commonwealth; and Colin F. Jackson, Steven Casey and Charles S. Young solely on the United States. At the same time, though, a rough chronological thread runs through the collection: Stueck and Yi concentrate on the years between 1945 and 1950; Shen looks at the first months of the war until Chinese intervention; Barnes examines the ensuing crisis; Jackson looks at the emergence of the military stalemate in the spring of 1951; Casey covers the war as a whole but does provide considerable detail regarding the middle years and Eisenhower's election campaign in 1952; and Young looks at the final eighteen months of the conflict and its aftermath.

Chapter 1 begins with William Stueck and Boram Yi examining the slow, and often difficult, emergence of the U.S.-South Korean alliance before,

INTRODUCTION

during and after the Korean War. One strand of their story is the controversial and hurried U.S. occupation of Korea south of the 38th parallel. Stueck and Yi tackle a number of familiar issues, including the United States Army Military Government in Korea's (USAMGIK) weak and inappropriate policies; General John Hodge's refusal to talk to popular Leftist groups and his reliance initially on the existing Japanese apparatus and then on the conservative landed elite; Washington's general lack of interest in Korea with more pressing Cold War priorities in Europe; the American military's desire to terminate its commitment as quickly as possible; the creation of the Republic of Korea (ROK) under UN auspices in 1948; and the withdrawal of American forces a year later. But they also go beyond traditional accounts by using Korean language sources and U.S. Army documents to provide original insights into the strained interaction between the occupiers – American officials as well as ordinary soldiers – and the occupied Korean population. They suggest that at the start of 1950 Washington had little interest in building closer bonds with the ROK.

Stueck and Yi emphasise that relations between the occupiers and occupied quickly soured. The USAMGIK's misguided and incoherent policies were partly responsible. But these policies also interacted with deep and existing socio-political divisions within the Korean society. Crucially, too Stueck and Yi emphasise how these policies were implemented on the ground. They look at the disrespectful and often criminal behaviour of U.S. troops toward Koreans. They uncover American soldiers' perceptions of Korea, from the notion that its people were deceitful and treacherous to the belief that Koreans only respected the rule of force. And they detail the common physical assaults inflicted upon ordinary Koreans, not to mention their lack of respect for Korean cultural norms, particularly when it came to approaching women. Stueck and Yi blame these problems on a variety of factors: the general low level of education amongst the soldiers; the fact many found it difficult to shift from the dehumanising experience of fighting to occupation duties; the lack of morale created by the perceived material impoverishment of serving in Korea; the poor quality officers who failed to discipline their inferiors; and inherent racist attitudes magnified by the victory over Japan. For their part the Korean people felt that Americans at all levels treated them as a conquered nation and did not take into account their legitimate desires for independence and unification.

Stueck and Yi finish by briefly examining U.S.-South Korean relations post-1948. They stress that Washington's reluctance to commit militarily to Seoul was based partly on greater Cold War priorities and partly on the poor relations that had developed during the occupation. In June 1950, this half-hearted U.S. commitment encouraged the North Korean invasion. In July, America's grudging intervention then 'derived more from concern about its potential impact on the reputation of the United States worldwide than on sympathy for ROK leaders or the Korean people'.

INTRODUCTION

Nevertheless, Stueck and Yi conclude that the Korean War had a deep psychological impact. It was, in particular, pivotal in forming a lasting alliance between the two countries that has withstood many upheavals in the international order. The 'second US occupation' and the sacrifice of American troops to protect the ROK allowed Washington to assume the new 'role of elder brother' in the Korean Confucian mindset. The U.S. Government, for its part, treated the ROK more seriously once its forces had proved their value and Seoul had become a major strategic Cold War partner. Even so, Stueck and Yi note that contemporary U.S.-South Korean relations, while culturally closer than ever, continue to be dogged by lingering resentments and prejudices that have grown as first-hand memories of the conflict have faded.

Alliance diplomacy also forms the core of Zhihua Shen's chapter. Shen examines the delicate triangular relationship that existed between the three Communist powers – the Soviet Union, China and North Korea – during the opening months of the Korean War. At the heart of his chapter are the controversial behind-the-scenes negotiations between Joseph Stalin, Mao Zedong and Kim Il Sung, leading up to Chinese intervention in Korea in October 1950. Using a range of new Soviet and Chinese records, Shen demonstrates that a constant feature of these discussions was whether Moscow would provide air cover for a Chinese invasion. While North Korea was enjoying successes on the battlefield, Stalin encouraged Mao's preparations to deploy forces to Korea, vaguely promising the use of the Soviet Air Force. At the time, the Soviet leader hoped that a quick victory would nullify this commitment. But this hope soon started to fade. In late August 1950 military fortunes shifted in the UNC's favour, prompting Kim to call for greater materiel support from both Moscow and Beijing. After the Inchon landings in mid-September Mao finally lost patience and stepped up military planning. Mao was determined to prevent an American conquest of North Korea, forcing Stalin to 'give the green light' to Chinese intervention and putting pressure on him to provide Soviet air cover.

Shen reveals that the ensuing weeks were a time of intense crisis inside the Communist camp. Stalin vacillated, first agreeing to Mao's demands but later informing Chinese Premier Zhou En-lai that the Soviet Air Force was in no position to provide cover. Shen maintains that Stalin had mixed motives. The Soviet leader feared being sucked into direct conflict with the United States. He was also wary of Mao's intentions and China's future regional influence. And he was unsure if the U.S./UN advance could be halted even if China intervened. Shen, while deeply critical of Stalin's inconsistencies, praises Mao's resolute decision to send Chinese forces into Korea despite the lack of air cover. He stresses that this action proved crucial, for once the Chinese had demonstrated their military effectiveness and anti-American credentials Stalin did finally commit the Soviet Air Force in early November 1950 to protect the Yalu River border area. As Shen concludes, while these developments sealed

INTRODUCTION

the short-term future of the Sino-Soviet-North Korean alliance, China was now the key player, while the Soviet Union was relegated to a supporting role.

Chapter 3 follows on both thematically and chronologically. Robert Barnes examines the diplomatic crisis within the Western alliance that unfolded at the UN following Chinese intervention. 'Historians', he observes, 'have lavished enormous attention' on events during these months, but they have failed to fully analyse the British Commonwealth's challenge to U.S. hegemony at the UN that temporarily constrained the Truman administration's plans to brand China an aggressor. Based on sources in American, British, Indian, Canadian, and Australian archival and private papers collections, Barnes argues that Commonwealth unity was essential to its success and explains that this occurred when four criteria were fulfilled: when the risk of a global conflict was at its greatest, when key Commonwealth personalities were prepared to exercise their influence in Washington, when coincidence brought the Commonwealth members together, and when the U.S. government was willing to bow to Commonwealth pressure.

Barnes' article starts by outlining the nature of the Commonwealth prior to June 1950, stressing its loose organisation and the inherent divisions between the 'Old Commonwealth' nations (Britain, Australia, Canada, New Zealand, and South Africa), and the postcolonial 'New Commonwealth' nations of India and Pakistan. Both groups had divergent national interests in the post-war world but Commonwealth membership remained an important aspect of each member's foreign policy for a range of sentimental and practical reasons. Fissures within the Commonwealth, though, were nowhere more evident than at the UN where the 'Old' members almost always bowed to U.S. dominance whereas India and, to a lesser extent, Pakistan had positioned themselves within the neutral camp. Still, Barnes emphasises that the severity of the crisis following Chinese intervention created the conditions necessary for Commonwealth unity as its members feared that the policy pursued by Washington at the UN might escalate the conflict into a global war.

Barnes then explores the various attempts made by the Commonwealth to find a means to reach a negotiated settlement. He demonstrates that despite the deteriorating military situation the Commonwealth persuaded the United States to allow two UN efforts to broker an armistice: first, the creation of the Cease-Fire Committee that unsuccessfully sought to negotiate terms with Beijing; and second, the adoption by the General Assembly of a set of cease-fire 'principles'. In both cases the Truman administration found the Commonwealth difficult to ignore because its members represented its key strategic partners in the Cold War as well as the leading Third World voice. But once the cease-fire 'principles' were rejected by the Chinese, under intense domestic pressure, Washington's willingness to bow to allied opinion evaporated. As a result, Commonwealth unity shattered with only Britain and India remaining steadfast. Importantly, though, British intransigence did prove sufficient to win one last concession. The U.S. Government altered its resolution so that after China was branded an aggressor one further attempt would be made to find a cease-fire before sanctions were considered. With their major aim achieved and with the military situation improving in late January 1951, all of the Commonwealth members except India now supported the U.S. resolution. Yet Barnes concludes that the Commonwealth challenge had sufficiently diluted American policy and delayed punitive action long enough so that the crisis had begun to pass and the risk of escalation had diminished.

In Chapter 4 Colin Jackson shifts attention to military strategy. His chapter critiques the so-called 'lessons' of Korea which shaped Washington's limited war strategy for much of the Cold War. Jackson does this be re-examining General James Van Fleet's often ignored proposal, made in the spring of 1951, for amphibious landings at Tongchon and an advance north to the narrow 'neck' of Korea stretching between Pyongyang and Wonsan. Basing his findings largely on new Soviet and Chinese evidence documenting cable traffic between Mao and Stalin, Jackson argues that Operation 'Detonate' was feasible on 'purely military grounds'. He states that the Communist forces had exhausted themselves during their failed Spring Offensives whereas the UNC enjoyed considerable firepower, mobility, and logistics advantages. The author thus contends that this episode represented a 'lost chance' to greatly weaken the enemy, place the UNC in a much stronger negotiating position once armistice talks began, deter the Communists from future aggression and undermine the Sino-Soviet alliance. Moreover, he claims there was little risk of escalation since Stalin was unlikely to commit Soviet forces to prevent such a limited advance.

Jackson is extremely critical of UN Commander General Matthew Ridgway and the Joint Chiefs of Staff for rejecting Van Fleet's proposal. He dismisses the arguments they presented after 1953, when they claimed Operation 'Detonate' would have been too costly, would have risked Soviet intervention and would have only gained territory that would have been later conceded during the armistice negotiations. Instead, Jackson believes their decision was political in nature. He claims Ridgway and the Joint Chiefs were especially cautious because of the domestic crisis revolving around UN Commander General Douglas MacArthur's recent dismissal and the concurrent Senate Hearings. The Joint Chiefs were also aware of the NATO allies' opposition to taking any new initiative in Korea, which Western European countries considered a strategic backwater. But Van Fleet's plan was not totally unrealistic. As Jackson points out, a month later Ridgway, realising his error, reconsidered the idea of an amphibious landing. By then, though, it was too late. The opportunity had passed.

In chapter 5 Steven Casey examines a very different aspect of the American experience during the Korean War. He explores how the U.S. public perceived the human cost of war – in terms of American battlefield deaths – and challenges John Mueller's widely influential thesis: 'as casualties mount, support decreases'. Casey argues that this formulation underestimates the reporting techniques used by the military and government to manage public opinion and fails to consider the role of political elites – namely the media and Congress – in scrutinising the official narrative. Taking these factors into account, Casey emphasises that casualty reporting is often the subject of intense political controversy, and as a result the public often has only a limited knowledge of the war's true toll. To demonstrate his argument, Casey looks at how the U.S. military publicised casualties in the midst of Korea's ongoing battles; what difficulties it encountered; the efforts it made to manage the public's reaction; how the media and Congress, in turn, used these figures to influence opinion; and when and to what extent any of these actions actually had an impact on public opinion towards the war. He concludes that during the first six months of the war, when the fighting was extremely fluid, the military struggled to produce accurate figures. Casey emphasises MacArthur's pivotal role. Initially, at least, MacArthur allowed war correspondents to roam the battlefield and imposed no formal censorship. But he did try to minimise UN casualty figures. It was hardly surprising that many in the media soon started to detect a discrepancy between MacArthur's communiqués and their correspondents' dispatches. In Washington the Republican opposition quickly seized on this discrepancy as part of its vicious partisan assaults on the Truman administration. When China intervened in the war, the public debate was already imbued with a sense of distrust about casualty figures. When the military was then unable to provide timely statistics in the midst of a big military setback—albeit largely for legitimate reasons of security—politicians and the press started to speculate about the likely death toll, often inflating the figure, increasing the sense of crisis, and undermining domestic support for the war in the process.

But the situation did improve. As Casey points out, in the spring of 1951 the UNC imposed limited censorship and restricted the movement of journalists in an effort to regain control over casualty reporting. These measures were easier to implement as the military situation solidified. Consequently, for over a year the authorities exerted a tighter control over casualty figures. Not until General Dwight D. Eisenhower in his 1952 presidential campaign began referring regularly to high casualties numbers did support for the war start to dip. As Casey concludes, 'In short, casualties are clearly important. But the specific impact they have on the home front depends on the complex interplay between the military's casualty reporting on the one hand and elite efforts to question the official narrative on the other'.

In Chapter 6 Charles Young uses memory to explore the war's conclusion and aftermath. Most Americans, he observes, do not view the Korean War as a pivotal episode. To them, Korea remains forgotten. This is partly because of the way the war ended. In contrast to victory in the two world wars—and defeat in Vietnam—the Korean armistice in 1953 was inconclusive. This ambiguous result gave few Americans a vested interest in either lauding its achievements or bemoaning its failures. But neither were Americans attracted by the war's other aspects: its limited nature, the lack of clear war aims, the military stalemate, the prolonged armistice negotiations, the media's disin-

INTRODUCTION

terest after the first year and Congressional dissent from both the Right and Left. Young highlights that while the United States had achieved its principal goal of containment, President Eisenhower in July 1953 could hardly have claimed a victory after three years of bitter fighting that left the peninsula divided along almost the same line as it had been in June 1950.

According to Young, however, the prisoner-of-war question did offer a perfect opportunity to forge a more positive memory of Korea. But it was a missed opportunity. In 1952 and 1953 the war was prolonged by eighteen months precisely because at the armistice talks the U.S. negotiators pushed for the principle of 'voluntary repatriation.' They refused to return prisoners to their homelands against their will. In 1953 China finally accepted these demands. This was, as Young writes, 'a significant concession from the Communists.' It was also a concession that the U.S. government might well 'have raised high on a banner', painting it as 'an epic humiliation' for the Cold War enemy, since 'tens-of-thousands of salt-of-the-earth peasant soldiers' were effectively turning their backs on Marxism. Borrowing from a famous MacArthur comment—later used as the title for Rosemary Foot's standard work on the armistice talks—Young argues that voluntary repatriation presented a possible 'substitute for victory'.[3]

But it was not used. After 1953 The Eisenhower administration was increasingly obsessed with waging the Cold War as a propaganda battle.[4] Yet it never made much of the clear-cut POW victory. Young blames this reluctance on the fact that voluntary repatriation remained a 'public secret' during and after the termination of the armistice negotiations. Both the Truman and Eisenhower administrations had never made voluntary repatriation a major public war aim. Their motive, as Young points out, was a deep fear that domestic support for the war would collapse if the public felt American soldiers were being killed in exchange for the freedom of Chinese and Korean ex-Communists.

While each of these chapters provides an exciting new outlook on the Korean War, they are all anchored in current historiographical debates. Thus, Stueck and Yi contribute significantly to the considerable body of literature on the origins of war, particularly those works that have examined the U.S. occupation of the southern part of the peninsula. Considerable disagreement has arisen on this issue over whether the USAMGIK should be assigned responsibility for the civil strife that led to the outbreak of fighting in 1950. Donald Boose, Choi Sang-Yong, Bruce Cumings, Jeon Sang-Sook, James Matray, as well as Stueck in an earlier work, have all argued that the US Army's miscalculations in working with Japanese authorities and the conservative elite while ignoring the Left, as well as the hasty end of the US occupation, left South Korea without a strong civil administration, creating conditions that led to the Korean War.[5] In contrast, Gregg Brazinsky, Donald Macdonald, Allan Millett, and Park Chan-Pyo, while acknowledging mistakes were made, have defended the USAMGIK's record. They stress that policies implemented during the occupation helped revive the South Korean economy, created an administrative infrastructure, instituted democracy, promoted land reform, and established a fledgling military.[6]

Shen adds to the controversy surrounding China's decision to intervene in the Korean War—a controversy that has received a thorough re-examination in recent years, as Soviet and Chinese records have become more readily available. The traditional argument, first put forward by Allen Whiting and later repeated by Russell Spurr and Hao Yufan and Zhai Zhihai, claims that Mao sent forces to Korea because the UNC advance to the Yalu constituted a grave threat to China's national security.[7] However, Chen Jian and Zhang Shuguang have recently contended that Beijing intervened for a range of other reasons: to restore China's Great Power status; promote the Communist revolution at home and abroad; and repay a debt to North Korea for the soldiers it had sent to fight in the Chinese Civil War. Moreover, both historians state that Mao was confident that his guerrilla tactics and the fighting spirit of the ordinary Chinese soldier could inflict a defeat upon the United States and China could withstand atomic attacks.[8] Furthermore, Shen's work builds on the research examining the difficulties experienced within the Communist camp during the Korean War, such as those by Sergei Goncharov, John Lewis, and Xue Litai, Alexandre Mansourov and Robert Simmons.[9]

Barnes' chapter is closely related to three categories of study: international histories of the Korean War, national histories of the role played by individual Commonwealth countries in the conflict, and histories of the UN's involvement. In terms of the first category, William Stueck has produced by far the most considered analysis of alliance diplomacy, paying particular interest to relations between the United States and its allies at the UN and beyond.[10] With regards to Commonwealth countries, the role of Britain has received considerable attention from Michael Dockrill, Anthony Farrar-Hockley, Rosemary Foot, Michael Hopkins, Peter Lowe and Callum MacDonald.[11] Two excellent national histories of Canada's experiences have been written by Denis Stairs and John Melady.[12] On Australia, Gavan McCormack and Robert O'Neill have provided the best contributions.[13] Ian McGibbon has written the only history of New Zealand in the Korean War.[14] And the best account of India's role remains Shiv Dayal's now dated book.[15] Graeme Mount has also considered relations between certain 'Old' Commonwealth countries and the United States during the conflict.[16] Finally, Barnes' research relates to the works of Tae-Ho Yoo and Leland Goodrich who have both examined the UN's role during the Korean War.[17]

Jackson builds upon the vast array of literature covering military aspects of the conflict. A large number of excellent official and unofficial histories have been written concerning the experiences of the various forces that were involved in Korea.[18] While these works are too numerous to consider at length here, it is important to point out that very few historians have challenged the orthodox view that by the late spring of 1951 relative parity existed, making any thought of taking the military initiative unrealistic and risky.

Jackson's chapter also touches upon a much bigger controversy. The Korean War has largely escaped the revisionism that has been such a part of the Vietnam War's military historiography. In examining why the United States lost in Vietnam, the likes of Harry Summers and Norman Podhoretz emphasise the constraints politicians placed on the military, which meant that the generals were forced to fight 'with one hand tied behind their backs'.[19] Jackson's claim that similar constraints operated during the Korean War has already generated a sharp response. Donald Boose and Allan Millett at least partially agree with Jackson's analysis that Van Fleet's proposal represented a 'lost chance' from a military standpoint although they are less critical of Ridgway and the Joint Chiefs. In contrast, James Matray, focusing more on political considerations, argues strongly that Operation 'Detonate' would not have brought a speedy end to the Korean War.[20] This chapter could well be the start of an impassioned new debate.

Casey's chapter provides a significant contribution to the small but growing body of literature assessing the Korean War's impact on U.S. domestic affairs. Casey himself has been the most prolific writer in this area in recent years, having published a book and a number of articles revolving around the ways the Truman and Eisenhower administration's attempted to 'sell' the Korean War to the American public and the government's relationship with the political elite[21]. Still, Ronald Caridi, Robert Ivie, Paul Pierpaoli and John Wiltz have all addressed related issues[22]. Casey's work is also directly connected to the considerable research into the internal workings of the U.S. Government during the Korean War. The best examples of this genre are the studies written by Foot and Burton Kaufman[23].

Young's work is also directly connected to the historiography focusing on the influence of the Korean War on U.S. domestic affairs. But as well as this Young makes an invaluable contribution to the body of work on the Korean armistice negotiations, in particular those books centred on the prisoner-of-war question. For a number of decades most historians argued that the motivation behind the inflexible refusal of the United States to return communist POWs to China and North Korea against their will was humanitarian, endorsing Truman's own explanation for his policy[24]. In recent years, however, Sydney Bailey, Barton Bernstein and Foot have insisted that the central factor in Truman's thinking was to win a propaganda victory in the Cold War. Moreover, these authors have doubted the legality of voluntary repatriation and been deeply critical of the UNC's use of Chinese Nationalist and South Korean guards and agents in the UN prisoner camps who used coercion and violence to force prisoners to refuse repatriation[25].

If at first glance, then, these essays appear an eclectic mix, this is only because a complex war deserves complex treatment. It needs to be examined from various angles: geographical, chronological, and methodological. Sixty years after its end, the Korean War continues to scar contemporary East Asian politics. The following chapters not only shed new light on various

INTRODUCTION

aspects of this important conflict; they also examine why the war remains so important to the politics of the region.

Notes

1 For Korea as the 'forgotten war' see Clay Blair, *The Forgotten War: America in Korea, 1950-53* (New York, 1987); Bruce Cumings and John Halliday, *Korea: The Unknown War* (London, 1988); Rosemary Foot, 'Making Known the Unknown War: Policy Analysis of the Korean War in the Last Decade', *Diplomatic History* 15 (1991), 411-31; Callum MacDonald, *Korea: The War Before Vietnam* (Basingstoke, 1986).

2 For detailed historiographical reviews of the Korean War see, for example, Lester Brune (ed.), *The Korean War: Handbook of the Literature and Research* (Westport, 1996); Foot, 'Making Known the Unknown War'; Kim Hakjoon, 'International Trends in Korean War Studies', *Korean War Studies*, 14:2 (1990), 326-70; James Matray, 'Korea's war at 60: A survey of the literature', *Cold War History* 11:1 (2011), 99-129; James Matray, 'The Korean War', in Robert Schulzinger (ed.), *A Companion to American Foreign Relations* (Malden, 2003); Allan Millett, 'A Reader's Guide to the Korean War', *Journal of Military History,* 61:4 (1997), 583-97.

3 Rosemary Foot, *A Substitute for Victory: The Politics of Peacemaking at the Korean Armistice Talks* (Ithaca, 1990).

4 Kenneth Osgood, *Total Cold War: Eisenhower's Secret Propaganda Battle at Home and Abroad* (Lawrence, 2006).

5 Donald Boose Jr., 'Portentous Sideshow: The Korean Occupation Decision', *Parameters* 25:4 (1995), 112-29; Choi Sang-Yong, "Trusteeship Debate and the Korean Cold War", in Oh Bonnie B. C. (ed.), *Korea Under the American Military Government, 1945–1948* (Westport, 2002); Bruce Cumings, *The Origins of the Korean War, Volume 1: Liberation and the Emergence of Separate Regimes, 1945-1947* (Princeton, 1981); Bruce Cumings, *The Origins of the Korean War, Volume 2: The Roaring of the Cataract, 1947-1950* (Princeton, 1990); Jeon Sang-Sook, "U.S. Korean Policy and the Moderates During the U.S. Military Government Era", in Oh Bonnie B. C. (ed.), *Korea Under the American Military Government, 1945–1948* (Westport, 2002); James Matray, 'Hodge Podge: US Occupation Policy in Korea, 1945-1948' *Korean Studies* 19 (1995), 17-38; James Matray, *The Reluctant Crusade: American Foreign Policy in Korea, 1941-1950* (Honolulu, 1985); William Stueck, *Road to Confrontation: American Policy Toward China and Korea, 1947-1950* (Chapel Hill, 1981).

6 Gregg Brazinsky, *Nation Building in South Korea: Koreans, Americans, and the Making of Democracy* (Chapel Hill, 2007); Donald Macdonald, *The Koreans: Contemporary Politics and Society* (Boulder, 1998); Alan Millett, *The War for Korea, 1945–1950: A House Burning* (Lawrence, 2005); Park Chan-Pyo, "The American Military Government and the Framework for Democracy in South Korea", in Oh Bonnie B. C. (ed.), *Korea Under the American Military Government, 1945–1948* (Westport, 2002).

7 Hao Yufan and Zhai Zhihai, 'China's Decision to Enter the Korean War: History Revisited', *The China Quarterly* 121 (1990), 94–115; Russell Spurr, *Enter the Dragon: China's Undeclared War Against the U.S. In Korea, 1950–1951* (New York, 1988); Allen Whiting, *China Crosses the Yalu: The Decision to Enter the Korean War* (Stanford, 1970).

INTRODUCTION

8 Chen Jian, *China's Road to the Korean War: The Making of the Sino-American Confrontation* (New York, 1994); Zhang Shuguang, *Mao's Military Romanticism: China and the Korean War, 1950–53* (Lawrence, 1995).

9 Sergei Goncharov, John Lewis, Xue Litai, *Uncertain Partners: Stalin, Mao, and the Korean War* (Stanford, 1993); Alexandre Mansourov, 'Stalin, Mao, Kim, and China's Decision to Enter the Korean War, Sept. 16-Oct. 15, 1950: New Evidence from Russian Archives', *Cold War International History Project Bulletin* No.6/7; Robert Simmons, *The Strained Alliance: Peking, Pyongyang, Moscow and the Politics of the Korean Civil War* (New York, 1975).

10 William Stueck, *The Korean War: An International History* (Princeton, 1995); William Stueck, 'The Limits of Influence: British Policy and American Expansion of the War in Korea', *Pacific Historical Review* 55:1 (1986), 65-95; William Stueck, *Rethinking the Korean War: A New Diplomatic and Strategic History* (Princeton, 2002).

11 Michael Dockrill, 'The Foreign Office, Anglo-American Relations, and the Korean War, June 1950-June 1951,' *International Affairs* 62:3 (1986), 459-476; Michael Dockrill, 'The Foreign Office, Anglo-American Relations and the Korean Truce Negotiations, July 1951-July 1953', in James Cotton and Ian Neary (eds.), *The Korean War in History* (Manchester, 1989), 100-119; Anthony Farrar-Hockley, *The British Part in the Korean War – Volume I: A Distant Obligation* (London, 1990); *The British Part in the Korean War – Volume II: An Honourable Discharge* (London, 1995); Rosemary Foot, 'Anglo-American Relations in the Korean Crisis: The British Effort to avert an expanded war, December 1950-January 1951', *Diplomatic History* 10:1 (1986), 43-57; Michael Hopkins, 'The Price of Cold War Partnership: Sir Oliver Franks and the British Military Commitment in the Korean War', *Cold War History* 1:2 (2001), 8-46; Peter Lowe, 'An Ally and a Recalcitrant General: Great Britain, Douglas MacArthur and the Korean War, 1950-1', *English Historical Review* 105:406 (1990), 624-653; Peter Lowe, *Containing the Cold War in East Asia: British policies towards Japan, China and Korea, 1948-1953* (Manchester, 1997), 167-269; Peter Lowe, 'Great Britain, Japan, and the Korean War, 1950-1951', *Proceedings of the British Association for Japanese Studies*, Volume 9 (1984), 98-111; Peter Lowe, 'Hopes Frustrated: The Impact of the Korean War Upon Britain's Relations with Communist China, 1950-1953', in T. G. Fraser and Keith Jeffery (eds.), *Men, Women and War* (Dublin, 1993), 211-226; Peter Lowe, 'The Frustrations of Alliance: Britain, the United States, and the Korean War, 1950-1951', in James Cotton and Ian Neary (eds.), *The Korean War in History* (Manchester, 1989), 80-99; Peter Lowe, The Settlement of the Korean War', in John Young (ed.), *The Foreign Policy of Churchill's Peacetime Administration, 1951-1955* (Leicester, 1988), 207-231; Callum MacDonald, *Britain and the Korean War* (Oxford, 1990).

12 John Melady, *Korea: Canada's Forgotten War* (Toronto, 1998); Denis Stairs, *The Diplomacy of Constraint: Canada, the Korean War, and the United States* (Toronto, 1974).

13 Gavan McCormack, *Cold War, Hot War: An Australian Perspective on the Korean War* (Sydney, 1983); Robert O'Neill, *Australia in the Korean War, 1950-53 – Volume I: Strategy and Diplomacy* (Canberra, 1991).

14 Ian McGibbon, *New Zealand and the Korean War – Volume I: Politics and Diplomacy* (Auckland, 1992).

15 Shiv Dayal, *India's Role in the Korean Question: A Study in the Settlement of International Disputes under the United Nations* (Delhi, 1959).

16 Graeme Mount, with Andre Laferriere, *The Diplomacy of War: The Case for Korea* (Montreal, 2004).

INTRODUCTION

17 Leland Goodrich, *Korea: A Study of US Policy in the United Nations* (New York, 1956); Tae-Ho Yoo, *The Korean War and the United Nations: A Legal and Diplomatic Historical Study* (Louvain, 1965).

18 Roy Appleman, *Disaster in Korea: The Chinese Confront MacArthur* (College Station, 1989); Roy Appleman, *East of Chosin: Entrapment and Breakout, 1950* (College Station, 1987); Roy Appleman, *Escaping the Trap: US Army X Corps in Northeast Korea* (College Station, 1990); Roy Appleman, *Ridgway Duels for Korea* (College Station, 1990); Clay Blair, *The Forgotten War: America in Korea, 1950-53* (New York, 1987); Conrad Crane, *American Airpower Strategy in Korea* (Lawrence, 2000); Ashley Cunningham-Boothe and Peter Farrar (eds.), *British Forces in the Korean War* (London, 1988); Alexander George, *The Chinese Communist Army in Action: The Korean War and its Aftermath* (New York, 1967); Walter Hermes, *Truce Tent and Fighting Front: The United States Army in the Korean War* (Honolulu, 1992); D. Clayton James, *Refighting the Last War: Command and Crisis in Korea, 1950-1953* (New York, 1993); Ian McGibbon, *New Zealand and the Korean War – Volume II: Combat Operations* (Auckland, 1996); Billy Mossman, *Ebb and Flow: November 1950 to July 1951* (Washington, 1990); Robert O'Neill, *Australia in the Korean War, 1950-53 – Volume II: Combat Operations* (Canberra, 1995); James Schnabel, *The US Army in the Korean War. Policy and Direction: First Year* (Washington, 1992); Zhang Shuguang, *Mao's Military Romanticism: China and the Korean War, 1950-1953* (Lawrence, 1995); Xiaoming Zhang, *Red Wings over the Yalu: China, the Soviet Union, and the Air War in Korea* (College Station, 2002).

19 Norman Podhoretz, *Why Were We In Vietnam* (New York, 1982); Harry Summers, *On Strategy: A Critical Analysis of the Vietnam War* (Novato, 1982).

20 Review by Donald Boose, *H-Diplo Roundtable Review* 11:41 (2010), 8-14; Review by James Matray, *H-Diplo Roundtable Review* 11:41 (2010), 15-23; Review by Allan Millett, *H-Diplo Roundtable Review* 11:41 (2010), 24-31.

21 Steven Casey, 'Selling NSC-68: The Truman Administration, Public Opinion, and the Politics of Mobilization, 1950-51,' *Diplomatic History* 29:4 (2005), 655-690; Steven Casey, *Selling the Korean War: Propaganda, Politics and Public Opinion* (Oxford, 2008); Steven Casey, 'Wilfred Burchett and the UNC's Media Operations during the Korean War, 1951-52', *Journal of Military History* 74:3 (2010), 821-845; Steven Casey, 'White House Publicity Operations during the Korean War, June 1950-June 1951', *Presidential Studies Quarterly* 35:4 (2005), 691-717.

22 Ronald Caridi, *The Korean War and American Politics: The Republican Party as a Case Study* (Philadeplhia, 1969); Robert Ivie, 'Declaring a National Emergency: Truman's Rhetorical Crisis and the Great Debate of 1951', in Amos Kiewe (ed.), *The Modern Presidency and Crisis Rhetoric* (London, 1994); Paul Pierpaoli, *Truman and Korea: The Political Culture of the Early Cold War* (Columbia, 1999); John Wiltz, 'The Korean War and American Society', in Francis Heller (ed.), *The Korean War: A 25-Year Perspective* (Lawrence, 1977), 112-58.

23 Rosemary Foot, *The Wrong War: American Policy and the Dimensions of the Korean Conflict, 1950-1953* (Ithaca, 1985); Burton Kaufman, *The Korean War: Challenges in Crisis, Credibility, and Command*, 2nd ed. (Philadelphia, 1997).

24 For traditional accounts of the Korean armistice negotiations see, for example, Wilfrid Bacchus, 'The Relationship between Combat and Peace Negotiations: Fighting While Talking in Korea, 1953-53', *Orbis* 17:2 (1973), 545-574; Allen Goodman (ed.), *Negotiating While Fighting: The Diary of Admiral C. Turner Joy at the Korean Armistice Negotiations* (Stanford, 1978); Hermes, *Truce Tent and Fighting Front*; William Vatcher, *Panmunjom: The Story of the Korean Military Armistice Negotiations* (Westport, 1958).

INTRODUCTION

25 Sydney Bailey, *The Korean Armistice* (Basingstoke, 1992); Barton Bernstein, 'The Struggle over the Korean Armistice: Prisoners of Repatriation', in Bruce Cumings (ed.), *Child of Conflict: The Korean-American Relationship, 1945–1953* (Seattle, 1983); Foot, *A Substitute for Victory*; Rosemary Foot, 'Negotiating with Friends and Enemies: The Politics of Peacemaking in Korea', in Kim Chull Baum and James Matray (eds.), *Korea and the Cold War: Division, Destruction, and Disarmament* (Claremont, 1993).

'An Alliance Forged in Blood': The American Occupation of Korea, the Korean War, and the US–South Korean Alliance

WILLIAM STUECK* AND BORAM YI**

*University of Georgia, USA, **University of Baltimore, USA

ABSTRACT The US occupation of Korea from 1945 to 1948 was not notable for its success. The volatile interaction between the occupiers and the occupied provided an important context for its relatively rapid conclusion and for Washington's ineffective employment of deterrence in the lead-up to the June 1950 North Korean attack on South Korea. This essay describes the volatile interaction between Americans and Koreans on the peninsula and the circumstantial, psychological, and cultural factors behind it. The essay concludes by analyzing the psychological impact of the Korean War on the relationship and how this and later cultural changes have made possible an enduring alliance between the United States and the Republic of Korea.

Concluded in the immediate aftermath of the Korean War, the alliance of the United States with the Republic of Korea (ROK) is now over a half-century old. It has survived by a generation the end of the Cold War, the ROK rapprochement with Russia and China, and the ROK's rise as a regional power. It has endured the tremors created by the emergence in Korea of a generation with no direct memory of the Korean War, the simultaneous tenure in office of ham-handed leaders George W. Bush and Roh Moo-hyun, and the evolution of US strategy in the post-9/11 world. Despite the continuing existence of detractors on both sides, it is tempting to view the alliance, if not its precise nature, as part of the natural order of things.[1]

With this in mind, we believe it useful to reexamine the shaky nature of the relationship of the United States and Korea in the years between World War II and the Korean War. In particular we will examine the attitudes, perceptions, and behavior of the American occupiers of Korea from September 1945 to August 1948, the reaction of the native population and its leaders to the US course, and the impact of the interaction on US policy in the lead-up to the outbreak of war in June 1950. This examination reveals some of the cultural and psychological differences between the two peoples and makes it clear that the alliance between the United States and the ROK was anything but inevitable. We conclude with some observations about how events on the peninsula from 1950 to 1953 impacted the relationship and why the military alliance that emerged in its aftermath has endured.

The Strategic Perspective

The United States engaged in four military occupations after World War II and the one in Korea was both the shortest and the least successful. When the occupation ended during the second half of 1948, Korea was a divided land with hostile indigenous governments, the US-sponsored ROK in the south and the Soviet-sponsored Democratic People's Republic of Korea (DPRK) in the north. Each of these governments claimed sovereignty over the entire peninsula and was headed by a man intent upon using whatever means were necessary to make his claim a reality. DPRK leader Kim Il-sung was in a much better position to do so, as his government was in firm control of territory above the 38th Parallel; in contrast, his rival to the south, Syngman Rhee, faced substantial and growing internal turmoil.

The DPRK's advantage reflected the relatively more successful Soviet occupation of the north than that of the United States in the south, at least for the short term. The Soviet zone possessed only half the population of the American and, from the start, the Soviet occupiers exercised a firm hand, immediately displacing Japanese colonial personnel, who had ruled the peninsula since 1910, supporting anti-Japanese natives, mostly exiles sympathetic to a revolutionary course, and then executing broad land reform. Uncooperative natives were either suppressed or pushed southward into the US zone.

---

[1]For a persuasive, largely optimistic analysis of the future of the alliance, see Scott Snyder, *China's Rise and the Two Koreas* (London: Lynne Rienner 2009).

In contrast, the poorly prepared Americans fumbled badly, at first retaining Japanese in positions of authority and then replacing them with Korean collaborators while retaining the colonial structure. Occupation authorities assisted in building an indigenous police force that replicated many practices of its despised Japanese predecessor and generated widespread animosity. The Americans also favored the political Right while encouraging political parties and free market activities, which facilitated neither cohesion nor material prosperity, and delayed extensive land reform until the spring of 1948, then redistributing only Japanese owned properties, a mere quarter of the total in the US zone. The ROK government that emerged in mid-August 1948 was dominated by the far Right and divided between an autocratic President Rhee and a Democratic Party of conservative landowners in the legislative branch, who believed the president should be a figurehead. In November, in the midst of stalemate between the executive and legislative branches in Seoul and expanding unrest in the countryside, US ambassador John J. Muccio wrote home that the new government was 'incompetent' and 'without strong public support'.[2]

The United States was far from firmly committed to stay the course in Korea. During 1947 the Joint Chiefs of Staff had concluded that the United States possessed no strategic interest in maintaining troops on the peninsula and Congress showed little inclination to expend major funds on Korea.[3] The State Department succeeded in delaying a final withdrawal of US military units, but by the end of 1948 the number of American soldiers there was down to 8,000. Persistent pressure from the Pentagon, combined with some improvement in conditions below the 38th Parallel, led to their departure in June 1949. Although the United States left behind some military equipment and 500 military personnel to assist in training ROK armed forces, Washington declined to make a commitment to South Korea's defense, as it was in the process of doing for Western Europe. What is more, Congress refused to move quickly to pass an economic aid program for the ROK. With the Communists in China marching toward victory in the civil war there, their northern armies manned in part by tens of thousands of

---

[2]US Department of State, F[oreign] R[elations of the] U[nited] S[tates], 1948 (Washington DC: Government Printing Office 1971), 6: 1326.
[3]For the Joint Chiefs' analysis, see FRUS, 1947, 6: 417–18. For the lack of congressional support for a large-scale aid program for Korea, see William Stueck, *The Wedemeyer Mission: American Politics and Foreign Policy during the Cold War* (Athens, GA: Univ. of Georgia Press 1984), 25–6.

ethnic Koreans well-positioned for redeployment in the DPRK, ROK prospects appeared anything but promising.[4]

How did the United States get to this discouraging point in Korea? The easy answer is that the situation grew out of a combination of the breakdown of US–Soviet relations in the aftermath of World War II, the bumbling of occupation authorities in South Korea, and a strategic reassessment of American interests in Korea in the midst of evolving conditions elsewhere, especially in Europe and the United States. That is, as Washington took on breathtaking and costly new peacetime responsibilities in Europe, Korea looked expendable, if grudgingly so given the confrontation there with the Soviet Union and its proximity to Japan. In the end the peninsula was not vital in terms of resources and Japan could be defended with air and naval power far more cheaply than with US troops on mainland Asia.

This explanation is essential to an understanding of events, but it ignores the context of direct American interaction with the Korean people from September 1945 onward. It is to this factor that we turn our focus.

Not a Pretty Picture: Americans and Koreans Getting to Know Each Other

US troops began arriving in large numbers in Korea on 8 September 1945, more than three weeks after the Japanese surrender. Over the next month and a half, the numbers rose to about 77,000, the peak for the occupation period.[5]

By the time American troops arrived, Koreans were deeply engaged in activity aimed at replacing the colonial regime and, they believed, establishing their independence. In mid-August Japanese

---

[4]For an analysis of US policy toward Korea from 1947 through June 1949, see William Stueck, *The Road to Confrontation: American Policy toward China and Korea, 1947–1950* (Chapel Hill: Univ. of North Carolina Press 1981), 75–110, 153–9. For coverage of evolving conditions in South Korea, see Bruce Cumings, *The Origins of the Korean War*, Vol. 2, *The Roaring of the Cataract 1947–1950* (Princeton, NJ: Princeton UP 1990), 185–290, and Allan R. Millett, *The War for Korea, 1945–1950: A House Burning* (Lawrence: UP of Kansas 2005), 159–85.

[5]'H[istory of] US A[rmy] F[orces[i[n] K[orea]' [henceforth 'HUSAFIK'] Part I, Ch. 6, 69. This unpublished manuscript written by American servicemen attached to the historical office of the US Command in Korea is available in the US Army Center for Military History, Ft McNair, Washington DC and the Historical Office of the US military base at Yongsan, Seoul, Republic of Korea. The organization is erratic, as 'Part' is used both for separate volumes and for sections of chapters. To avoid confusion, we identify the largest organizational category as 'Volume' and a separately labeled section of a chapter as 'Part'.

Governor-General Abe Nobuyuki, anticipating his country's surrender, aware that the Soviets had entered the peninsula after declaring war on 8 August, and fearing that Koreans would respond by attacking the more than 378,000 Japanese civilians and 163,000 Japanese military personnel residing in Korea, moved to engage a native elite in a transitional process that would ensure order.[6] After a moderate nationalist rejected his overture, Abe approached Yo Un-hyong, a non-Communist Leftist whose demands for freedom of action were reluctantly accepted. Thus in Seoul Yo established the Committee for the Preparation of Korean Independence (CPKI) and began setting up a governmental framework for Korean self-rule. At the local level people's committees sprouted up, often at the behest of the CPKI. These bodies frequently gained backing from native soldiers who had recently deserted the Imperial Japanese Army and armed youth groups (*ch'iandae*) and private armies that included thousands of prisoners – both political and criminal – freed by the CPKI.[7]

Yo sought to recruit people of all political stripes, but most conservatives refused to cooperate, resulting in a Leftist-dominated organization. Korea in those days, according to one authoritative account, was 'a maelstrom of old and new classes, political groups, and ideologies'. Four in five natives farmed for a livelihood, overwhelmingly as tenants. Japanese-directed economic development had added to the mix 'an assortment of capitalists, white-collar professionals, [and] factory wage workers'. Wartime mobilization had produced increasing, often forced, internal migration and a draconian system of assimilation that sought to root out all vestiges of Korean culture, including names and language. While open resistance was impossible, Koreans accommodated their Japanese masters to varying degrees, producing resentments within the native population that promised to surface with liberation. Broadly speaking, political groupings divided into Right and Left.

Most Koreans with property and education had engaged in some collaboration with the Japanese, and they stood on the Right in opposing far-reaching change, such as comprehensive land reform or other instruments for redistributing wealth. Joining them were less educated, less prosperous people who had served in the colonial regime, including in the notorious police force, which was nearly 40 percent Korean.

---

[6]Millett, *War for Korea*, 43.
[7]Key secondary sources include ibid., 43–52, and Bruce Cumings, *The Origins of the Korean War*, Vol. 1, *Liberation and the Emergence of Separate Regimes 1945–1947* (Princeton, NJ: Princeton UP 1981), 68–100.

On the Left were a variety of groups – intellectuals, peasants, workers, and students – who lay in wait to rise up against the government. Groupings were far from static. On the Left the Communists were the best organized and possessed some connection to the Soviet Union through its Seoul consulate, but they were neither dominant nor initially unwilling to work with others.[8]

By early September Pak Hon-yong, the most prominent Communist in the south, exercised considerable influence in the CPKI and conservatives, anticipating the arrival of American troops, organized a countermovement. On the eve of US arrival, CPKI leaders called a meeting in Seoul of hundreds of sympathizers from the provinces and declared the formation of the Korean People's Republic (KPR). Controlled by Leftists, the meeting nonetheless appointed to top positions several Rightists, including patriots residing abroad such as Syngman Rhee, the most influential fighter for Korean independence in the United States, and Kim Ku, head of the Korean Provisional Government (KPG) in Chungking. Unfortunately, such appointments occurred without the knowledge or approval of the appointees themselves and at a time when US relations with the Soviet Union were deteriorating.[9]

Leading American troops who entered Korea in September 1945 was Lieutenant General John R. Hodge, the tough, straight-talking, combat-hardened commander of the XXIV Corps. Hodge lacked experience in administration and politics, knowledge of Korea, and detailed guidance from Washington or his immediate superior, General Douglas A. MacArthur, the US Far Eastern Commander and head of the occupation of Japan. His primary understanding of events in Korea was through wire communications with Japanese officials in Seoul, which began on 29 August. Alarmed by the activities of the CPKI and other Leftist organizations and suspecting that the Soviet consulate was advising the Communists, Japanese authorities reasserted themselves while urging the Americans to hasten their arrival. With mounting strikes and assaults on police by Koreans, the Japanese warned of possible attacks on American troops as they landed and suggested a delay in the 'dismemberment of Japanese forces and the transfer of administrative organs from the Japanese hand'.[10] General MacArthur initially directed Hodge to treat Koreans as 'liberated people' and Hodge's letter to his subordinate commanders of 28 August adopted this view while cautioning them on 'matters of security'. With several

---

[8]Carter Eckert, Ki-baik Lee, Young Ick Lew, Michael Robinson, and Edward W. Wagner, *Korea Old and New: A History* (Seoul: Ilchokak 1990), 199–236.
[9]Cumings, *Origins*, 1: 68–100.
[10]'HUSAFIK', Vol. 1, Ch. 1, 51–2, 57–8, 83–4.

hundred thousand Japanese on the peninsula and Koreans divided into 'several political factions', he warned, the Americans must 'be wary of Oriental favors and on the alert for a double cross'.[11]

A week later, however, General Hodge referred to Korea as 'an enemy of the United States ... subject to the provisions and the terms of the surrender'.[12] On 1 and 5 September he had leaflets dropped on Seoul, Pusan, and Inchon informing residents of the impending arrival of US troops and urging Koreans to avoid disorder and prepare for a gradual transition from Japanese governance to self-rule.[13] Profoundly conservative and focused on maintaining order in what seemed to be highly volatile conditions, Hodge devoted little thought to the manipulative aspects of Japanese communiqués deriving from the natural desire to hold on to as much of the peninsula's wealth as possible.

General Hodge's refusal to treat Koreans as 'liberated' was consistent with much thinking in Washington. Prior to the Japanese takeover, Korea had governed itself for over a millennium, but American planners thought the people there required tutelage before enjoying full independence. The declaration at Cairo of the United States, Great Britain, and China in November 1943 that, 'in due course', the peninsula would become 'free and independent' reflected this thinking.[14] Conscious that Korea's internal turmoil at the turn of the century had helped bring on two wars in northeast Asia and that the Japanese had dominated all the top positions in the government since 1910, American policymakers were disinclined to leave Koreans to their own devices after Japan's defeat. The preferred course, one analysis concluded, was a promise of eventual independence 'after a period of self-government under international trusteeship'.[15]

American planners ignored the consistent stand of Korean exiles against any kind of transition to independence. After Pearl Harbor leaders of the KPG quickly began lobbying for recognition and aid.[16] Noting the divisions in the KPG and among exile groups in the United

---

[11]Ibid., 67.

[12]Hodge's directive of 4 Sept. 1945, as quoted in Han-mu Kang, 'The United States Military Government in Korea, 1945–1948: An Analysis and Evaluation of its Policy' (PhD diss., Univ. of Cincinnati 1970), 34–5.

[13]'HUSAFIK', Vol. 1, Ch. 1, 68–71.

[14]*Department of State Bulletin 9* (4 Dec. 1943), 393.

[15]N[ational] A[rchives, College Park, MD], [State Department Records] RG 59, Records of Harley A. Notter, 1939–45, box 63, 'Korea: Economic Developments and Prospects', April 1943.

[16]See, for example, report by Roy P. McNair, Jr, 17 Dec. 1942, assistant military attaché to China, in Records of the Department of State Relating to the Internal Affairs of Korea, 1940–44 (microfilm edition), Reel 2.

States, the uncertain roots of the KPG among Koreans at home, the unlikelihood that Koreans could provide any significant assistance to the war effort against Japan, and the complications recognition of the anti-Communist KPG would create with the Soviet Union, the United States never granted recognition. KPG efforts continued, however, giving Americans every reason to believe that Korean exiles, at least those in the United States and Nationalist China, stood as one on immediate independence after the war.[17]

Yet US leaders still talked of a multi-power Korean trusteeship and thought they had agreement in principle of their Soviet and British colleagues for the approach. The war ended more quickly than anticipated and, with the disappearance of common enemies, amid increasing distrust between the United States and the Soviet Union. On the eve of Japan's surrender and with Soviet troops already on the peninsula in the extreme northeast, Washington proposed the 38th Parallel as the dividing line between Soviet and American occupation zones and Moscow quickly agreed, but no agreement existed on Korea's road to independence. The trusteeship approach remained alive in Washington, grounded in the assumption that for the moment Koreans were incapable of governing themselves. That assumption joined with a growing desire to contain Soviet expansion and evolving conditions on the ground in Korea to dictate policy.[18]

Koreans' failure to contribute significantly to the defeat of Japan was also a factor in Hodge's initial actions on the peninsula. The Commanding General's only prior exposure to Koreans had been with the tens of thousands who either had fought in Japan's armies in the Pacific War or had provided much of the labor for them behind the lines.[19] Within days of his arrival in the country Hodge was widely quoted as referring to Koreans as 'the same breed of cat as the Japanese'.[20] The quote was inexact and taken out of context, but Hodge's attitudes, not to mention those in Washington, derived in part

---

[17]James I. Matray, *The Reluctant Crusade: American Foreign Policy in Korea, 1941–1950* (Honolulu: Univ. of Hawaii Press 1985), 20–1.

[18]For a recent account of American maneuvering on Korea during the war, see Seung-Young Kim, *American Diplomacy and Strategy toward Korea and Northeast Asia, 1882–1950 and After: Perception of Polarity and US Commitment to a Periphery* (New York: Palgrave Macmillan 2009), 73–131.

[19]On the use of Korean manpower by the Japanese during World War II, Richard Frank provided us with key information. For the revealing experience on this matter of a young US Marine officer during the Saipan campaign of 1944, see Gregory Henderson, *Korea: The Politics of the Vortex* (Cambridge, MA: Harvard UP 1968), 416n29.

[20]Richard E. Lauterbach, *Danger from the East* (New York: Harper & Row 1947), 201; *FRUS, 1945*, 6: 1135.

from a belief that Koreans had done nothing to earn immediate independence.

Despite Japan's intense wartime propaganda against the United States and the brutal behavior of Soviet troops in the north, American soldiers received an enthusiastic reception from most Koreans.[21] Due to the actions of Japanese police, Koreans at Inchon on 8 September were subdued as the US 7th Infantry Division began landing in force.[22] Yet days before hundreds of Koreans residing in villages between Inchon and Seoul had gathered along the route of an advance team of American military police to adorn their vehicles with flowers.[23] The larger units that followed, one American journalist who accompanied them later wrote, 'were like shining knights descended straight from heaven to strike away a people's shackles'. As American soldiers fanned out across the southern half of the country to assume their occupation duties, they were almost uniformly welcomed as heroes.[24]

The honeymoon was short. Within days of General Hodge's arrival in Seoul, the police were in disarray and the streets seethed with tension.[25] Soviets in the consulate there were suspected of encouraging agitators and, as one American remarked, were 'the roughest, toughest aggregation of people he had ever seen'.[26] The State Department representative to the occupation reported 'critical shortages [of] coal and food cereals' and widespread unemployment, in part due to collapse of Japanese war industries, in part because many Koreans had chosen to take 'a prolonged holiday' after the announcement of Japan's surrender.[27] *New York Times* correspondent Richard J. H. Johnston,

---

[21]For Korean perspectives, see Sonny Che, *Forever Alien: A Korean Memoir, 1930–1951* (Jefferson, NC: McFarland 2000), 143–6 and *Maeil Sinbo*, 9 Sept. 1945. For a recent account of the early behavior of Soviet troops in the north, see Ronald H. Spector, *In the Ruins of Empire: The Japanese Surrender and the Battle for Postwar Asia* (New York: Random House 2007), 143–6.

[22]'HUSAFIK', Vol. 1, Ch. 4, 6; *New York Times*, 9 Sept. 1945. See also the recollections of an American officer in 'My Most Memorable Day: Korea, Sept. 8, 1945', *Monadnock Ledger*, 24 May 2001.

[23]Lawrence E. Gelfand to Yi Boram, 22 Sept. 2005. Gelfand was a member of the unit. See also the description of Col. Brainard E. Prescott, who arrived at Inchon on 6 Sept. 1945 and soon became the Civil Administrator of the occupation, in *Department of State Bulletin* 24 (27 Jan. 1946), 106.

[24]Harold R. Isaacs, *No Peace for Asia* (New York: Macmillan 1947), 81–3; see also 'HUSAFIK', Vol. 1, Ch. 6, 10, 15–16, 51–2.

[25]NA, [Records of GHQ Far East Command, Supreme Commander Allied Powers and United Nations], RG 554, Entry A1 1378, box 21, 'Notes on Corps Staff Conference', 13 Sept. 1945.

[26]Ibid.; 'Notes of Staff Conference', 15 Sept. 1945.

[27]*FRUS, 1945*, 6: 1050–1.

who accompanied US forces entering Korea, remarked that 'here is an unprecedented situation for the Allied liberators'.[28]

The version of the Cairo declaration that circulated in Korea translated the phrase 'in due course' into 'the equivalent of "in a few days"', but General Hodge quickly made it clear that independence would not be granted immediately and that Japanese would be kept in government positions, high and low alike, until Koreans acquired the skills necessary to replace them. He urged Koreans to show patience, to 'demonstrate to the democratic nations of the world and to me as their representative your capacities and abilities as a people and your readiness to accept an honored place in the family of nations'.[29] Historian Bruce Cumings remarks that Hodge's initial actions, combined with the cordial relations apparent between the Americans and Japanese, now 'cooperative, orderly, and docile', suggested that the Americans 'liked the Japanese better than the Koreans', who seemed 'headstrong, unruly, and obstreperous'.[30] Hodge's announcement created such an uproar among Koreans that MacArthur intervened, leading to the immediate replacement of Governor-General Abe and his top subordinates.[31]

Realizing that Korean sentiment dictated the rapid replacement of Japanese in government positions, General Hodge turned for advice to better educated Koreans who were often Christians, had extensive past experience with Americans, usually through missionaries, and spoke at least some English. The English-speakers often took jobs with the American military government as translators. Unfortunately, Hodge, in part because he was not authorized to recognize an indigenous Korean government, but mostly because he tended to view anyone to the left of center as unreliable, chose to ignore the KPR and to favor conservatives in the KDP, which included many Koreans resented by their countrymen for having done comparatively well under the Japanese.[32] The result was to reinforce divisions on the peninsula, among Koreans, who needed all the encouragement they could get to cooperate with each other, and between Americans and Soviets, the latter of whom were already well ensconced above the 38th Parallel. While not recognizing the Seoul-based KPR, the Soviets did work extensively with the people's committees at the local level in their zone.

Despite General Hodge's refusal to recognize the KPR or to consult extensively with its members, the group refused to retreat from its claim

---

[28]*New York Times*, 10 Sept. 1945.
[29]'HUSAFIK', Vol. 1, Ch. 4, 17; *FRUS, 1945*, 6: 1049.
[30]Cumings, *Origins*, 1: 138–9.
[31]*FRUS, 1945*, 6: 1045.
[32]For example, see 'HUSAFIK', Vol. 3, Ch. 2, 16.

to be a government and it continued to draw considerable support from the local press and the public. In early October, in an effort to undermine the KPR while at the same time showing sensitivity to the need to consult Koreans on a formal basis, the US military governor, Major General Archibald V. Arnold, appointed an Advisory Council of eleven Korean elders, nine of whom were conservatives.[33] A few days later General Arnold issued a scathing statement ridiculing the pretensions of KPR leaders and the behavior of much of the press, which wrote positively about them and criticized US actions. The remarks were particularly offensive in their use of such words as 'amateur', 'venal', 'self-styled', 'boyishness', and 'puppet' to characterize many Koreans who were of considerable age and stature in a society that placed high value on seniority and 'face'. Adding injury to insult, he ordered newspapers to publish his remarks.[34] The American occupation's campaign to prop up conservatives continued with efforts to arrange for the return of Rhee from the United States and KPG leaders from China. As a result, Rhee arrived in Korea during the third week of October and top KPG personnel appeared in late November and early December.[35]

As conservatives with reputations in their homeland and lacking any hint of collaboration with the Japanese, these men appeared to Hodge to be potential uniters of Rightist parties in the quest for stability and to squelch the Left. Yet the Commanding General got less than he had bargained for. Both Rhee and Kim Koo proved fiercely independent – of the United States as well as of each other. In particular, Rhee's open antagonism toward the Left and the Soviet Union strengthened the trend toward the division of the peninsula and the polarization of politics below the 38th Parallel. In late November William Langdon, the State Department's political adviser to the occupation, who had served in Korea during the 1930s, wrote home that 'in the Korean people are certain bad traits that cannot be overcome except by actual experience of their evil consequences: Division, obsequiousness, inordinate self seeking, strong sectional rivalries and intolerance of opposition'. He proposed that the United States move expeditiously toward creating an independent government in Korea and a joint withdrawal of occupation forces.[36]

---

[33]Richard D. Robinson, 'Betrayal of a Nation', 57. This unpublished manuscript was written by a member of the US occupation in the fall of 1947, immediately after he left Korea. It is available at the Harvard-Yenching Library, Cambridge, MA.

[34]Ibid., 55–6; 'HUSAFIK', Vol. 1, Ch. 8, 55–8.

[35]Cumings, *Origins*, 1: 188–93.

[36]*FRUS, 1945*, 6: 1131.

By mid-December 1945 General Hodge was so frustrated with conditions in south Korea, a result in his mind of the division of the peninsula into separate occupation zones and the disinclination of most Koreans to cooperate with either each other or the Americans, that he recommended to Tokyo and Washington 'serious consideration to an agreement' for joint foreign withdrawal from the country, thus leaving it 'to its own devices and an inevitable internal upheaval for its self purification'.[37] Four months later his frustrations boiled over in a report to Tokyo. Koreans were 'the most difficult of all peoples I have ever encountered', he declared. 'Independence' was their 'one common idea', and to them it meant 'that all should be freed from any distasteful work and from any and all restraint on actions or words'. 'Stubborn, ... highly contentious among themselves, ... highly volatile and unpredictable, ... [possessing] low individual integrity ... [and] low capacity for citizenship', they were 'pro self and anti most everything else'. 'Their history as a corruptly governed hermit nation before Japanese domination', Hodge continued, 'plus the years as a slave nation of Japan and the high illiteracy rate, operate[d] greatly against their capacity for competent self-rule in modern times'. '[T]here will be a real blood purge in Korea at some stage of her reestablishment', he predicted, and it could come during the American occupation. 'Pressed hard enough', the Commanding General warned, Koreans 'would happily open guerrilla warfare against occupying troops of any nation'.[38]

This diatribe included elements of truth, but General Hodge ignored the fact that some of his problems were rooted in American missteps, including his early encouragement of political groupings, however small, his disastrous effort to create a free market for rice that produced widespread hoarding and shortages, and Washington's effort against his advice to impose a multilateral trusteeship on Korea.[39]

To his credit, General Hodge initially did not insist on suppression of the people's committees at the local level. American officers in the provinces possessed considerable flexibility to work with those groups, which was often essential in maintaining order given the breakdown in authority of the Japanese police and the limited number of US troops available.[40] Had Hodge adopted as a more systematic and sustained policy of cooperation with the people's committees, he would have

---

[37]Ibid., 1148.

[38]As quoted in 'HUSAFIK', Vol. 1, Ch. 1, 143–4.

[39]On the encouragement of political groups and its impact, see Henderson, *Korea*, 113–36; on efforts to create a free rice market, see Cumings, *Origins*, 1: 202–206

[40]E. Grant Meade, *American Military Government in Korea* (New York: King's Crown Press 1951), 60–1.

greatly reduced the tasks of American forces, tasks made all the more difficult by the need to replace Japanese personnel as rapidly as possible and by the absence until the second half of October 1945 of a sizable group of civil administrators from the United States.

The need to work through local organizations was reinforced by the lack of training for Korea of both the tactical army commands and civil administrators. The latter had received some preparation for Japan, but had been reassigned once MacArthur decided in late September that it would be possible to depend on indigenous personnel there. None of the American administrators knew the Korean language and few knew anything about the people they were now supposed to help govern. E. Grant Meade, a civil administrator assigned to South Cholla province in the extreme southwest of the peninsula, later recalled that, in nine months of training prior to his October arrival in Korea, his sole exposure to the peninsula was in one one-hour lecture.

Lack of training aside, Meade estimated that, for reasons of limited intelligence and/or faulty character, over one in three of the men originally assigned to civil affairs were 'more of a liability than an asset'. Arrogance and condescension frequently accompanied ignorance and incompetence in the makeup of Americans in the occupation.[41]

Donald S. Macdonald, another civil affairs officer who wound up in South Cholla, recounted an incident involving a US major who served as commander of the military government in Kwangju, the provincial capital. One day a group of Koreans visited his office to suggest the name of a man to serve as the city's mayor. The American replied indignantly, 'Mayor? You must be kidding. We came here to kill all you people.'[42]

Although Koreans lived in a Confucian culture that respected rank, their experiences with US officers poorly versed in their immediate surroundings and often unconcerned about the feelings of those they were charged with governing undermined the authority of the American occupation.[43] Compounding the problem was the fact that the shortage of adequate officer personnel to serve in positions of authority meant that US enlisted men in their late teens and early twenties often found themselves giving orders to Koreans of considerably greater age and stature in their own communities, a circumstance that caused further strains between occupier and occupied. Such strains became magnified

---

[41]Ibid., 48–51.

[42]Macdonald Oral History, 'Frontline Diplomacy', <http://memory.loc.gov/ammen/collections/diplomacy/>.

[43]See, for example, Chon Suk-hi, 'Memory of August 15, 1945: Oral History of Forty Koreans' (Seoul: Hangilsa 2005), 109–10.

in early 1946, when Hodge began campaign to dismantle the people's committees.[44]

From the start the behavior of many rank-and-file US soldiers helped to erode Korean confidence in the occupation. Prior to 1945 the direct experience with Americans of most Koreans had been with the hundreds of missionaries who had flocked to the peninsula from the mid-1880s onward, and that experience had been largely positive.[45] US soldiers during the occupation, however, were a very different breed than the missionaries. One of the sources of their misbehavior, General Hodge would claim in early 1947, was the rapid replacement of 'those splendid combat soldiers' who had defeated the Japanese with poorly trained 'replacement troops who never fired a shot at the enemy'.[46] The 7th, 40th, and 6th US Army Divisions that occupied Korea did experience considerable turnover in the months leading up to September 1945, in part because they suffered substantial casualties in fighting the Japanese in Okinawa or the Philippines and required replacements, in part because the most battle-hardened infantrymen who survived were the most likely to be released from service first once the war ended. Even so, many American soldiers who entered Korea in September and October 1945 had fought the Japanese and the behavior of some of them was far from exemplary.[47]

By December 1945 most of the specific acts with which the US command contended as the occupation proceeded – open expressions of disrespect toward Koreans, lack of care in avoiding Korean pedestrians while driving American military vehicles, offensive advances toward Korean women, looting and larceny – were common. Brigadier General Donald J. Myers observed that, while there were always 'a few men with criminal tendencies' who discredited 'thousands of conscientious and trustworthy soldiers', many others made 'false step[s]' that led to courts-martial. He cited two men he had interviewed recently, one of whom 'had robbed a Korean of a worthless wristwatch', the other of whom had stolen 'a few worthless Japanese yen'. One of them had a wife and child in the United States, the other

---

[44]Meade, *American Military Government*, 8.

[45]Young Ick Lew, Byong-kie Song, Ho-min Yang, and Hy-sop Lim, *Korean Perceptions of the United States: A History of Their Origins and Formation*, trans. Michael Finch (Seoul: Jimoondang 2006), 1–306.

[46]RG 554, Entry A1 1370, box 50, 'Message from the Commanding General, US Armed Forces in Korea', attached to Col. Charles Ennis, Adjutant General, 'Distribution A', 17 Jan. 1947.

[47]In the 6th Division, for example, many officers and enlisted men who, theoretically, had accumulated enough points to be released immediately after Japan's surrender, were required to go to Korea in late September. See 'HUSAFIK', Vol. 1, Ch. 6, 35.

'a superior combat record'.[48] In the cases in which official records of courts-martial are available for crimes committed during the first three months of the occupation, two of the soldiers involved in misconduct entered the army in 1942. The entry date for the others remains uncertain.[49] On 8 December General Hodge wrote to a subordinate in charge of a key area between Seoul and Inchon that he was 'increasingly concerned about the behavior and seeming lack of integrity on the part of our soldiers ..., [including] many of the officer personnel'. In particular he mentioned 'licentiousness', 'hold-ups and robberies', and the acceptance of bribes from Koreans seeking possession of goods in Japanese warehouses. The General believed that such activities were sufficiently widespread to 'jeopardize the success of our occupation'.[50]

The fact is that qualities that make a person effective on the battlefield differ substantially from those needed for service in an occupation of foreign peoples, and the experience of war often diminishes any prior feelings of sympathy for others. The experience generally begins in a military training facility in the United States. One veteran of the Pacific War and the Korean occupation described Camp Hood in Texas, his site for basic training in late 1944, as an 'American concentration camp ... where young boys were robbed of their innocence and trained to do the killing necessary to finish the war'. He remembered one captain telling his unit that 'my main purpose in life ... is to change your attitude so that you will want to close with the enemy and kill him with your bare hands', and the officer conducted numerous drills to ensure success.[51]

The experience of war reinforced soldiers' training with a vengeance. Journalist Harold R. Isaacs, who spent much of the early 1940s in Asia and the Pacific and accompanied US forces to Korea in September 1945, later wrote that American combatants generally 'did not like' the Asian peoples with whom they came into contact, and the feeling was reciprocated. 'It could hardly have been otherwise', he noted, as 'war in general fosters callousness and indifference to suffering and

---

[48]RG 554, Entry A1 1370, Box 1, Brig. Gen. Donald J. Myers to Col. Edwin A. Henn, 12 Dec. 1945.

[49]The cases are Howard L. Waldron, 5 Nov. 1945, Box 241; Jerry L. Whitecotton, 13 Nov. 1945, Box 241; William J. Smith, 12 Jan. 1946, Box 238; Paul Jones, 24 Jan. 1946, Box 230; all in RG 554, General Courts-Martial.

[50]RG 554, Entry A1 1370, Box 1, Hodge to Maj. Gen. Gilbert R. Cheeves, 8 Dec. 1945.

[51]Russell E. McLogan, *Boy Soldier: Coming of Age During World War II* (Reading, MI: Terrus Press 1998), 21–2.

death ... [and] grotesquely deforms all human relations'. What is more, the American soldier:

> came from a life of gadgets and movies, schools, mass production, more or less good food, cars, juke boxes, radios, and corner drugstores. He was wrenched from all this and plunged abruptly into the midst of primitive misery. He vaguely expected the Orient to be a lush, glamorous, exciting, and somehow mysterious place. What he found was squalor and poverty and degradation.

American combatants had increasing difficulty viewing 'these Asiatics as men and women. Only some subhuman species could live as they did, submit as they did.... Pity usually gave way to indifference, impatience, contempt, and even hatred.'[52]

American veterans of the Pacific War who entered Korea in September and October 1945 possessed a sense of achievement for having defeated the Japanese in a prolonged and brutal conflict, as well as an understanding that they were liberating the peninsula from Japan's rule. As Isaacs observed, they had little preparation in their upbringing or education 'to be citizens of the world'. Their notion of themselves as part of a melting pot contributed to their pride, as did the sense that their country possessed 'the most, the best, the biggest, the tallest, the greatest, the finest, the deepest, the superlative in everything', which sheltered them from self-awareness, from the reality of their 'provincial' outlook. 'Profoundly convinced that everything not American is inferior', they regarded their task as achieved and longed to be home, out of the army. Such sentiments impeded empathy.[53]

So did the appearance of Koreans, distinctive in skin color and facial features, diminutive in stature, and clothed in white cotton jackets, pullover tops, and baggy pants tied around the ankles, all without buttons or zippers and with few if any pockets. Add to this the smell of the land, where open sewers flowed through the streets and human feces served as the primary fertilizer, and of the food, the main staple of which, other than rice, was *kimchi*, a marinated cabbage aged in garlic

---

[52]Isaacs, *No Peace in Asia*, 7–8. In a survey of early 1944 in Great Britain, American soldiers often expressed shock at the 'backwardness' of the English and their 'lower standard of living', responses that provide insight into how their compatriots in the Pacific theater felt in experiencing the far more primitive conditions there. See NA, [Office of Secretary Defense Records] RG 330, Headquarters, European Theater of Operations, US Army, Research Branch, SSD, Box 1015, 'What American Enlisted Men in England Think of the English', 21 March 1944.

[53]Isaacs, *No Peace in Asia*, 8–9.

and hot peppers, and American soldiers were well on the way toward an unhappy, contentious sojourn.[54]

Resentful of being held abroad after the war and aware that they were doing Koreans a great favor in removing the Japanese, American soldiers initially tended to be friendly to their hosts, especially children, but they expected deference in return.[55] When they did not get it – and as time passed they increasingly did not – they responded in a less than kindly fashion. Given the widespread poverty of the native population and the habits built up over two generations of relations with their Japanese masters, many Koreans engaged in petty theft against the occupying troops and their supply depots. Some native women resorted to prostitution to provide income for themselves and their families. While many American soldiers happily availed themselves of this service, they were not deterred from making overt passes at more 'respectable' Korean women, which violated local mores and sparked resentment and sometimes open antagonism in Korean men.

In October a printed warning circulated, revealing both the resentment of Korean men and the receptiveness of some Korean women to the overtures of American men. 'We could not overlook you, womanhood', the English translation of the document began, 'when you fool around with westerners in just showing your vanity and worldly devices, which is nothing but scandalous, while you should put all your strength on establishing the state of new Korea.' It went on to identify several 'scandalous actions' that Korean women were urged to avoid lest they 'be insulted right in front of public' by better behaved Koreans among them. These included 'riding automobiles with westerners', winking and greeting them with friendly words, chewing gum in public, 'whispering to westerners in the night', and going to dance halls frequented by westerners to enjoy 'coffee and chocolate'.[56] The document illustrates both the restrictiveness of relations between the sexes outside the family among respectable Koreans and the exclusiveness and protectiveness against outsiders of the prevailing

---

[54]For a description of Korean attire, see *National Geographic Magazine* 88 (Oct. 1945), 436. For examples of American soldiers' reaction to the smell of Korea, see McLogan, *Coming of Age*, 306; W. L. Dixon, 'Recollections of Korea', *Baltimore and Ohio Magazine* Aug. 1950, 8–9; and Richard A. Ericson, Jr., Oral History, 'Frontline Diplomacy', < http://memory.loc.gov/ammen/collections/diplomacy/ >.

[55]'HUSAFIK', Vol. 1, Ch. 8, 64.

[56]As quoted in 'HUSAFIK', Vol. 1, Ch. 8, 66. Chon Sang-in, 'haepang kong' ganui sahoesa' [Political geography and social history of Korea, 1945–1950], in Park Chi-hyang *et al.* (eds.), *haepangchonhusaui/chaeinsik (chaeinsik)* [The New Interpretation of Korean History between Liberation and the Korean War], (Seoul: Ch'aeksesang 2006), Vol. II, 159.

insular, patriarchal culture. Rape charges by Koreans against the occupying troops were common, in part because Koreans, at least when American males made passes at native women, defined rape in a manner that involved what they considered inappropriate overtures but not necessarily physical contact.[57]

US occupiers of Germany and Japan behaved much the same way as their countrymen in Korea, but those countries were defeated nations whose people possessed far different psychologies and cultures than Koreans. In Japan, for example, authorities went to considerable lengths to prepare 'comfort facilities' for the sexual gratification of American soldiers once they arrived. To be sure, resentments did develop among Japanese and German males over the aggressiveness of the occupying troops toward native women, but to a significantly lesser degree. In part the depleted male populations in Japan and Germany as a result of the huge war casualties explains this difference. In Korea, in contrast, men were at least as plentiful as women.[58]

If US combat veterans did their fair share to diminish the American reputation with Koreans, they received plenty of help from newer recruits. Certainly they lacked the training and discipline of their predecessors in the Army while possessing all the provincialism and sense of superiority of their older comrades, if not their dehumanizing experience in fighting the Japanese. When in mid-December 1945 Hodge ordered his top subordinates to intensify their educational efforts 'on propriety, behavior and conduct of officers and men' in his command and 'strong punitive action against offenders', the need was manifest among a broad range of soldiers.[59]

---

[57]Lawrence Gelfand to William Stueck, 27 Feb. 2009. Rapes by Western standards did occur and, when reported, sparked considerable outrage among Koreans. In Jan. 1946, for example, four armed GIs raped three Korean female passengers in a railroad compartment while threatening the lives of other passengers. All the perpetrators were captured, tried by court martial, convicted, and sentenced to life imprisonment. For expressions of outrage over the incident in the Korean press, see *Choson Ilbo*, 10 and 12 Jan. 1946. For the conviction and sentencing, see *New York Times*, 6 March 1947.

[58]Japanese census reports on Korea from 1940 and 1944 both indicated a slightly larger male population than female. See George M. McCune, *Korea Today* (Cambridge, MA: Harvard UP 1950), 328. On the interaction of American GIs with German women after the war in the context of a shortage of German men, see Petra Goedde, *GIs and Germans: Culture, Gender, and Foreign Relations, 1945–1949* (New Haven, CT: Yale UP 2003). On American GIs and Japanese women, see John Dower, *Embracing Defeat: Japan in the Wake of World War II* (New York: W.W. Norton 1999), 121–67; on Japanese war casualties, see John Dower, *War Without Mercy: Race and Power in the Pacific War* (New York: Pantheon Books 1986), 296–9.

[59]In addition to the documents cited in footnotes 44 and 46 above, see RG 554, Entry A1 1370, Box 1, Maj. Gen. C. E. Hudris to Hodge, 14 Dec. 1945.

General Hodge's efforts had limited impact, in part because of an increasing shortage of officers, particularly ones of high character and experience.[60] In March 1946, in the face of evidence of growing distaste among Koreans about the actions of US soldiers, Hodge again admonished his forces to behave themselves, and even authorized Korean police to apprehend and deliver to American authorities US personnel caught in serious criminal acts.[61] In November 1946 the Commanding General launched a courtesy drive, among other things listing ten specific acts by American soldiers about which Koreans complained.[62]

Yet persuading – or forcing – American troops to treat Koreans with respect was no easy task. The fact was that what limited interaction had occurred between the average US soldier and low-level officers and the average Korean had not endeared the one to the other. American journalists who visited Korea picked this up immediately. In mid-October 1946, after landing at Kimpo Airport outside Seoul, Mark Gayn was escorted in a 'sedan' into the city by a 'young lieutenant', who 'spoke of the Koreans with contempt' as 'dirty and treacherous'. 'We were watching a flight of [US] fighter planes cavorting over villages to the west', Gayn recorded in his diary. 'The planes dived in a mock attack, re-formed in the sky, and then dived on a new target'. '"Psychological warfare", the lieutenant said. "That's the only way to show these gooks we won't stand for any monkey business".' Late that night, in walking through the streets of Seoul with Roy Roberts, an Associated Press correspondent, Gayn was 'amazed . . . [by] the number of drunk Koreans and GIs. I saw an American arguing with a Korean. The soldier was holding the Korean by the lapels of his coat and shouting, "I'll show you, you goddamned gook!"' After intervening to break up the confrontation, Roberts told Gayn, 'such incidents are frequent and generate much resentment against Americans'.[63]

At the end of 1946, Walter Simmons of the *Chicago Tribune* engaged in conversation American military men aboard a ship transporting them from Korea to Japan. 'How do you like Korea?' the GIs in the ship lounge were asked. An army sergeant from Michigan 'snorted' that 'there is as much difference between Japan and Korea as . . . between the United States and Japan', and the comparison did not favor Korea.

---

[60]On the shortage of experienced officers, see RG 554, Entry A1 1370, Box 1, Brig. Gen. Donald J. Myers to Col. Edwin A. Henn, 12 Dec. 1945, and Maj. Gen. C.E. Hudris to Hodge, 14 Dec. 1945.

[61]Ibid., Hodge to USAFIK, 3 March 1946, and Hodge to major commanders, 3 March 1946.

[62]See ibid., Box 24, Circular 'Courtesy Drive', 6 Nov. 1946.

[63]Mark Gayn, *Japan Diary* (Rutland, VT: Charles E. Tuttle 1981), 349, 354.

A private from Oklahoma chimed in that 'the worse you treat the Korean, the more he likes you. The only things they understand are the ball bat and pick handle.' Another private, this time from Pennsylvania, remarked that 'the Japanese are friendly. The Koreans are hostile.... You treat the Korean nice and he cheats you. You leave anything around, and the next minute it is gone'. 'This outpouring ... continued for a long time', Simmons reported, 'and no GI had a kind word to say for the Koreans'. A long-silent army captain eventually confessed to Simmons that 'I've spend over a year in Korea and I am afraid we are failing in the job of making friends with the people. The GI is wrong in some ways, but on the whole I am afraid he is justified in his attitude.'[64]

General Hodge's sternest missive to his troops came on 17 January 1947. 'I get increasing expression from Koreans in all walks of life', he told them, 'to the effect that the American officers and men ... are incurring disfavor ... because of poor behavior and because of their 'superior attitude'. After describing five types of soldier who created a negative image of the United States among Koreans – from ones who 'walk five or six abreast down the street shouldering aside the citizens of the town with great contempt' to 'rapists, murderers, hold-up men, and thieves' – he admonished his troops 'to learn something about Korean customs' and 'to respect them in your dealings with Koreans'. 'Take your shoes off when you enter a Korean's home', he urged, and 'keep your hands off Korean women'. Stop 'laughing *at*' Koreans, calling them by 'derogatory' names, and treating them as members of a 'conquered nation': 'we are here to help the Korean People not run over them', the commander declared. The Korean 'bows and speaks deferentially because he is polite, not because he is currying favor. He has a long proud history (4,000 years) back of his nationality, and though polite and friendly, he is very proud', Hodge noted. 'Openly misjudging him' produced 'resentment', and if he is pushed too far, 'you'll find yourself on the receiving end of a club, knife, or brickbat'. The General concluded with a plea for self-examination on the part of his troops and for them to 'give a helping hand to the new arrivals as they come in and afterward'.[65]

There is no reason to believe that the behavior of American troops improved dramatically as a result of General Hodge's efforts. One reason was the ongoing poor morale of US soldiers produced by the relatively harsh material conditions they faced. These conditions derived partly from the general poverty of Korea, which was

---

[64]*Chicago Tribune*, 16 Dec. 1946.
[65]RG 554, Entry A1 1378, Box 50, 'Message from the Commanding General, US Armed Forces in Korea', attached to Col. Charles Ennis, Adjutant General, 'Distribution A', 17 Jan. 1947.

exacerbated by its ongoing division into occupations zones that were economically complementary but increasingly isolated from each other as relations between the Soviets and the Americans deteriorated. Yet a weak supply system from the United States and within the US zone greatly worsened the problem. Complaints about conditions in Korea from soldiers there and their loved ones at home surfaced before the end of 1945 and grew to such proportions in late 1946 and early 1947 that they drew substantial attention from American legislators.

In September 1946, after visiting US military installations abroad with a group of colleagues, Congressman John Sheridan (Democrat, Pennsylvania), the acting chairman of the House Military Affairs Committee, singled out the American occupation in Korea for criticism. Troop morale there was the lowest anywhere in the world, as soldiers faced conditions in which even fruit juice and toothpaste were luxuries. The politician called for the removal of Hodge from his command.[66]

In early November 1947 an American civilian attached to the US Army in Pusan told journalist Mark Gayn that supplies had improved somewhat in 'some of the bigger towns' after the congressional visit, but were still abysmal in more remote areas. 'This is not a disciplined war army', Gayn was told, but 'a peacetime army of boys 18 and 20, who have had only eight weeks of basic training before they came here'. Little was being done outside the 'big towns ... to keep up their morale. No radios, few movies, little athletic equipment'.[67] Mail from home to US soldiers, which often included food items, was terribly slow in arriving. During the holiday season that followed Gayn's visit, 3,991 bags of mail headed to Korea were lost at sea, a further blow to morale.[68]

The New Year 1947 brought little relief for the American command in Korea. Rhee had arrived in Washington to lobby against US occupation policies and one of his supporters, the energetic Robert T. Oliver, a professor on leave from Syracuse University in upstate New York, informed the State Department that he planned to urge members of Congress to provide no more appropriations to continue military government on the peninsula.[69] With the executive branch engaged in an in-depth review of US policy toward Korea, General Hodge returned home for consultations. Arriving in Washington in mid February,

---

[66]Lauterbach, *Danger from the East*, 225.

[67]Gayn, *Japan Diary*, 409–10.

[68]NA, [War Department Records] RG 165, box 249, 'Letter from a civilian contractor to her family', 25 Dec. 1946.

[69]RG 59, 740.00119 CONTROL (KOREA)/1-2047, Box 3825, Memorandum of Conversation on Korea between Dr Robert T. Oliver and John Z. Williams, 20 Jan. 1947.

THE KOREAN WAR AT SIXTY

Hodge brought with him extensive reports to address the growing correspondence received by the War Department from Capitol Hill complaining about conditions in Korea. 'The primary causes of discontent', one report concluded, ranged from inadequate food – in quality and quantity – a lack of potable water, primitive housing, scarce entertainment, and the limited opportunity to attend church services. The gist of Hodge's response was, as one of his subordinate officers wrote, that 'many of the complaints are ... groundless, beyond the control of this command, [a]natural result of lack of facilities or resources, or ... plain ignorance'. 'The American people have come to accept their comforts and relatively high standard of living', the officer continued, 'without giving thought to the effort that goes into providing those facilities and comforts. The result is a complaining, whining individual when they are not available.'[70]

Hodge's reports did not curb the complaints. On 21 March, General Dwight D. Eisenhower, the Army Chief of Staff, wrote to General MacArthur in Tokyo that 'a steadily increasing number of congressional inquiries concerning alleged unsatisfactory conditions in Korea', mostly an outgrowth of letters from soldiers there, might result in a formal investigation by the legislative branch. 'I believe that this matter is [of] sufficient importance to warrant a thorough investigation by your HQ [Headquarters]', Eisenhower advised.[71]

MacArthur, who rarely devoted much attention to Korea, avoided a congressional investigation only by following Eisenhower's advice and dispatching a 'high-powered staff group' to the peninsula. Arriving on 15 March 1947, from the start the group was favorably disposed toward Hodge. But its members conducted a thorough, two-and-a-half-week tour of the US occupation zone, visiting dozens of bases and interviewing hundreds of officers, enlisted men, and draftees. They concluded that, while earlier in the winter morale had been low, the cause was not poor leadership in Korea; rather it was the arrival as the coldest weather set in of 30,000 inexperienced replacement troops – the third major turnover of personnel since September 1945 – most of whom had been seriously misled by army recruiters at home about the conditions they could expect in Korea. Yet despite the erratic 'internal distribution of available stocks', 'a primitiveness in sewage disposal and other sanitary processes', a frequent scarcity of potable water, and the absence of many other amenities available stateside, food was more than adequate, the health of the troops was 'excellent', and their morale was on the upswing. The inspectors reported that 'the majority of

---

[70]RG 554, Entry A11378, Box 83, Col. Charles Ennis, 'Complaints to Members of Congress', 12 Feb. 1947.
[71]RG 554, Entry A1 1370, Box 2, Eisenhower to MacArthur, 21 March 1947.

recent complaints ... coming to ... the War Department and the press through soldiers' letters to their parents ... have exaggerated actual conditions to the point of fantasy and falsity'. Insofar as problems had arisen and continued to exist, responsibility, the inspectors hinted, rested at least as much with the War Department at home as the leadership in the field.[72]

Although the report was not a total whitewash of the occupation, it did diverge sharply from views expressed by many of the soldiers in Korea and their loved ones at home. One letter signed by 11 soldiers, who sarcastically labeled themselves 'Just a bunch of Sissies', was written sometime during the spring of 1947. This group began by declaring that 'we did not join the army expecting to find a bed of roses. But we did expect to live like civilized people, ... at least as good as the Occupation troops in nearby Japan or Germany.' Self-righteous, yet conscious that their protest would reach at least some unsympathetic eyes, they queried, 'Is it expecting too much to desire a shower more than once in four weeks? Is it expecting too much to have as our *only* recreation to get drunk once in a while? ... Is it being a Sissy to expect to have your blackest washed once in seven months?' This was merely the beginning of a litany of complaints: 'the mail service stinks', 'most of the food isn't fit for dogs', there are no 'light bulbs or brooms for our huts', and medical care is sparse and delinquent.[73]

Fred Ottoboni, a 19-year-old from Santa Rosa, California, who arrived in Korea in January 1947 and was stationed outside Kunsan on the west coast nearly 200 miles via rail and road from Seoul, noted a half-century later that by springtime his normal weight of 150 pounds, at which he 'had been called skinny', was down to 120. Food had become increasingly scarce as supplies had not kept up with the influx of soldiers into the base. Overall, conditions were so bad that in early March a group of soldiers in the camp briefly 'staged what might be called a mutiny'. Ottoboni sympathized with the mutineers, although he confined his complaints to conversations with fellow soldiers and letters home to his mother, who complained to the War Department.[74] A group of mothers from Dearborn, Michigan, also lodged a complaint. Just because Korea 'is supposed to be the end of the supply

---

[72]The report is quoted extensively in Col. Charles H. Donnelly, 'Autobiography', 869–71, unpublished manuscript, US Military History Institute, Carlisle Barracks, PA, Donnelly Papers.

[73]RG 554, Entry A1 1370, Box 2, Attachment to Hodge to Maj. Gen. Floyd L. Parks, 8 June 1947.

[74]Fred Ottoboni, *Korea Between the Wars: A Soldier's Story* (Sparks, NV: Vincente Books 1997), 128–33. The only point on which Ottoboni's account disagrees with that of the 'Sissies' is medical care, which Ottoboni considered adequate and timely.

line is no excuse for lack of properly prepared food and the necessary medical attention for the boys there', they asserted. They went on to question the need for the United States to maintain troops on the peninsula: 'Why can't the Korean occupation forces be recalled?'[75]

To most Americans who had even heard of the occupation of Korea, the answer to that question was far from obvious. American troops sent to that country understood little more, except that the United States was liberating it from Japan. By 1947 the Japanese in Korea had returned home, thus making US purposes all the more dubious.

The 'Sissies' and mutineers among American troops in Korea, though vocal, represented a distinct minority. True, most soldiers lacked the discipline of those in the wartime army, had enlisted to become eligible for GI benefits, and had been misled by recruiters regarding the conditions to expect in service abroad, particularly in Korea.[76] Yet they had grown up during the Great Depression, many of them on farms on which amenities such as electricity, indoor plumbing, and bountiful food were exceptions and hard work an everyday routine. Carl Vipperman, an 18-year-old from West Virginia, was one such recruit, arriving in Korea in January 1947 on a 16-month tour. Stationed in a rural area not far from the 38th Parallel, he reflected in 2008 that he and his fellow soldiers considered their sojourn 'a great adventure'. Conditions were rugged, of course, but not altogether unlike their childhood experiences. His strongest negative memory was of treatment at the hands of some officers, who often behaved as 'horse's asses'.[77]

In fact, the poor quality of officers at the unit level and above, if not at the top, was more the rule than the exception in Korea. Ottoboni recalled that most of the young men with whom he enlisted already had graduated from high school and wanted to attend college, but needed government assistance through the GI bill to do so. They 'were curious young adults who thought a great deal about many things', he wrote in his memoir, and they were taken aback by 'an almost total lack of communication between the people in charge and the enlistees about the what, where, and why of our

---

[75]RG 554, Entry A1 1370, Box 2, 'Communistic Letter from "Moms" of America', [undated].

[76]In the aftermath of the Japanese surrender, local draft boards often failed to meet their quotas, thus placing pressure on army recruiters to entice young men to enlist. See unpublished manuscript in the Office of the Chief of Military History, Ft McNair, Washington DC, OCMH-66, 'The All-Volunteer Army of 1947–1948'.

[77]Stueck interview with Carl Vipperman, 29 July 2008. Vipperman subsequently used his GI benefits to pursue a higher education, including a PhD in history. Eventually he became a professor of history at the University of Georgia.

tour of duty'. Concerned about their poor training at home, they questioned early on in their stay in Korea if the Army was 'serious about anything'. The poor management of supplies and equipment in transit, they came to realize, was a notable source of the shortages that produced their discomfort. On the 30-mile trip by truck on bumpy dirt roads from the railroad station in Ili to the base outside Kunsan, for example, many of the soldiers' duffel bags were poorly stored and lost, leaving many of the men with inadequate clothing to maintain warmth or good hygiene through the cold Korean winter. Later, in a visit to Kunsan, Ottoboni and others in his unit purchased from Koreans a variety of food items of US Army origin, an indication that many of the supplies that entered Inchon, their main port of entry, did not reach their intended destination. The reason? They were stolen by Koreans or sold by American supply officers and soldiers to Koreans for resale on the black market.

Resentments in the rank-and-file in rural areas built up as well over the superior lifestyles of the officers that commanded them, not to mention over that of the soldiers fortunate enough to be stationed in the Seoul area. Rumor had it that General MacArthur's command in Tokyo made sure that the best officers sent to the western Pacific went to Japan and that those who performed poorly there often wound up in Korea.[78] Historical records suggest the truth of the rumor.[79] Furthermore, as the occupations proceeded word spread among officers in the United States that there were three things to avoid if sent to the western Pacific, 'gonorrhea, diarrhea, and Korea', so the more resourceful and better connected ones undoubtedly maneuvered to avoid being assigned to the peninsula.[80]

Although overt malcontents represented a small minority of American soldiers in Korea, they did make the occupation more difficult to sustain. As General Hodge remarked in one of his letters to critics in the United States, 'each of them makes a noise like a pig under

---

[78]Ottoboni, *Korea Between the Wars*, 78–9, 85, 129–30, 140, 146–7.

[79]On the poor general quality of officers in Korea and/or the inclination of the Tokyo command to keep the best in Japan, see RG 554, Entry A1 1370, Box 2, Paul S. Anderson to Hodge, 27 June 1947; Box 1, Hodge to Maj. Gen. Cheeves, 8 Dec. 1945; Box 1, Brig. Gen. Donald J. Myers to Col. Edwin A. Henn, 12 Dec. 1945; Box 2, Hodge to major commanders, 3 Jan. 1948. See also Lauterbach, *Danger from the East*, 223–4; Meade, *American Military Government in Korea*, 87–9; William C. Sherman Oral History, 27 Oct. 1993, 3, 'Frontline Diplomacy', <http://memory.loc.gov/ammen/collections/diplomacy/>; and Robert Smith, *MacArthur in Korea: The Naked Emperor* (New York: Simon & Schuster 1982), 18.

[80]The quoted phrase was allegedly uttered publicly by Hodge as a widespread perception in Japan in Nov. 1947. See Harry G. Summers, 'The Korean War: A Fresh Perspective', *Military Affairs*, April 1996, 2.

a gate', and that noise clearly reached Capitol Hill.[81] After a series of flare-ups during the first half of 1947, Hodge's efforts to orient troops once they arrived in Korea and his and the Pentagon's public relations measures directed at concerned citizens in the United States appear to have reduced overt discontent among US soldiers on the peninsula.[82]

Negative reports from higher-ups on the behavior of Korean political elites joined with complaints from the field by rank-and-file soldiers to provide an important context within which the Pentagon pressed for an early end to the occupation and a final withdrawal of US troops and Congress proved reluctant to appropriate funds to sustain what were considered minimal American interests in Korea.[83] Rhee and his allies maneuvered furiously from early 1946 onward to prevent an agreement between the United States and the Soviet Union to end the artificial division of Korea, which they feared would doom the peninsula to domination by the Communists. By the middle of 1946 they were campaigning for creation of an independent government in the south, and this campaign often included advocacy of a joint withdrawal of foreign troops. Hodge tried to counter the campaign. For example, in January 1947, amid growing agitation among Koreans and discontent among his own troops, he issued a press release defending US policy and asserting that his country remained determined to stay 'to bring about the unification of a free and democratic Korea'. Despite his own private reservations, he defended the agreement on Korea made at Moscow in December 1945 by the Soviet, American, and British foreign ministers. While including the possibility of a multipower trusteeship, the agreement called for a joint Soviet–American commission to create a united Korean provisional government. Through this decision, Hodge asserted in a none-to-subtle reminder of the circumstances leading to Japan's departure, 'the Allied Powers assured the world that [the] blood, lives, and resources expended by them in making possible ... [Korean's liberation] would not be wasted, and that Korea would be independent'. He scolded the 'certain elements' who, 'through lack of knowledge or through malicious intent', were deceiving the people in 'creating the impression that the United States now favors and is actively working toward a separate government in

---

[81]RG554, A1 1370, Box 2, Hodge to Cecil Brown, 10 June 1947.

[82]Much of the effort by Hodge and his command is documented in correspondence in ibid., Boxes 1–3. Hodge also wrote 'With the US Army in Korea', which appeared in the June 1947 issue of the popular magazine *National Geographic*, 829–40.

[83]Gen. William O. Reeder, an army supply officer in Washington during this time told Stueck in an interview on 21 Oct. 1974 that the chief reason for the withdrawal of troops from Korea was the constant complaints of American soldiers and their loved ones to the Pentagon and Congress.

Southern Korea'.[84] Hodge's efforts came to naught. Because a Communist Korea was also anathema to the United States, it refused to suppress the Rhee forces and eventually executed a plan that in August 1948 left them in a dominant position in an independent government below the 38th Parallel.

Yet the weakness of that government relative to the emergent regime in North Korea now led Rhee to lobby for the continued presence of US Army units. His campaign came to a head in May 1949, when the US State Department finally ended its resistance to Pentagon efforts to remove the remaining American troops. On 7 May the ROK government released a statement that sought either the continued presence of those forces or a public assurance of US protection against outside attack. In this quest the statement distorted the circumstances under which the country had become divided, implying that it was the fault of the United States that Communists were in Korea and threatened the ROK and omitting the role Rhee had played in sabotaging the American effort to reach agreement with the Soviets on creation of a national provisional government.[85] ROK leaders received neither a reversal of the decision to withdraw forces nor an assurance of protection. Rather, US diplomats warned them that they must do more to put their own house in order, including a buildup of their own army, and to avoid provocations along the tense 38th Parallel boundary, where skirmishes between the ROK and DPRK armies were commonplace. When the ROK ambassador in Washington noted with concern to American officials that the United States was distancing itself from the Nationalist government in China as the Communists advanced there, he was told that South Koreans should learn from that case that US aid could not stem the Communist tide unless indigenous forces put up a stiff resistance.[86]

Among other things, the exchange revealed the deep psychological chasm existing between officials of the two governments. On the one hand were people representing the richest, most powerful nation on earth, who were attempting to cobble together a new global order in the face of concerted opposition from without and only limited acquiescence from many of their countrymen. To US officials dealing with Korea, ROK leaders were a contentious, willful group that showed little appreciation for the American role in freeing their country from Japan, had enormously complicated the American task in the

---

[84]*Department of State Bulletin*, 19 Jan. 1947, 128.

[85]*FRUS, 1949*, 7: 1011–12.

[86]See documents in ibid., 1013–21; also Ambassador Muccio's oral history at the Harry S. Truman Library, Independence, MO. Muccio gave a similar account in his interview with author Stueck on 27 Dec. 1973 in Washington DC.

recent occupation, and now presided over a corrupt, autocratic, and often inept government facing active resistance from a significant portion of the South Korean populace. That regime constantly sought aid, resisted any strings attached, and attempted to maneuver the United States into an open-ended commitment to its survival. Such a pledge was out of the question, not the least because it might encourage ROK belligerence toward the North – unnecessarily provoking a conflict that was contrary to American interests – and/or discourage the government from pursuing domestic policies that would broaden public support and enhance prospects for economic development. Under the circumstances, the overt ROK campaign for a clear US commitment simply underscored its absence, thus undermining a more modest effort to deter an outside attack.

On the other hand were people from a small nation that had for centuries sought to isolate itself from the outside world. It had largely succeeded in doing so through a loose attachment to a benevolent, unobtrusive China, in the Confucian worldview its 'elder brother'. In the late nineteenth century Korea was dragged unwillingly into relations with the larger world, was fought over by the three great powers surrounding it, and then, early in the twentieth century, was conquered by the strongest among them. Their country too weak to win independence on its own, Korean exiles sought the assistance of stronger powers, but divided over their preferred patron. When they finally escaped the Japanese grasp in 1945, it was at the price of occupation by two other great powers, both of whom held interests and perceptions that conflicted with Koreans' desire for immediate independence. In the end, those who became ROK leaders chose to postpone unity so as to grasp independence under conditions in which they dominated half the country. Having achieved that objective, partly through manipulation of the United States, they found themselves in the uncomfortable position of resenting their sponsor for its condescension and its failure in 1945 to prevent Soviet entry into the North, yet expecting it to play the 'elder brother' role in providing protection against hostile outside forces.[87]

Given those divergent perspectives, it hardly should be surprising that the United States failed to employ measures adequate to deter an outside attack on the ROK. Even Ambassador Muccio, a patient diplomat more sympathetic than most Americans to South Korean leaders, was distrustful enough to ensure that the allocation of US military aid to the ROK was sufficiently piecemeal to discourage adventurism toward the North.[88] In the summer of 1950, the strong

---

[87]Lew *et al.*, *Korean Perceptions of the United States*, 315–18.
[88]Stueck interview with Muccio, 27 Dec. 1973, Washington DC.

American response to the DPRK military offensive derived more from concern about its potential impact on the reputation of the United States worldwide than on sympathy for ROK leaders or the Korean people.[89]

Creating and Sustaining an Alliance

It would be a distortion to suggest that the Korean War completely transformed the attitudes toward each other of the peoples or policy elites of the United States and South Korea. Evidence is not hard to find after 1953 to demonstrate continuing condescension, frustration, and even disdain on the part of Americans toward South Koreans. Nor is it difficult to unearth evidence of resentment, outrage, and resistance among South Koreans toward their allies across the Pacific. Yet such feelings did not influence the relationship to the degree that they had during the American occupation from 1945 to 1948, and this is the case even though the firing stopped in July 1953 with over 300,000 American troops on the peninsula, a figure that declined to under 60,000 three years later but then held at over 40,000 until the late 1970s, at 37,000 until the second Bush administration, and now has stabilized at around 27,000. The second American occupation of Korea that began in July 1950 in response to the North Korean attack proved more acceptable to both sides than the first. The question is, why?

The answer is in some ways straightforward. Unlike during the first American occupation, South Koreans now possessed their own government. The ROK grudgingly conceded elements of its sovereignty to accommodate foreign soldiers on its soil and confronted often unwelcome advice on their political, economic, and military affairs, but these paled by comparison to the humiliation of being lectured to by General Hodge and his subordinates on the need for patience on the road to self-government. Furthermore, for over three years the United States had fought side-by-side with South Koreans to defend the ROK, providing massive materiel support and suffering over 150,000 casualties. South Koreans had seen the result of the US withdrawal in 1949, they appreciated the American willingness to help save them from 1950 to 1953, and they understood that a continued US presence, both for military protection and for economic recovery, was essential for their continued survival. The United States had finally played the role of elder brother to the Koreans and its sacrifices had raised the peninsula to a significance in US strategy that was unthinkable prior to June 1950. The ROK and its people were taken far more seriously in

---

[89]Stueck, *Road to Confrontation*, 185–90.

Washington than ever before, and they knew and appreciated the fact.[90]

The psychology on the American side shifted as well, partly because the sacrifices of war had been shared, partly because Korea had become a major theater in the Cold War. While Koreans had contributed little to their liberation from the Japanese, the ROK Army played an essential role in defending the Pusan perimeter against the North Korean onslaught in August 1950 and by the end of the war manned over 70 percent of the front line units in the United Nations Command. Between 1950 and 1953, the ROK Army suffered over three and one-half times the battlefield deaths of US armed forces.[91] In addition, the war produced a major growth in US military preparedness and, with Korea now enjoying a far higher priority among American officials and the public, the most competent and ambitious members of the armed forces had little reason to avoid service there.[92] Not only could they anticipate major support from home if sent to the peninsula; they could be confident that service in Korea was a likely stepping-stone to career-advancement. Thus morale among American soldiers in Korea never reached the depths after the war that it had during the first occupation, and the level of competence and efficiency was much higher.

To be sure, the United States remained a country with more than its share of racial prejudice and sense of cultural superiority. If insensitivity toward Koreans on the part of American soldiers gradually diminished during the second occupation, it never disappeared. During the 1980s, anti-Americanism surfaced as never before in South Korea,

---

[90]For an elaboration on this point, see William Stueck, *Rethinking the Korean War: A New Diplomatic and Strategic History* (Princeton, NJ: Princeton UP 2002), 192–206.
[91]John Kie-chiang Oh, 'The Forgotten Soldiers of the Korean War', in Mark F. Wilkinson (ed.), *The Korean War at Fifty: International Perspectives* (Lexington: Virginia Military Institute 2004), 101–15. Jack Cox, who graduated from West Point in 1949 and served in the Korean War as an army lieutenant from Oct. 1950 to Feb. 1952, recalled recently that he heard all kinds of negative stories about Koreans before he went to the peninsula, including that they would constantly steal from Americans and would never truly be friends with foreigners. He took about three months to develop a positive attitude toward Koreans. The realization that South Koreans really cared about their country, were willing to fight and die for it, and were more often than not willing to police each other to contain pilfering from their foreign benefactors produced the change. Stueck interview with Cox, 26 Nov. 2007, Fayetteville, NC.
[92]In stark contrast to the situation prior to the war, 'by 1953', historian Steven Casey concludes, 'South Korea could count on an enormous amount of sympathy inside the United States'. See Steven Casey, *Selling the Korean War: Propaganda, Politics, and Public Opinion 1950–1953* (New York: OUP 2008), 352–3. On Korean War rearmament in the United States, see William Stueck, 'Reassessing US Strategy in the Aftermath of the Korean War', *Orbis* 53 (Fall 2009).

now well advanced toward a modern economy, populated increasingly by people with little or no direct memory of the Korean War, and still saddled with an autocratic government supported by the United States. Democracy flourished after 1987, of course, but as the first decade of the twenty-first century progressed public opinion polls in the ROK frequently revealed a high level of distrust of and even animosity toward the United States and the presence of its forces on the peninsula.[93]

Yet that presence continues, and is likely to do so indefinitely. Ongoing concerns about regional stability and the security of a small nation surrounded by giants surely provide the major impetus here, but cultural and psychological factors deserve a place in any explanation of the enduring alliance. Failed marriages often occur because one partner changes while the other remains static, or because changes in both partners move in opposite directions. In the cases of the United States and South Korea since the first American occupation, the movement has been more toward convergence than distance. Whether in the smell of the land, the accessibility of the food, or the dress, linguistic range, educational achievements, modes of transportation, production, and entertainment of the people, South Korea has become much more similar to the United States. True, the surface convergence sometimes hides deeper, enduring differences and it has made South Koreans less willing to tolerate American arrogance, either in the behavior of US soldiers on the streets or in the bars of Seoul and other towns and cities in their land or of US generals, diplomats, and politicians in the councils of government.

Still, accompanying the convergence has been a steady if gradual shift in responsibility and power within the alliance – for example, toward granting the ROK justice system control over off-duty US soldiers who break the laws of the land, toward complete ROK control over its own armed forces, and toward ROK assumption of a larger share of the cost of maintaining US forces on the peninsula and of defending military positions on the ground north of Seoul. Indeed, the evolution of power and responsibility within the alliance since the 1960s inspires confidence that the changing psychological and cultural needs of both sides can be adjusted to accommodate the enduring if also changing strategic rationales for the alliance.

---

[93]See, for example, Yoichi Funabashi, *The Peninsula Question: A Chronicle of the Second Korean Nuclear Crisis* (Washington DC: Brookings 2007), 218; Mike Chinoy, *Meltdown: The Inside Story of the North Korean Nuclear Crisis* (New York: St Martin's Press 2008), 100, 154–5, 160, 190, 202; Chae-jin Lee, *A Troubled Peace: US Policy and the Two Koreas* (Baltimore: Johns Hopkins UP 2006), 193, 226–7, 247.

Bibliography

Casey, Steven, *Selling the Korean War: Propaganda, Politics, and Public Opinion 1950–1953* (New York: OUP 2008).

Che, Sonny, *Forever Alien: A Korean Memoir, 1930–1951* (Jefferson, NC: McFarland 2000).

Chinoy, Mike, *Meltdown: The Inside Story of the North Korean Nuclear Crisis* (New York: St. Martin's Press 2008).

Chon Sang-in, 'haepang kong' ganui sahoesa' [Political geography and social history of Korea, 1945–1950] in Park Chi-syang *et al.* (eds.), *haepangchonhusaui chaeinsik (chaeinsik)*, [The New Interpretation of Korean History between Liberation and the Korean War] (Seoul: Ch'aeksesang 2006).

Cumings, Bruce, *The Origins of the Korean War*, 2 vols. (Princeton, NJ: Princeton UP 1981 and 1990).

Dixon, W.L., 'Recollections of Korea', *Baltimore and Ohio Magazine*, Aug. 1950, 8–9.

Dower, John, *War Without Mercy: Race and Power in the Pacific War* (New York: Pantheon Books 1986).

Dower, John, *Embracing Defeat: Japan in the Wake of World War II* (New York: W.W. Norton 1999).

Eckert, Carter, Ki-baik Lee, Young Ick Lew, Michael Robinson, and Edward W. Wagner, *Korea Old and New: A History* (Seoul: Ilchokak 1990).

Funabashi, Yoichi, *The Peninsula Question: A Chronicle of the Second Korean Nuclear Crisis* (Washington DC: Brookings 2007).

Gayn, Mark, *Japan Diary* (Rutland, VT: Charles E. Tuttle 1981).

Goedde, Petra, *GIs and Germans: Culture, Gender, and Foreign Relations, 1945–1949* (New Haven, CT: Yale UP 2003).

Henderson, Gregory, *Korea: The Politics of the Vortex* (Cambridge, MA: Harvard UP 1968).

Isaacs, Harold R., *No Peace for Asia* (New York: Macmillan 1947).

Kang, Han-mu, 'The United States Military Government in Korea, 1945–1948: An Analysis and Evaluation of its Policy' (PhD diss., Univ. of Cincinnati 1970).

Kim, Seung-Young, *American Diplomacy and Strategy toward Korea and Northeast Asia 1882–1950 and After: Perception of Polarity and US Commitment to a Periphery* (New York: Palgrave Macmillan 2009).

Lauterbach, Richard E., *Danger from the East* (New York: Harper & Row 1947).

Lee, Chae-jin, *A Troubled Peace: US Policy and the Two Koreas* (Baltimore: Johns Hopkins UP 2006).

Lew, Young Ick, Byong-kie Song, Ho-min Yang, and Hy-sop Lim, *Korean Perceptions of the United States: A History of Their Origins and Formation*, trans. by Michael Finch (Seoul: Mimoondang 2006).

McCune, George M., *Korea Today* (Cambridge, MA: Harvard UP 1950).

McLogan, Russell E., *Boy Soldier: Coming of Age During World War II* (Reading, MI: Terrus Press 1998).

Matray, James I., *The Reluctant Crusade: American Foreign Policy in Korea, 1941–1950* (Honolulu: Univ. of Hawaii Press 1985).

Meade, E. Grant, *American Military Government in Korea* (New York: King's Crown Press 1951).

Millett, Allan R., *The War for Korea, 1945–1950: A House Burning* (Lawrence: UP of Kansas 2005).

Oh, John Kie-chiang, 'The Forgotten Soldiers of the Korean War', in Mark F. Wilkinson (ed.), *The Korean War at Fifty: International Perspectives* (Lexington: Virginia Military Institute 2004).

Ottoboni, Fred, *Korea Between the Wars: A Soldier's Story* (Sparks, NV: Vincente Books 1997).

Smith, Robert, *MacArthur in Korea: The Naked Emperor* (New York: Simon & Schuster 1982).

Snyder, Scott, *China's Rise and the Two Koreas* (London: Lynne Rienner 2009).

Spector, Ronald H., *In the Ruins of Empire: The Japanese Surrender and the Battle for Postwar Asia* (New York: Random House 2007).

Stueck, William, *The Road to Confrontation: American Policy toward China and Korea, 1947–1950* (Chapel Hill: Univ. of North Carolina Press 1981).

Stueck, William, *The Wedemeyer Mission: American Politics and Foreign Policy During the Cold War* (Athens, GA: Univ. of Georgia Press 1984).

Stueck, William, *Rethinking the Korean War: A New Diplomatic and Strategic History* (Princeton, NJ: Princeton UP 2002).

Stueck, William, 'Reassessing US Strategy in the Aftermath of the Korean War', *Orbis* 53 (Fall 2009).

Summers, Harry G., 'The Korean War: A Fresh Perspective', *Military Affairs*, April 1996.

US Department of State, *F[oreign] R[elations of the] U[nited] S[tates], 1948* (Washington DC: Government Printing Office 1971).

China and the Dispatch of the Soviet Air Force: The Formation of the Chinese–Soviet–Korean Alliance in the Early Stage of the Korean War

ZHIHUA SHEN

Center for Cold War International History Studies, East China Normal University, China

ABSTRACT China's entry into the Korean War, together with the involvement of the Soviet Air Force, constituted not only the base of Chinese and Soviet joint assistance to North Korea but also the formation of the Sino-Soviet–North Korean triangular alliance. Recently declassified Russian Defense Ministry archives show that Stalin wavered on dispatching the Soviet Air Force for fear of a direct confrontation with the US/UN forces. It was 12 days after Chinese troops entered the war that Stalin finally allowed the Soviet Air Force to provide air cover. New documents that shed light on this enormously significant historical process demonstrate that the Sino-Soviet–North Korean triangular relationship was extremely delicate and weak.

With the declassification of many Russian and Chinese archives and documents, it is now possible to explore how the Soviets, Chinese and North Koreans established their alliance and what kind of alliance they formed. The Korean War was clearly a pivotal moment in this process. At this early stage of the alliance's development, two main threads ran through the story: one concerned the dispatch of Chinese troops to

---

An early version of this article was translated by Yang Jingxia and Douglas A. Stiffler, Juniata College. Yafeng Xia, Long Island University, molded the article to its final form.

assist North Korea, the other related to the process of Soviet military assistance to North Korea. Identifying the interconnections between these two threads reveals the complex relationships between the three allies.

China's intervention in October 1950 transformed the Korean War. The peninsula became a field for confrontations and conflicts between the two blocs, and, in the end, the conflict determined Cold War-era arrangements throughout Asia. Because of its vital importance, the Chinese leader Mao Zedong's decision to dispatch the Chinese troops to North Korea has become one of the most interesting topics in Korean War history. But less is known about the dispatch of the Soviet Air Force. With the opening of Soviet archives, we now know that the US and Soviet Air Forces fought at close quarters during the Korean War.[1] During the entire Cold War struggle, this was the one and only time that the United States and the Soviet Union engaged each other in face-to-face acts of war. Even though both sides clearly understood the nature of their military engagements, they chose to cover up the fact for over 40 years.[2] As this article demonstrates, the dispatch of the Soviet Air Force to North Korea is directly linked to China's strategic decision to dispatch troops.

Stalin's Promise to Commit the Soviet Air Force

The launching of the Korean War was originally Moscow's and Pyongyang's idea. Both the Soviet leader, Joseph Stalin, and the North Korean leader, Kim Il-sung, were confident that the United States would not enter the war and that South Korea would be easily defeated

---

[1]The earliest research on this topic was based mainly on oral history materials. See Jon Halliday, 'Air Operations in Korea: The Soviet Side of the Story', in William J. Williams (ed.), *A Revolutionary War: Korea and the Transformation of the Postwar World* (Chicago: Imprint Publications 1993), 149–70. Later, Russian scholars sporadically made some archival materials public. See A.S. Orlov, 'Sovetskaia aviatsiia v Koreiskoi vaine 1950–1953gg.', *Novaia i noveishaia istoriia* 4 (1998), 121–46. See also Shen Zhihua, 'The Soviet Air Force during the War to Resist America and Aid Korea', *Zhonggong Dangshi Yanjiu* [Studies of CCP History], 2 (2002), 69–74; Zhang Xiaoming, *Red Wings over the Yalu: China, the Soviet Union and the Air War in Korea* (Texas A&M UP 2002).

[2]In fact, the US CIA inferred as early as 27 Nov. 1950 that 'if the UN air force attacks targets in Manchuria', the Soviets would very much likely participate in the war secretly. See N[ational] A[rchives, College Park, MD], Fiche 22 Item 100 NIE 2/2. On 30 July 1952, the CIA further concluded based on 'numerous indications' that the Soviets participated extensively in 'enemy air operation'. See H[arry] S. T[ruman] L[ibrary, Independence, MO,] Harry S. Truman Papers, PSF Intelligence File NIE-55/1.

without China's help. But both men were wrong. To their intense surprise, within days of the North Korean invasion, the United States immediately declared that it would intervene.[3]

The US/UN entry into the war quickly resulted in enormous losses to the North Korean military, with air and naval forces the first to be affected. According to a report of the Soviet Army General Staff headquarters, by 3 July (only a few days after the start of hostilities) 36 North Korean aircraft and five naval vessels had been attacked and destroyed.[4] At this point, Stalin realized that the war was not going to proceed smoothly. He now pondered the question of how to boost support to North Korea while making sure that such support would not come directly from Moscow.

Before the war, Soviet assistance had mainly revolved around the training of North Korean troops, the provision of weaponry and the drawing up of battle plans. Stalin had absolutely forbidden Soviet soldiers from crossing the 38th Parallel and directly participating in the upcoming battle. Instead he had thought that the Chinese Army could provide assistance, if necessary. Of course, when and how such assistance would be provided would depend on the fortunes of war.

Chinese leaders paid careful attention to the US intervention. On 2 July, Zhou Enlai, the Chinese premier and foreign minister, called in the Soviet ambassador, Nikolai Roshchin, to request that he inform Moscow of the Chinese assessment of the Korean situation. Zhou pointed out that in order to prevent US troops from landing in Korea, the North Korean People's Army (NKPA) should accelerate its drive to the south, attack and occupy the southern harbors and station strong defense forces at places like Inchon. He emphasized that if the Americans crossed the 38th Parallel, the Chinese Army would engage the American forces in the guise of volunteers wearing the uniforms of the NKPA. To prepare for this eventuality, China would deploy three armies totaling 120,000 men to the Northeast area. Zhou ended the meeting by inquiring whether the Soviet Air Force would provide cover for these armies.[5]

---

[3]Concerning the Soviet leaders' estimate of the prewar US position, see Shen Zhihua, *Mao Zedong Sidalin yu Chaoxian Zhanzheng* [Mao, Stalin and the Korean War] (Guangzhou: Guangdong Renmin Chubanshe 2003), 147–58.

[4]TsAMORF(Tsentral'nyi Arkhiv Ministerstva Oborony Rossiiskoi Federatsii), f.16, op.3139, d.17, p.37.

[5]AVPRF(Arkhiv Vneshnei Politiki Rossiiskoi Federatsii) (ed.), *Khronologiia osnovnykh sobytii kanuna i nachal'nogo perioda koreiskoi voiny ianvar' 1949–oktiabr' 1950 gg.*, 35–7.

Zhou made all of these points before the Chinese government had taken a formal decision. China only established its Northeast Border Defense Force a few days after this meeting, and its troop deployments would not be completed before 5 August.[6] Obviously Zhou wanted Stalin to know that the Chinese leaders were willing to assist North Korea. He was also keen for Stalin to understand that China expected the Soviet Union to provide coordinated air cover for Chinese ground forces.[7]

Stalin responded straight away, wiring back on 5 July: 'We think it is correct to concentrate nine Chinese divisions on the China–Korea border so that the volunteers can enter North Korea for battles when the enemy crosses the 38th Parallel. We will try our best to provide air cover.'[8] Having received no further information from China, on 13 July Stalin again asked Roshchin to convey this message to Zhou or Mao:

> We are not clear about whether you have decided to deploy nine Chinese divisions on Sino-Korea border. If you have already made such a decision, we will then prepare to send an air force division equipped with 124 jet fighter planes to cover these armies. We plan to have our pilots train Chinese pilots for two to three months and then pass on all the equipment to your pilots. We plan to have the Shanghai air force division do the same thing.[9]

As these two documents indicate, in order to urge the Chinese to make the decision and prepare to dispatch troops to Korea as soon as possible, Stalin clearly promised that – besides assisting the Chinese in

---

[6]Zhongyang wenxian yanjiushi (ed.), *J[ianguo] Y[ilai] M[ao] Z[edong] W[engao]* [Mao Zedong's Manuscripts since the Founding of the PRC] 15 vols. (Beijing: Zhongyang Wenxian Chubanshe 1987–1999), 1: 428.

[7]See B.T. Kulik, 'SShA i Taivan' protiv KNR 1949–1952 Novye arkhivnye materialy', *Novaia i noveishaia istoriia* 5 (1995), 32–3; Zhongyang Wenxian Yanjiushi (ed.), *Jianguo Yilai Liu Shaoqi Wengao* [Liu Shaoqi's Manuscripts since the Founding of the PRC] 4 vols. (Beijing: Zhongyang Wenxian Chubanshe 2005), 1: 472; Pang Xianzhi and Jin Chongji (eds.), *Mao Zedong Zhuan 1949–1976* [A Biography of Mao Zedong] (Beijing Zhongyang Wenxian Chubanshe 2003), 49; V.P. Naboka, 'Sovetskie letchiki-istrebiteli v Kitae v 1950 godu', *Voprosy istorii* 3 (2002), 139–41.

[8]APRF (Arkhiv Prezidenta Rossiiskoi Federatsii), f.45, op.1, d.334, p.79.

[9]Ibid., 85. For China's response and arrangements made, see Zhongyang Wenxian Yanjiushi (ed.), *J[ianguo] Y[ilai] Z[hou] E[nlai] W[engao]* [Zhou Enlai's Manucripts since the Founding of the PRC] [henceforth *JYZEW*](Beijing Zhongyang Wenxian Chubanshe 2008), 3: 61–9, 90–1.

air force training and equipment – he would also provide air cover for Chinese troops that 'entered North Korea for combat'.[10]

Moscow in No Hurry for China to Send Troops

US air bombing created a tense situation in Pyongyang, despite the early success of the North Korean ground campaign. On 7 July, Kim met the Soviet ambassador to North Korea, Terentii Shtykov, requesting that Soviet military advisors be deployed to Seoul as soon as possible in order to participate in the military command of all army groups. If not, the NKPA could be faced with 'failure' and 'collapse'. Kim also said that he was receiving many phone calls, all reporting severe damage done by US air strikes, including the destruction of railway terminals and many bridges. According to Shtykov's observation, this was the first time that Kim looked 'emotionally upset and somewhat depressed' since the beginning of the war.[11] Stalin again directed his attention to China. On 8 July he instructed Roshchin to ask Mao to send representatives to contact the North Koreans.[12]

In fact, China was already making its own active preparations. While Chinese troops were being deployed to the northeast on a large scale, Chinese leaders were speeding up their Korean battle planning. On 12/13 July, Zhou told Kim that China would not tolerate the US intervention in Korea, and that the Chinese government was ready to provide, to the best of its ability, all assistance needed by North Korea in the war. Meanwhile, China requested that the North Koreans 'provide 500 each of Korean maps with the scales of 1:100,000; 1:200,000 and 1:500,000 ... and send over samples of the NKPA uniforms as soon as possible'. Kim immediately informed the Soviet ambassador of these requests, asserting: 'now that countries like the United States have already entered the war on Syngman Rhee's side, democratic countries like Czechoslovakia and China could also use their own armies to assist North Korea'. But Shtykov deliberately avoided proffering a response.[13]

On 19 July, Kim informed the Soviet embassy of the details of a meeting between his representative in Beijing and Mao, especially the

---

[10]See A.M. Ledovskii, 'Stalin Mao Tszedun i koreickaia voina 1950–1953 godov', *Novaia i noveishaia istoriia* 5 (2005), 100–1; Alexandre Y. Mansourov, 'Stalin, Mao, Kim and China's Decision to Enter the Korean War Sept.16–Oct.15 1950: New Evidence from the Russian Archives', *Cold War International History Project* Bulletins 6–7 (Washington DC: Winter 1995–96), 105.

[11]TsAMORF, f.5, op.918795, d.122, pp.193–4.

[12]APRF, f.45, op.1, d.334, p.82.

[13]TsAMORF, f.5, op.918795, d.122, pp.303–5.

fact that Mao thought the United States would be involved in the war for a long time and would throw in more forces. Mao ended by stating that if North Korea needed help, China 'could send her own army to Korea. For this purpose, the Chinese side had already mustered four armies totaling 320,000 men'. Kim was keen to discover Moscow's reaction. But though Shtykov duly asked Moscow for its opinion on the question of China sending troops, Stalin never replied.[14] After raising this question several times, Kim seemed to understand Stalin's thinking on this issue – in his view, Stalin's reluctance to respond indicated that the Soviet leader had growing doubts about sanctioning such a course.

Shtykov continued to keep Moscow informed of the rapidly changing Korean situation. On 18 July he wrote that the steady advance of the NKPA had stimulated the activation of the southern guerrilla movement, concluding that North Korea's leaders and its citizens had rid themselves of their initial panic and now had a renewed confidence in victory.[15] In August, the Soviet embassy in North Korea submitted another report that reached the same conclusion. It mentioned in passing, however, that North Korean cadres and the masses were now expressing their discontent at the USSR's inability to mobilize its air force in time to prevent US bombing.[16]

Based on these optimistic estimates of the war situation, Stalin decided that, for the time being, China did not need to send in troops. But Mao still seemed keen. This Chinese eagerness to dispatch its forces into Korea at a time when victory seemed likely aroused Stalin's suspicions. He thought such an outcome would expand China's status and influence in Korea, which in the long run would not be to the Soviet Union's advantage.

Mao was indeed carefully considering the issue of sending in troops, especially after the Soviets promised to provide air assistance. On 22 July, he replied to Stalin's 13 July telegram:

> Concerning the jet plane division you are going to use for covering my army, we intend to deploy them in Shenyang area, among which two regiments are going to be deployed at Anshan and one regiment at Liaoyang. This will help complete the task of providing air cover for our army and the Shenyang, Andong and Fushun industrial areas with the help of our fighter plane air regiment of the mixed air force brigade stationed in the Andong area.

---

[14]Ibid., 352–5.
[15]AVPRF, f.0102, op.6, p.21, d.47, pp.29–40.
[16]Ibid., d.48, pp.109–69.

At the same time, Mao discussed the arrangement for training Chinese pilots. The plan was to take over all military materials from two Soviet air divisions, while also quickly completing all the work of re-equipping and training. On these matters, the Soviets expressed complete agreement.[17] In fact, just the day before (i.e. 21 July), the Soviet Council of Ministers had already passed a related resolution. On the basis of this resolution, on 22 July Soviet Defense Minister Marshal Aleksandr M. Vasilevskii instructed Soviet military advisors in China, Krasovskii and Batitskii to give all the planes from Batitskii's forces stationed at Shanghai to China. By 10 August, moreover, the 151st Soviet Fighter Air Division would also complete the task of assembling at Shenyang, Liaoyang, Anshan, and other places.[18]

On the question of sending Chinese troops, though, Mao remained in the dark about Stalin's preferences. With the North Koreans first stalling and then failing to give a definite reply to China's offer, Mao raised his tentative plan through a different channel. On 19 and 28 July, he talked twice about the Korean War with the Soviet Philosopher-Academician Pavel Yudin, who was in Beijing helping to edit 'The Selected Works of Mao Zedong'. Mao mentioned two possibilities: If the Americans continued to use only their current armed forces in Korea, they would then soon be driven out of the peninsula and would never come back. But if Washington was determined to win, it would have to send 30 to 40 army divisions, which would make it very hard for the North Koreans to cope. In this situation, Kim would need direct assistance from China, whose forces could annihilate the 30 to 40 US divisions. Mao was confident that such an outcome would postpone the outbreak of the third world war[19] – a message he clearly intended to be passed on to Moscow.[20] But Stalin would not be swayed.

Kim's Anticipation of Air Support from Other Countries

By mid-August, with the NKPA's offensive halted on the line of the Naktong River, Kim began to exhibit signs of anxiety and disappointment.

On 19 August, he dispatched his private secretary, the Korean-born Soviet citizen Mun Il, to see Shtykov to request Soviet air assistance. But Shtykov still lacked instructions from Moscow. The Soviet

---

[17]AVPRF, f.45, op.1, d.334, pp.88–9, 90.

[18]TaAMORF, f.16, op.3139, d.16, pp.1–2; APRF, f.45, op.1, d.334, pp.88–9; Naboka, 'Sovetskie letchiki-istrebiteli', 141.

[19]AVPRF, *Khronologiia osnovnykh sobytii kanuna* ... 45, 47.

[20]See Shen, *Mao Zedong Sidalin yu Chaoxian Zhanzheng*, 169–76.

ambassador could only continue to be evasive, suggesting that the NKPA 'quickly harness the army's military strength and throw reserve forces into battle in order to advance quickly'. Later, Shtykov reported to Moscow that 'Kim Il-sung had been somewhat depressed lately', and 'worried somewhat about whether the People's Army could hold out longer at the front'.[21]

On the evening of 26 August, Kim told Shtykov through Mun Il that he was 'still thinking about the idea of asking the Chinese comrades to send troops to aid Korea because the current frontline conditions of the People's Army are too difficult'. But Shtykov remained unforthcoming. He did report to Moscow that, in recent days, Kim had appeared increasingly pessimistic about relying on his own strength to win the war. And he made numerous attempts to get approval from the Soviet embassy to request assistance from the Chinese. But Kim now took the hint. After sounding out the Soviets through Mun Il – and having received no clear reply – the North Korean leader never mentioned this question again.[22]

All the while, the military situation continued to deteriorate. In addition to the NKPA's inability to dislodge the Americans from the Naktong River line, Kim also received ominous information, probably from the Chinese, that the United States planned to launch a counter-attack at Inchon. In a telegram to Stalin on 2 October, Mao wrote:

> As early as April this year, when Kim Il-sung came to Beijing, we told him to seriously pay attention to the possibility of the foreign reactionary armies invading Korea. In mid-July, late-July and early-September, we asked the Korean comrades three times to keep an eye on the danger of the enemy's advancing from the sea to Inchon and Seoul and cutting off the route of retreat of the People's Army.[23]

Mao's message was a reminder to Kim that, based on experience, he needed to depend on immediate assistance from the Chinese Army if he was to achieve victory. In early September, after Mao's repeated urgings, the military planned to increase the strength of the Northeast Border Defense Force to 700,000, in addition to 200,000 replacement troops, while also boosting the amount of weaponry.[24] China was obviously preparing for any possible actions the Americans might take.

---

[21]TsAMORF, f.5, op.918795, d.122, pp.621–3.

[22]Ibid., 666–9.

[23]Cited from Pang Xianzhi and Li Jie, 'Mao Zedong, and Resisting America and Aiding Korea', *Dang de Wenxian* [Party Historical Documents] 5 (2000), 39.

[24]*JYZEW*, 3: 247–51.

Given the deteriorating military situation, Stalin could no longer ignore Kim. But he still rejected North Korea's request for international assistance. On 28 August, he told Kim: 'the Central Committee of the Communist Party of Soviet Union (CPSU) has no doubt at all that the foreign interventionists will be driven out of Korea soon'. Then, he comfortingly advised: 'Do not feel restless because (you) did not gain continuous victories in the fight with foreign interventionists. Victories sometimes are accompanied by some setbacks, even local failure. There are no continuous victories in a war like this.' At the end, Stalin promised Kim that 'if necessary, we can provide Korea with attack planes and fighter planes again'.[25] Having heard Stalin's opinions directly, Kim 'felt very happy and expressed his thanks many times'.[26] He continued to place all his hopes on Moscow.[27]

But Stalin, fearing a direct confrontation with the United States, soon became even more cautious. Not only did he fail to provide air support to North Korea in a timely manner, but he also halted the already-determined provision of air cover for Chinese troops. On 28 August, Soviet Defense Minister Vasilevskii reported that, due to air attacks and strafing carried out by US airplanes in residential areas and train stations in northeast China on 27 August, the Ministry of Military Affairs had requested that the already-deployed 151st Fighter Air Division assume the task of providing air cover for Chinese Northeast Border Defense Army. He also asked that a draft order be approved and transmitted to the division commander Belov. The next day, however, Vice Chair of the Council of Ministers Nikolai Bulganin only noted on the document: 'Return to A. M. Vasilevskii', and no order followed. On 31 August, Vasilevskii submitted another report, asking: 'whether it is necessary to order the 151st Fighter Air Division, which was training Chinese pilots, to also provide air cover for the People's Liberation Army in that area'. This time, Bulganin was straightforward and crossed out the query in red.[28] Bulganin's action was obviously permitted – and most likely even suggested – by Stalin.

A few days later, Stalin also decided to move the air forces deployed in the Shenyang area to augment the strength of the USSR's Lushun naval base (on the Port Arthur peninsula). In accordance with a 13 September CPSU Politburo resolution, the Ministry of Defense ordered that the 151st Fighter Air Division should finish training the Chinese

---

[25]APRF, f.45, op.1, d.347, pp.5–6, 10–11.

[26]Ibid., 12–13.

[27]See Shen Zhihua, 'Sino-North Korean Conflict and its Resolution during the Korean War', *Cold War International History Project*, Bulletins 14/15 (Winter 2003–Spring 2004), 9–24.

[28]TsAMORF, f.16, op.3139, d.16, pp.1–2, 4–5.

pilots in the Shenyang area by 1 February 1951; it could then move two of its regiments and the commanding organs to the Lushun naval base. Together with the 177th Regiment and the Air Mechanics Battalion of the 303rd Air Division, transferred from Vladivostok on 6 October, they would form a new MiG-15 Fighter Air Division.[29]

This transfer order to the Soviet Air Force in China was obviously related to the 4 September incident in which US planes attacked and shot down a Soviet bomber on a training run at the Lushun naval base.[30] In the wake of this incident, Stalin's priorities were crystal clear: while he clearly valued the Soviet position at Lushun harbor,[31] he no longer emphasized the importance of air support to the Chinese Army, which was about to fight in Korea. But the dramatically changing war situation soon disrupted Stalin's plans.

Mao's Eagerness to Send Troops to Aid Korea

From 14 to 18 September, Stalin continuously received battlefield reports on the American landing at Inchon, which was transforming the Korean War situation.[32]

The Chinese leaders' response was immediate. On 18 September, Zhou Enlai called in Roshchin and Soviet military advisors Kotov and Konov. Zhou pointed out with annoyance that North Korea rarely provided the Chinese with information on military affairs. China had offered to send military technicians to Korea to observe the battlefield situation, but so far had not got any reply from Pyongyang. The Chinese knew nothing about either the battle plans of the NKPA or the true situation on the battlefield. According to official sources, Zhou suggested that, if North Korea had insufficient reserve forces (100,000 people), they should withdraw the main force to the north to establish strike forces that could be used in a decisive battle. On behalf of Mao, Zhou also asked the Soviet government to provide more accurate information. Finally, Zhou claimed that because Western countries had not prepared for a long-term and large-scale war, they were likely to be very worried that the Soviets and Chinese might participate in the Korean military conflict. Zhou said: '[We] should take advantage of the feeling of fear and take steps that can demonstrate our intentions. To

---

[29]Ibid., 170–1.

[30]*Vneshniaia politika Sovetskogo Soiuza Dokumenty i materialy 1950 god* (Moskva: GPL 1953), 214–16; I.F. Stone, *Chaoxian Zhanzheng Neimu* [The Hidden History of the Korean War], trans. Nan Zuoming etc. (Hangzhou: Zhejiang Renmin Chubanshe 1989), 131.

[31]See Shen, *Mao Zedong, Sidalin yu Chaoxian Zhanzheng*, 143–6.

[32]TsAMORF, f.16, op.3139, d.17, pp.156–7, 158, 159–60, 161–2, 163–4.

this end, moving Chinese troops from the south to the northeast will be enough to make the British and American governments nervous.' Zhou requested that the Soviet government be informed of these opinions, and that he would await its reply.[33]

On 20 September, Moscow responded that the Koreans ought to provide military intelligence in a timely manner, but explained away their earlier lapse by referring to the government's youth and inexperience. With respect to China's suggestion on the Korean battle plan, the Soviets agreed immediately to move the main force of the NKPA to the north and to build a defense line around Seoul. Significantly, though, Stalin did not respond to Zhou's query about sending Chinese troops.[34]

As a result Zhou could only suggest that Kim concentrate his military strength to protect the 38th Parallel and 'stick to the general policy of relying on one's own efforts and striving over a long period of time'.[35] On 21 September, Liu Shaoqi again told Roshchin that the Chinese leaders thought the 'Chinese revolution has not yet ended', [but] if the United States won an advantage in Korea, 'China is obligated to help the Korean comrades.'[36]

Zhou also asked North Korea for its opinion. On 19 September, Zhou called in Yi Chu-yon, the North Korean ambassador to China and told him about the conversation he had with Roshchin the previous day, before asking: 'what requests would the Korean government have for China' in the aftermath of the Inchon landing?[37] The next day, Kim Il-sung reported to the Soviet ambassador the content of Zhou's conversation and explained that China and Korea had an agreement that if the enemy landed in the rear area, the Chinese would use their own army to help Korea. Kim then asked Shtykov how to reply to the Chinese. After the Soviet ambassador replied in diplomatic language, 'no comment', Kim immediately said that the Chinese Army was excellent and had battle experience, but with the continuous, intense, and random bombing by so many US planes, it would be hard to say how these troops would perform. All North Koreans on the scene observed that, 'If (we) let Chinese army enter the war in Korea without air cover, then the battles would still be rather difficult.' Minister of

---

[33]APRF, f.45, op.1, d.331, pp.123–6; A.V. Torkunov, *Zagadochnaia voina: koreiskii konflikt 1950–1953 godov* (Moskova RPE 2000), 106–8.

[34]Shen Zhihua (ed.), *Chaoxian Zhanzheng Eguo Danganguan de Jiemi Wenjian* [The Korean War: Declassified Documents from the Russian Archives] (Taipei Institute of Modern History Academia Sinica 2003), 542–5.

[35]*JYZEW*, 3: 311–12.

[36]APRF, f.45, op.1, d.331, pp.133–5; Torkunov, *Zagadochnaia voina*, 109–11.

[37]APRF, f.45, op.1, d.331, p.131; Torkunov, *Zagadochnaia voina*, 109.

Foreign Affairs Pak Hon-yong then clearly expressed a 'hope to have China participate in the war'. Due to lack of instructions from Moscow, Shtykov once more 'avoided answering this question'.[38] Kim could only continue to try to read Stalin's mind,[39] assuming that the Soviet leader still did not want China to enter the war until the final moment, that is the moment when the enemy crossed the 38th Parallel.

On 30 September, Moscow received a report from Shtykov that Seoul was probably already lost, that the road for the main force of the NKPA to retreat north had been blockaded and that communications had been cut off. Kim was worried that the enemy would cross the 38th Parallel and that the North Koreans would have no way of building a new army for effective resistance. The Korean Politburo discussed the situation and drafted a letter to Stalin asking the Soviets to provide air support. They also drafted a letter to Mao, which hinted at asking for help. Panicked and lacking confidence, they did not know what to do. That same night, Kim sent a letter earnestly requesting that Stalin provide 'direct military assistance', and if that was not workable to 'form an international volunteer army of China and other people's democratic countries'.[40]

Facing this emergency situation, Stalin finally gave the green light to the Chinese entry to the war. On 1 October, he asked Mao to intervene with Chinese troops as volunteers, adding that they should begin by organizing defenses in the area north of the 38th Parallel. Stalin also rather disingenuously stated: 'I have not mentioned this to the Korean comrades and do not intend to mention it. But I have no doubt that they will be very happy after they hear this.'[41]

The morning after Mao received this telegram he hurriedly drafted a reply tentatively agreeing to send troops. After vigorous advocacy by Mao and Peng Dehuai, on 5 October the Enlarged Meeting of the Chinese Communist Party (CCP) Politburo adopted the resolution to send troops to Korea. Soon, the Chinese People's Volunteers (CPV) command was formally established and the Army entered its final pre-war preparation stage.[42]

Although the decision to send troops had already been made, Chinese leaders continued to hesitate and worry. If they had sent troops before the Inchon landing, then these forces could have helped defend the rear areas to ensure the victory of the main force of the NKPA in the front. Alternatively, if they had sent troops just after the Inchon landing, then

---

[38]TsAMORF, f.5, op. 918795, d.125, pp.86–8.

[39]Ibid., 89–91.

[40]APRF, f.45, op.1, d.347, pp.41–5, 46–9.

[41]APRF, f.45, op.1, d.334, pp.97–8.

[42]See Shen, *Mao Zedong Sidalin yu Chaoxian Zhanzheng*, 179–90.

such forces could have built a defense line along the 38th Parallel to prevent the enemy from continuing to advance north. But now it was too late to do either. By early October, when the main force of the NKPA had been practically wiped out, the opportune moment for China's entry had been lost.

The Chinese Army's weakness was obvious. As Mao explained in a draft telegram to Stalin on 2 October, its weapons were backward and it lacked air cover.[43] Although this telegram was never sent, Stalin received the gist of the message through other channels. On 7 October, Matveev, Stalin's personal representative in North Korea, reported that Pak Il-u, the Interior Minister had returned from Beijing on 5 October. Pak Il-u was received twice by Mao and CCP leaders during his stay in Beijing, and they talked at length, sometimes for as long as ten hours. Mao stated that China should do its best to help Korea, but could not dispatch troops for the time being. His reasons were straightforward: the dispatch of Chinese troops would drag the Soviets into the war, which would lead to a third world war, and though the Chinese Army was sizeable, it did not have modern weapons, an air force or a navy.[44]

In direct talks with Soviet representatives Mao was even blunter. On 6 October Mao told Roshchin that he was gratified by Stalin's comment that the Chinese and Soviets would fight the Americans side-by-side. As to the question of China sending troops, Mao emphasized that the Chinese Army's technology and equipment were so backward that it would have to 'completely depend on Soviet assistance'. During this conversation, Mao 'especially paid attention to the air force issue', pointing out that in order to send out troops, China 'must have an air force'. Its task would be to protect the Chinese ground force sent to Korea, to participate in frontline fighting and to protect the major industrial centers of China. At the end, Mao stated that, in order to report on the situation and to exchange opinions, he needed to send Zhou Enlai and Lin Biao, a high-ranking Chinese general, to the Soviet Union immediately.[45] As these sources indicate, Stalin undoubtedly knew about Zhou's purpose and requirements before he headed to the Soviet Union for the negotiations.

On 8 October, Mao informed Kim and Stalin respectively that the CPV would be entering Korea around 15 October. After 8 October, Moscow and Pyongyang also exchanged information. Everybody seemed relieved that China had decided to send troops. Kim was

---

[43]*JYMZW*, 1: 540.

[44]TsAMORF, f.5, op.918795, d.121, pp.705–6.

[45]RGASPI (Rossiiskii Gosudarstvennyi Arkhiv Sotsial'noi i Politicheskoi Istorii), f.558, op.11, d.334, pp.126–8; Shen, *Chaoxian Zhanzheng Eguo Danganguan de Jiemi Wenjian*, 588–90.

beside himself with joy, and even went so far as to make arrangements concerning when, where and how the Chinese army would deploy in Korea.[46] But such planning was premature: Stalin was already reconsidering the issue of sending in the Soviet Air Force.

Stalin's Refusal to Provide Air Cover for the Volunteer Troops

On 11 October, Zhou Enlai and his retinue flew via Moscow to Stalin's summer villa near the Black Sea, where they met with the Soviet leaders that same afternoon. Zhou briefed the Soviets on the CCP Politburo's deliberation on the Korean situation and the question of sending troops. He explained that China's dispatch of troops faced major practical difficulties and emphasized that the Soviets must provide weapons, equipment and air support. Stalin pointed out that he could meet all Chinese needs for military equipment like airplanes, tanks and artillery. However, the Soviet Air Force was not yet ready and could not go into action for two to two-and-a-half months. After extended discussions, both sides agreed that since neither was ready, they had to give up Korea and inform Kim to arrange a retreat as soon as possible. After the meeting, Stalin and Zhou sent Mao a joint telegram. Because the air force would not be in a position to provide air cover for at least two months, and Chinese forces needed at least six months to equip and train, it would be pointless to try to assist Korea. The telegram concluded by stating that Stalin and Zhou awaited Mao's decision.[47]

Stalin's claim that the Soviet Air Force was not yet ready was obviously just an excuse. At the very least, the Belov Air Division that had been assembled in the Shenyang area was already prepared and awaiting further instructions. Moreover, about ten days earlier, Vasilevskii had reported to Stalin that the 304th Regiment of the 32nd Air Attack Division (including two anti-aircraft battalions and other supplementary troops) were ready to be moved from the Binhai border areas to Pyongyang. They would only take five to six days to get into position, and could 'start carrying out the combat mission of protecting Pyongyang' on 3 October.[48]

---

[46]Pang and Li, 'Mao Zedong and Resisting America/Aiding Korea', 3–4; RGASPI, f.558, op.11, d.334, p.132; TsAMORF, f.5, op. 918795, d.121, pp.711–13.

[47]Shi Zhe, *Zai Lishi Juren Shengbian: Shi Zhe Huiyilu* [Together with Historical Giants: A Memoir of Shi Zhe] (Beijing: Zhongyang Wenxian Chubanshe 1991), 495–8; Mansourov, 'Stalin, Mao, Kim', 94–107; RGASPI, f.558, op.11, d.334, pp.134–5. See also Shen, *Mao Zedong Sidalin yu Chaoxian Zhanzheng*, 192–7.

[48]APRF, f.3, op.65, d.827, pp.81–2. Due to the rapid deterioration of the Korean situation, this task was not executed.

Upon closer scrutiny, Stalin had three reasons for not wanting the Soviet Air Force to go into battle along side Chinese ground forces. First, the Soviet leader always forbade his military from directly engaging with US forces, even if it was only to provide air cover in rear areas. On the morning of 2 October, Stalin received a report that an advance party of South Korean soldiers had crossed the 38th Parallel.[49] This meant that the northern part of Korea would become a war zone. Stalin's cautious instincts were immediately to the fore, for he did not want to give any sign of an impending public confrontation between the Soviet Union and the United States. Moscow's reaction to the US air attack on a Soviet airfield near the border illustrates this point. On 8 October, two US fighter planes intruded into the territorial air space of the Soviet coastal area, flew at a low altitude, and strafed a Soviet military airport about 100 kilometers from the border, causing the destruction of seven planes. Not only did the Soviets fail to react militarily; they even remained silent when their diplomatic protest was rejected.[50] It was against this backdrop of caution that Stalin adopted an evasive approach to Zhou's requests.

Second, Stalin still had hopes of solving the Korean problem peacefully through secret diplomatic channels. At the critical moment on 27 September when the 38th Parallel was about to be crossed, Soviet Foreign Minister Andrei Vyshinskii, who was in New York, sent a telegram stating that Lancaster, a pro-Soviet US entrepreneur had stated to the Soviet representative to the UN that he could arrange a meeting with US Assistant Secretary of State or ambassador to the UN to discuss ways for solving the Korean issue peacefully. The CPSU Politburo called a meeting the same day and decided to send someone to meet with the US side and listen to its opinion.[51]

As the battlefield situation then worsened, the Soviet Union made another move. On 4 October, a Soviet employee at the UN secretariat invited the Norwegian representative to the UN for lunch, hoping that he could serve as an intermediary to pass a message to the US government: If General Douglas MacArthur agreed to stop at the 38th Parallel, the Soviet Union would persuade the North Koreans to lay down their arms and allow a UN committee to enter North Korea to organize a general election.[52] If this secret diplomacy had been

---

[49]TsAMORF, f.16, op.3139, d.17, pp.185–6.

[50]TsAMORF f.16, op.3139, d.16, pp.102–3. Also see Shen Zhihua, 'More on Stalin, Mao Zedong and the Korean War', *Shixue Jikan* [Collected Papers of History Studies], 1 (2007), 62–5.

[51]APRF, f.3, op.65, d.827, pp.86–7, 84–5.

[52]*Foreign Relations of the United States 1950* (Washington DC: Government Printing Office 1976), 7: 877–8.

successful, then the question of Chinese intervention would have become moot – and it would not have been necessary for the Soviets to run the risk of war with the United States.

Finally, the transformation of the battlefield situation had also altered Stalin's calculations about the likely impact of China's intervention. Before UN forces had crossed the 38th Parallel, Stalin had been in no doubt that China could have effectively changed the balance on the battlefield, but he had worried that a Chinese victory would lead to a dissipation, and perhaps even removal, of Soviet influence on the peninsula. Now that UN forces were pushing into North Korea, however, Stalin's goal of controlling the peninsula was fading for another reason: the even more disturbing prospect of an American victory. Stalin therefore wanted China to defend North Korea. But he now fretted that Chinese wavering demonstrated that the Chinese leaders themselves had doubts about victory. So Stalin now decided to bide his time before committing the Soviet Air Force. He wanted a breathing space to see if the Chinese Army could stand its ground in Korea.[53]

After receiving the Stalin–Zhou telegram from the Black Sea, Mao was sunk in deep thought. At 3.30pm on 12 October, when he first read it, his reaction was: 'I agree with your decision.' At 10.22pm, Mao sent another telegram to inform the Soviets that the Chinese Army had not yet entered Korea, and orders had been given to 'stop the implementation of the plan to enter Korea'. Stalin then sent a telegram to Pyongyang to tell Kim the result of the Black Sea meeting and to ask him to organize a retreat.[54]

In fact, Mao was not as resolute as he sounded in his telegram. His actual instruction to Peng Dehuai was 'to temporarily suspend implementation of the 9 October order' and 'to temporarily delay [the army's] dispatch'. He also asked Peng and Gao to come to Beijing for consultation.[55] After the Politburo meeting on 13 October, when his comrades fully endorsed the decision to intervene, Mao's policy became clearer. He immediately called in Roshchin and announced that the CCP Central Committee had decided that 'we should help the Koreans'.[56] Mao also mentioned that China hoped to pay for the weaponry provided by the Soviets by means of a loan.[57]

---

[53]Pang and Li, 'Mao Zedong, and Resisting America and Aiding Korea', 13–14.

[54]RGASPI, f.558, op.11, d.334, pp.140–3.

[55]Pang and Li, 'Mao Zedong, and Resisting America and Aiding Korea', 5–6; *JYMZW* 1: 552–3.

[56]RGASPI, f.558, op.11, d.334, p.145.

[57]APRF, f.45, op.1, d.347, p.77 and d.335 pp.1–2.

In a telegram sent to Zhou at 10pm on 13 October, Mao clearly explained the arrangements and requests concerning China's reconsideration of sending in the army. To begin with, after entering Korea, the Chinese Army would engage in battle only with South Korean armies and establish bases in order to raise the morale of the troops; Chinese troops would not attack American armies before the arrival of Soviet air volunteers and weaponry. Mao also asked Zhou to try to arrange for China to lease the weaponry to be provided by the Soviets, as well as asking the Soviets to send out a volunteer air force in two to two-and-a-half months to support Chinese combat operations in Korea. At 3am on the 14 October, Mao sent yet another telegram to Zhou, reiterating his requests for Soviet assistance.[58] The key issue was the entry of the Soviet Air Force into the conflict.

By this time, Zhou had returned to Moscow from where he sent a letter to Stalin conveying Mao's opinion, mentioning especially the question of the critical relationship between 'the Soviet volunteer air force' and the Chinese volunteers.[59] But Stalin remained suspicious of China's motives in sending troops. He stated that, even if the Soviet Air Force was sent out, it could only operate north of the Yalu River and would not enter Korea to cooperate in military operations with the Chinese volunteers.[60] This poured cold water on the Chinese plan. On 17 October, Mao sent urgent telegrams to Peng Dehuai and Gao Gang to ask them to come to Beijing for consultation and to postpone the date of sending troops. As a result of a discussion at the meeting on 18 October, China decided that troops would still be sent into Korea on 19 October.[61]

It was not until 25 October, after, the first engagement between the CPV and the United Nations Army, that Stalin truly believed that the CCP was not a nationalist or 'pro-American element'.[62] On 29 October, M. V. Zakharov, the Soviet chief military advisor in China informed Zhou that Moscow had agreed that the Soviet Air Force 'is in charge of air defense at Andong', adding that it could fly across the

---

[58]Pang and Li, 'Mao Zedong, and Resisting America and Aiding Korea', 6–8, 10; *JYMZW*, 1: 564.

[59]*JYZEW*, 3: 404–5.

[60]See Shi, *Zai Lishi Juren Shenbian*, p.502; Pang and Li, 'Mao Zedong, and Resisting America and Aiding Korea', 9, 14; Li Ping *et al.*, *Zhou Enlai nianpu, 1949–1976* [A Chronology of Zhou Enlai] (Beijing: Zhongyang Wenxian and Renmin Chubanshe 1997), 1: 86–7.

[61]Pang and Li, 'Mao Zedong, and Resisting America and Aiding Korea', 11.

[62]See AVPRF, f.0100, op.50a, d.1, p.423; B.T. Kulik, *Sovetsko-kitaiskii rackol: prichiny i posledctviia* (Moskva IDV RAN 2000), 95; Zhongyang Wenxian Yanjiushi (ed.), *Zhou Enlai Xuanji* [Selected Works of Zhou Enlai] (Beijing Renmin Chubanshe 1980) 2: 302.

China–Korea border, while also agreeing to move the base from Shenyang to Andong in ten days.[63] On 1 November, for the first time, the Soviet Air Force threw itself into the battle over the Yalu River.[64]

Conclusion

The Korean War was a fire started by Moscow. When it started to get out of control, Stalin ultimately wanted Mao to pull his chestnuts out of this fire and agreed to send the Soviet Air Force for assistance. Yet Stalin's motivations and actions were highly complex. Suspicious of Mao's and the CCP's true intentions, Stalin did not want China to have a hand in Korean affairs before the UN troops crossed the 38th Parallel. He was keen to ensure that the Chinese would not harm Soviet interests in the Far East or intensify the Soviet–US conflict. And when the crisis finally arrived and China did enter the war, Stalin initially went back on his promise and placed Mao in an awkward predicament.

But at this critical moment of the war, North Korea could only count on assistance from China. Kim, for his part, did not trust Mao and was also worried about Stalin's obvious suspicions of Beijing. Without approval from Moscow, Kim would never have dared to agree to the request to have Chinese troops enter the conflict.

China had hoped to dispatch troops to Korea at an earlier date. It wanted to end the fighting near its northeast borders as soon as possible, but this plan had come to naught because of Stalin's and Kim's suspicions. For China to send troops, the Soviets would have to guarantee to provide weapons and air cover. But neither side fully trusted the other. In Beijing, as the Korean situation worsened, Mao worried that Stalin would go back on his word. At the Black Sea talks, when Zhou suggested that Chinese entry to war would depend on the Soviet air cover, Stalin's own suspicions were heightened another notch.

If Mao had agreed to the decision reached at the Black Sea talks, then all of Korea would undoubtedly have been occupied by US troops, China's security would have been threatened and the Sino-Soviet alliance would have existed in name only. Taking into consideration the adverse circumstances China confronted, not to mention its position and responsibility in the socialist camp, Mao decided to risk everything and fight with his back to the wall. His decision to enter the war brought together China, the Soviet Union and North Korea to fight the enemy. China's dispatch of troops, therefore, was a key step in turning the Sino-Soviet alliance from a paper alliance into a real one. It

---

[63]*JYZEW* 3: 427.
[64]APRF, f.45, op.1, d.335, pp.71–2.

was also the precondition for the Soviet Union to send in its air force to assist Korea. These were necessary steps in establishing the China–Soviet–North Korea Alliance during the war.

In sum, the Soviet Air Force's entry into the conflict was always tangled up with the issue of Chinese entry to the Korean War. Examination of this enormously significant event demonstrates the complicated and subtle relations of alliance between the Chinese, the Soviets and the North Koreans. Before the outbreak of the Korean War, the Sino-Soviet relationship had been based on a very weak foundation. Just five years before, Jiang Jieshi (Chiang Kai-shek) had been Stalin's chosen partner in Asia, while Mao had placed his hopes on the US for aid. In 1949, Stalin had been forced to alter Soviet policy toward China when the CCP was winning in the Chinese Civil War, while Mao, for his part, had come to rely on Soviet support to consolidate the CCP's political power in China. Nonetheless, during the protracted CCP-Soviet negotiations for the Sino-Soviet alliance treaty in 1950, the Soviet Union had been forced to make concessions to China, and Stalin had become even more suspicious of Mao's true color.[65]

These tense relations underpinned events during the early stages of the Korean War. Before China dispatched its troops, Moscow had always been on its guard against Beijing, while Kim had been at Stalin's beck and call. However, with China's intervention in the Korean War, this situation was fundamentally changed. China became the main force of this alliance. And in the numerous subsequent disagreements between Beijing and Pyongyang, Moscow on the whole supported China's stand and opinions – a situation that was to endure to the end of the war.[66]

Bibliography

Foreign Relations of the United States 1950 (Washington DC: Government Printing Office 1976).

Halliday, Jon, 'Air Operations in Korea: The Soviet Side of the Story', in William J. Williams (ed.), *A Revolutionary War: Korea and the Transformation of the Postwar World* (Chicago: Imprint Publications 1993), 149–70.

Kulik, B.T., 'SShA i Taivan' protiv KNR 1949–1952 Novye arkhivnye materialy', *Novaia i noveishaia istoriia* 5 (1995), 29–38.

Kulik, B.T., *Sovetsko-kitaiskii rackol: prichiny i posledctviia* (Moskva IDV RAN 2000).

Ledovskii A. M., 'Stalin Mao Tszedun i koreickaia voina 1950–1953 godov', *Novaia i noveishaia istoriia* 5 (2005), 92–109.

---

[65] Shen Zhihua, 'From Xibaipo to Moscow: Mao Zedong Declared "Lean-to-one-side" Policy', *Zhonggong dangshi yanjiu* 5 (2009), 14–33.

[66] For details, see Shen Zhihua, 'The Soviet Factor in Decision-making in the War to Resist America and Aid Korea', *Dangdai zhongguo shi yanjiu* [Contemporary China History Study] 1 (2000), 28–39; Shen, 'Sino-North Korean Conflict'.

Li Ping *et al.*, *Zhou Enlai nianpu, 1949–1976* [A Chronology of Zhou Enlai] (Beijing: Zhongyang Wenxian and Renmin Chubanshe 1997).

Mansourov, Alexandre Y., 'Stalin, Mao, Kim and China's Decision to Enter the Korean War Sept.16–Oct.15 1950: New Evidence from the Russian Archives', *Cold War International History Project* Bulletins 6–7 (Washington DC: Winter 1995–96), 94–119.

Naboka, V.P., 'Sovetskie letchiki-istrebiteli v Kitae v 1950 godu', *Voprosy istorii* 3 (2002), 136–48.

Orlov, A.S. 'Sovetskaia aviatsiia v Koreiskoi vaine 1950–1953gg.', *Novaia i noveishaia istoriia* 4 (1998), 121–46.

Pang, Xianzhi and Jin Chongji (eds.), *Mao Zedong Zhuan 1949–1976* [A Biography of Mao Zedong] (Beijing: Zhongyang Wenxian Chubanshe 2003).

Pang, Xianzhi and Li Jie, 'Mao Zedong, and Resisting America and Aiding Korea', *Dang de Wenxian,* [Party Historical Documents] 5 (2000), 32–43.

Shen, Zhihua, 'The Soviet Factor in Decision-making in the War-to-Resist America and Aid Korea', *Dangdai zhongguo shi yanjiu* [Contemporary China History Study] 1 (2000), 28–39.

Shen, Zhihua, 'The Soviet Air Force during the War to Resist America and Aid Korea' *Zhonggong Dangshi Yanjiu*, 2 (2002), 69–74.

Shen, Zhihua, *Mao Zedong Sidalin yu Chaoxian Zhanzheng* [Mao, Stalin and the Korean War] (Guangzhou: Guangdong Renmin Chubanshe 2003).

Shen, Zhihua (ed.), *Chaoxian Zhanzheng Eguo Danganguan de Jiemi Wenjian* (Taipei Institute of Modern History Academia Sinica 2003).

Shen, Zhihua, 'Sino-North Korean Conflict and its Resolution during the Korean War', *Cold War International History Project* Bulletins 14/15 (Winter 2003–Spring 2004), 9–24.

Shen, Zhihua, 'More on Stalin Mao Zedong and the Korean War', *Shixue Jikan* 1 (2007), 58–67.

Shen, Zhihua, 'Alliance of "Tooth and Lips" or Marriage of Convenience? The Origins and Development of the Sino-North Korean Alliance, 1946–1958', *Working Paper Series* 2008–09, The US-Korea Institute at SAIS, Dec. 2008.

Shen, Zhihua, 'From Xibaipo to Moscow: Mao Zedong Declared "Lean-to-one-side" Policy', *Zhonggong dangshi yanjiu* 5 (2009), 14–33.

Shi, Zhe, *Zai Lishi Juren Shengbian: Shi Zhe Huiyilu* [Together with Historical Giants: A Memoir of Shi Zhe] (Beijing: Zhongyang Wenxian Chubanshe 1991).

Stone, I.F., *Chaoxian Zhanzheng Neimu*, trans. Nan Zuoming etc. (Hangzhou: Zhejiang Renmin Chubanshe 1989).

Torkunov, A.V., *Zagadochnaia voina: koreiskii konflikt 1950–1953 godov* (Moskova RPE 2000).

Vneshniaia politika Sovetskogo Soiuza Dokumenty i materialy 1950 god (Moskva: GPL 1953), 212–20.

Zhang, Xiaoming, *Red Wings over the Yalu: China, the Soviet Union and the Air War in Korea* (Texas A &M UP 2002).

Zhongyang Wenxian Yanjiushi (ed.), *Jianguo Yilai Mao Zedong Wengao* [Mao Zedong's Manuscripts since the Founding of the PRC] (Beijing: Zhongyang Wenxian Chubanshe 1987–1999), 15 vols.

Zhongyang Wenxian Yanjiushi (ed.), *Zhou Enlai Xuanji* (Beijing Renmin Chubanshe 1980).

Zhongyang Wenxian Yanjiushi (ed.), *Jianguo Yilai Liu Shaoqi Wengao* [Liu Shaoqi's Manuscripts since the Founding of the PRC] (Beijing: Zhongyang Wenxian Chubanshe 2005), 4 vols.

Zhongyang Wenxian Yanjiushi (ed.), *Jianguo Yilai Zhou Enlai Wengao* [Zhou Enlai's Manuscripts since the Founding of the PRC] (Beijing: Zhongyang Wenxian Chubanshe 2008), 3 vols.

Branding an Aggressor: The Commonwealth, the United Nations and Chinese Intervention in the Korean War, November 1950–January 1951

ROBERT BARNES

International History Department, London School of Economics and Political Science, UK

ABSTRACT The crisis following China's intervention in the Korean War led to a significant rift between the United States and the Commonwealth at the United Nations (UN). This article examines the conditions under which the Commonwealth became united and was able to directly influence UN decision-making. It concludes that, when united, the Commonwealth could not easily be ignored by Washington, and thereby acted as an agent of constraint upon the Western superpower.

China's intervention in the Korean War in November 1950 precipitated the biggest crisis of the early Cold War period. Because of its importance, historians have lavished enormous attention on both the Truman administration's political and military responses and on the diplomatic manoeuvring that occurred inside the United Nations (UN).[1] But they have largely overlooked the role played by the

---

[1]See, for instance, Rosemary Foot, *The Wrong War: American Policy and the Dimensions of the Korean Conflict, 1950–1953* (New York: Cornell UP 1985); William Stueck, *Rethinking the Korean War: A New Diplomatic and Strategic History* (Princeton, NJ: Princeton UP 2002); William Stueck, *The Korea War: An International History* (Princeton, NJ: Princeton UP 1995).

Commonwealth.[2] This is a significant gap, for during this crisis the Commonwealth not only challenged US hegemony at the world organisation but also directly influenced UN actions. Essential to the Commonwealth's success was the unity of its members. This article argues that Commonwealth unity occurred when the risk of a global conflict was at its greatest, when key Commonwealth personalities were prepared to exercise their influence, when coincidence brought the Commonwealth members together, and when the US government was willing to bow to Commonwealth pressure. After these conditions were removed, the Commonwealth members put their other allegiances ahead of Commonwealth loyalty. Crucially, no single Commonwealth country, not even Britain, had sufficient influence to constrain US policy, but as a unit the Commonwealth wielded considerable moral authority, not to mention influence in Washington.

The British Commonwealth and the United Nations before Chinese Intervention

Before the Singapore Declaration of 1971 the Commonwealth had neither a formal organisational structure nor a set of unifying principles.[3] It remained largely defined by its founding document, the 1931 Statute of Westminster, which effectively established the legislative independence and equality of the then six Dominions – Australia, Canada, the Irish Free State, Newfoundland, New Zealand, and the Union of South Africa – who became known as the 'Old' Commonwealth members. The Statute also defined the Commonwealth as being 'a free association ... united by common allegiance to the

---

[2]There have been works on the role played by individual or a selected few Commonwealth members. See Shiv Dayal, *India's Role in the Korean Question: A Study of the Settlement of International Disputes Under the United Nations* (Delhi: S. Chand & Co. 1959); Anthony Farrar-Hockley, *The British Part in the Korean War, Volume I: A Distant Obligation* (London: HMSO 1990); Anthony Farrar-Hockley, *The British Part in the Korean War, Volume II: An Honourable Discharge* (London: HMSO 1995); Callum MacDonald, *Britain and the Korean War* (Oxford: Blackwell 1990); Robert O'Neill, *Australia in the Korean War, 1950–53. Volume 1: Strategy and Diplomacy* (Canberra: The Australian War Memorial and the Australian Government Publishing Service 1981); Ian McGibbon, *New Zealand and the Korean War – Volume 1: Politics and Diplomacy* (Auckland: Oxford UP 1992); Graeme Mount, *The Diplomacy of War: The Case of Korea* (Montreal: Black Rose Books 2004).

[3]For good accounts of the Commonwealth see Patrick Gordon-Walker, *The Commonwealth* (London: Secker & Warburg 1962); Hessel Hall, *The Commonwealth: A History of the British Commonwealth of Nations* (London: Van Nostrand Reinhold 1971); and Liz Paren, *The Commonwealth: A Family of Nations* (London: Commonwealth Secretariat 2003).

Crown'. From the outset, therefore, the Commonwealth was a loosely-defined intergovernmental organisation of independent states united by a shared Head of State. The only official contact its members had with each other beyond normal diplomatic channels were at sporadic meetings on specific issues and roughly bi-annual Commonwealth Prime Ministers' Conferences held in London in which common problems were dealt with informally.

World War II undoubtedly marked the pinnacle of Commonwealth cooperation. Although Britain's inability to offer adequate protection led to periodic spats, for the most part all the Commonwealth members, with the exception of Ireland, united against the dire threat posed by the Axis Powers, and London became the focal point of wartime planning. But the post-war world soon proved more complex. The composition of the organisation expanded with India, Pakistan and Ceylon[4] accepting Commonwealth membership when they gained independence.[5] These states became known as the 'New' Commonwealth members. Then in 1949 two members left the Commonwealth. Newfoundland joined Canada while Ireland became a republic, a path that India seemed likely to follow. But India was too important to lose. And so, rather than accepting its departure when it became a republic, the Commonwealth Prime Ministers agreed on the London Declaration. This allowed members who simply recognised the British Sovereign as Head of the Commonwealth, while also dropping the word 'British' from the organisation's title. These actions demonstrated the flexibility of the Old Commonwealth members, particularly Britain, not to mention their strong desire to retain close relations with the new partners.

Still, the importance of the Commonwealth to each of its members depended greatly on their foreign-policy priorities. The British Labour government was not overly sentimental towards the Empire. But Prime Minister Clement Attlee, Foreign Secretary Ernest Bevin and Secretary of State for Commonwealth Relations Patrick Gordon-Walker did realise that a united Commonwealth helped to perpetuate Britain's Great Power status, despite growing indications of post-war decline. Moreover, the British government hoped that by maintaining close relations with the New Commonwealth members, especially India, it could influence events in the emerging Third World and help prevent the spread of Communism in Asia. Bevin, though, was wary of using

---

[4]Ceylon was not a member of the UN until 1955 and so will not be considered in this article.

[5]Burma opted against Commonwealth membership when it gained independence in 1948.

the Commonwealth as a counterweight to American influence. His focus was on securing US aid and military support in Europe.

After Britain, Australia and New Zealand were the most emotionally attached members of the Commonwealth. The conservative Australian and New Zealand Prime Ministers, Robert Menzies and Sidney Holland, were both fervent Anglophiles and looked to Britain to provide leadership. Yet Menzies and Holland disliked the admission of the non-white Commonwealth members and their respective Ministers for External Affairs, Percy Spender and Frederick Doidge, placed greater emphasis on courting American support for a Pacific security pact than Commonwealth loyalty. In contrast, Canada and South Africa displayed much greater independence from Britain. Canada had its own 'special' relationship with the United States, while its Francophone population, including Prime Minister Louis Saint Laurent, had few emotional ties to the Empire. Lester Pearson, Canada's foreign minister and a true internationalist, also thought the Commonwealth anachronistic but still maintained close relations with his Commonwealth colleagues, both Old and New. Meanwhile, the South African government of Daniel Malan, pursuing a policy of Afrikaner nationalism and racial segregation, had little desire to promote the multi-ethnic British Commonwealth.

After independence, the governing elites in India and Pakistan retained close cultural and personal ties with Britain and above all respected the British democratic tradition. Their economies also remained inextricably connected to the other Commonwealth members, particularly the British. Politically, the New Commonwealth governments were hopeful that the Commonwealth could be used to counterbalance US dominance of the non-Communist world. Ironically, India and Pakistan also used Commonwealth membership as a way of checking each other's global influence. With Kashmir a constant threat to regional stability, Jawaharlal Nehru and Liaquat Ali Khan hoped that the Commonwealth could provide a forum both for building bridges and for keeping an eye on each other.

The Commonwealth's role at the UN inevitably reflected the views of its individual members towards the world organisation. Britain's initial hopes for the UN had evaporated with the breakdown of the wartime Grand Alliance. The Attlee government, therefore, was generally content to follow the US lead at the UN, although some debates there had strained Anglo-American relations, most notably the initial wrangling over Palestine. By 1950, the only significant difference between London and Washington revolved around the former's desire to maintain the support of the neutral members whenever possible. The Australian, New Zealand and South African governments, for their parts, had little faith in the UN and preferred to remain quiet and support the Anglo-American position. The Canadian government, however, felt that as a Middle Power Canada could play a useful mediatory role at the UN. Yet Canada always supported the American position when push came to shove.[6]

The Indian position was very different. Nehru, much to the irritation of the Americans, was convinced that the world organisation could be utilised to reconcile Cold War issues. As a result India styled itself as the leader of the Arab-Asian 'neutral' bloc, albeit one that always kept a wary eye on Pakistan.

Inside the UN, then, while the Heads of the Commonwealth delegations met informally to discuss policy, the Old and New Commonwealth members rarely acted as a single unit. Significantly, a partial exception came at the very start of the Korean War. In the wake of North Korea's sudden and brazen invasion, all the Commonwealth members endorsed a US-sponsored Security Council resolution condemning North Korea and calling for the withdrawal of its forces north of the 38th Parallel.

But beyond this, the Commonwealth states soon followed different paths, even during the period of great military uncertainty during the summer of 1950 when a North Korean conquest of the peninsula was a very real possibility. In the Security Council India, the only Commonwealth member represented except Britain, refused to vote on the second US-sponsored resolution calling for the members of the UN to furnish such assistance to South Korea necessary to repel the North Korean armed attack and restore international peace and security. It was only after intense British pressure that Nehru agreed to 'accept' the resolution as a natural progression of the UN action.[7] Still, the Indian Prime Minister refused to sanction the British-sponsored but American-authored third resolution that placed the US government in control of the Unified Command in Korea – a resolution that transferred the Security Council's powers of military coordination to Washington.

On the other hand, the Old Commonwealth members rallied behind US leadership in the UN, particularly the British who were closely consulted by the Truman administration. These Commonwealth governments also talked among themselves regarding what contributions they could make to the UN action. Within days these governments pledged to provide military assistance to the UN action, despite their

---

[6]Lester Pearson, *Memoirs – Volume 2: The International Years, 1948–1957* (London: Gollancz 1974), 121–3.

[7][New Delhi, India] N[ational] A[rchives of] I[ndia], M[inistry of] E[xternal] A[ffairs], CJK Branch, 67-CJK/50, Secretary-General for External Affairs [Gopal Menon]-Rau, New Delhi, 29 June 1950.

reluctance to commit ground forces in light of their domestic and global defensive commitments. Moreover, after the rapid reversal in military fortunes following UN Commander General Douglas MacArthur's successful amphibious counter-attack at Inchon, the older members supported a resolution in the General Assembly, jointly sponsored by the United States and Britain, which effectively permitted the UN Command to unify the peninsula by force.

It was a position that was anathema to the Indians. In Beijing, the Indian ambassador, Sardar K. M. Panikkar, had repeatedly been warned that the new People's Republic of China (PRC) would intervene if UN forces crossed the 38th Parallel. And Nehru's government thought a UN move into North Korea entailed an unacceptable risk of escalation. It proved to be a significant piece of foresight.

Limited Chinese Intervention

On 6 November 1950, with UN forces approaching the Chinese border, the Security Council received a special report from MacArthur stating that 'hostile contact' had been made 'with Chinese communist military units'.[8] While this news came as a great shock to the international community, the American response was moderate. US Secretary of State Dean Acheson formulated a draft resolution, which simply called on the Chinese forces to cease their activities in Korea and withdraw to allow the UN Command to complete the unification of Korea.[9]

The British Delegation immediately agreed to co-sponsor this proposal along with four other members of the Security Council. But divergence between the Commonwealth and the United States had already begun to surface. The British Permanent Representative Gladwyn Jebb, with the support of Rau, insisted that as a preliminary measure the Security Council invite the PRC to send a representative to clarify China's objectives in Korea.[10] Behind this request was the belief held by the Commonwealth governments, particularly Britain and India, that China might have intervened to protect her interests in the border zone, particularly the hydro-electric power stations on the Yalu river. Implicit in this conclusion was a sense that the United States was in some way responsible for the alarming turn of events.

---

[8]U[nited] N[ations] S[ecurity] C[ouncil], Official Records, Fifth Year Supplement for Sept. through Dec., S/1884, 6 Nov. 1950.
[9]F[oreign] R[elations of the] U[nited] S[tates], 1950, 7: 1053.
[10]U[nited] N[ations] S[ecurity] C[ouncil] Fifth Year, No.62 – 520th Meeting, New York, 8 Nov. 1950.

When China rebuffed the Anglo-Indian overture, Bevin became alarmed. He now feared that the PRC was planning a large-scale invasion of Korea. And to head it off he proposed the creation of a buffer zone south of the Korean–Chinese border. The Foreign Secretary hoped this would avoid a costly war without having to make any significant territorial or political concessions to the Chinese. Even so, Bevin grudgingly backed down when the Truman administration revealed it would only accept a buffer zone in Manchurian territory.[11] Acheson was opposed to taking any action that would hinder MacArthur's forthcoming 'end-the-war' offensive to reunify the whole of Korea.[12] Clearly, Bevin was already more willing than Acheson to placate Beijing, which was hardly surprising given that the British had strong economic ties with China through Hong Kong.

Massive Chinese Intervention

On 24 November 1950 MacArthur launched his 'end-the-war' offensive confident that neither the PRC nor the USSR would intervene on a large scale. Yet within days his forces had encountered approximately 200,000 Chinese troops in northern Korea, and were now in rapid retreat.[13]

The Truman administration's reaction to this news was emphatic. In the UN, the US Permanent Representative Warren Austin openly accused the Chinese Communists of committing aggression in Korea and pressed for an immediate vote on the Six-Power draft resolution.[14] Although nine members voted for this resolution, its adoption was blocked by the Soviet veto, forcing the US government to switch debate to the General Assembly.[15]

Washington's decisive response brought all the Commonwealth members into play. But rather than meekly follow the US lead, as many had done in the summer, this time the Commonwealth swiftly united behind an effort to constrain the Truman administration and prevent the US Delegation from convincing the General Assembly to take precipitate action that might escalate the crisis.

---

[11][Kew,] UK, [The] N[ational] A[rchives,] CAB[inet Papers] 128/18, C.M.(50)73rd Conclusions, 13 Nov. 1950; and C.M.(50)76th Conclusions, 20 Nov. 1950.

[12]*FRUS 1950*, 7: 1212.

[13]Ibid., 1237.

[14]*UNSC Fifth Year*, No.68 – 526th Meeting, New York, 28 Nov. 1950.

[15]*UNSC Fifth Year*, No.72 – 530th Meeting, New York, 30 Nov. 1950; N[ational] A[rchives, College Park, MD], [State Department, Foreign Service Post Files Records] RG 84/350/82/5/7 E.1030-H, Box 4, 1950, Tel Incs US-December, Acheson to Austin, Washington DC, 4 Dec. 1950.

What united the Commonwealth states was their shared fear that an American effort to brand the PRC an aggressor would result in the implementation of the UN Charter's collective security provisions. From the Commonwealth perspective, such an outcome would be utterly disastrous. Although the various members had different strategic priorities, none relished the prospect of a wider war. The Indians, for instance, feared that another global conflagration would create both external and internal threats to their recently won independence, while Australia and New Zealand thought that such a war would leave them further isolated in the Pacific region. Canada felt more secure due to her proximity to the US and NATO membership but was unwilling to increase her military spending or deploy large numbers of troops overseas unless this was absolutely essential. And in London, Attlee's government concluded that any collective security measures against the PRC would divert resources away from Europe, trigger Chinese retaliatory action against Hong Kong or Indochina, and drag the Soviet Union into the fight, producing a global conflict.

Determined to restrain the United States, the Commonwealth states employed various techniques. Initially, the Indian and British delegations sought to find out through General Wu Hsiu-chuan, the Chinese representative in New York, whether Beijing had intervened in Korea for aggressive purposes or simply to defend its borders. But though Jebb managed to meet once with the Chinese representative, Wu simply stressed that the Chinese soldiers in Korea were volunteers and the only peaceful solution was the withdrawal of all US forces from the Far East.[16] Meanwhile, the Indian Permanent Representative, Benegal Rau, was scarcely more effective. Though he got to see Wu on several occasions, Rau was given no indication that China would support a ceasefire.[17]

Stymied here, the Commonwealth players switched their attention to the Truman administration. In early December, in the wake of Truman's off-the-cuff press conference comments that the use of atomic weapons was under active consideration, Attlee flew to Washington to meet the President. The British Prime Minister, desperate to stave off a backbench rebellion, received full support from other Commonwealth members to discuss the situation in the Far East.[18] But he had little joy. Once in Washington Attlee was unable to

---

[16]UK NA, F[oreign] O[ffice Papers] FO 371/84105, Jebb to Bevin, New York, 5 Dec. 1950.

[17]UK NA, FO 371/84106, British High Commissioner to India (Archibald Nye) to Gordon-Walker, New Delhi, 5 Dec. 1950.

[18]UK NA, CAB 128/18, C.M.(50)80th Conclusions, London, 30 Nov. 1950.

convince Truman to agree to an immediate ceasefire, let alone a commitment to discuss other Far Eastern issues, such as China's admission to the UN or the future of Taiwan after the fighting had ceased. Instead, the two leaders simply agreed to back the Six-Power draft resolution in the General Assembly.[19]

After Attlee departed from Washington, the focus shifted back to New York. Here the Heads of the Commonwealth delegations were decidedly unimpressed with the American stance. Meeting on 6 December, they concluded that the Six-Power draft resolution was outdated, divisive, and would be rejected by the PRC. In such circumstances the United States would inevitably press for an aggressor resolution, with all that this entailed. The Commonwealth members thus launched their most important diplomatic gambit. They all agreed to support the British suggestion for a resolution calling for a ceasefire.[20]

Nehru, who felt most strongly that a cessation of hostilities should take place immediately and was the least concerned with upsetting the Americans, took up the mantle. His draft resolution proposed a ceasefire at the 38th Parallel, the creation of a demilitarised zone, and the prospect of negotiations with the PRC on Korea and Taiwan after the cessation of hostilities.[21] Although Nehru's draft garnered general support from other Commonwealth members, Acheson immediately rejected it. But the Commonwealth's leverage over the United States was nevertheless beginning to take hold. Acheson recognised that Britain was Washington's only true global partner, while the other Commonwealth members represented its key allies in North America and the Pacific, together with the leading voice in the emerging neutral bloc.

Indeed, Acheson was in a difficult position. His initial instinct was clearly to reject Nehru's draft out of hand, convinced that the West ought to hang tough in response to Chinese aggression and acutely aware of the intense domestic political pressure to brand it an aggressor. But he also recognised that a united Commonwealth was far more difficult to ignore than its constituent members, even Britain, when they acted alone. Crucially, therefore, in an effort to maintain US-Commonwealth unity, Acheson proposed that the President of the

---

[19]UK NA, FO 371/84105, British Ambassador USA (Oliver Franks) to Bevin, Washington, 5 Dec. 1950.

[20]UK NA, FO 371/84124, Record of Meeting Heads of Commonwealth Delegations, New York, 6 Dec. 1950.

[21]UK NA, PREM[ier Papers] PREM 8/1405 Part 4, Record Conversation Gordon-Walker to Indian High Commissioner UK (Krishna Menon), London, 11 Dec. 1950.

General Assembly, along with two people he would designate, be empowered to confer with the Unified Command and the PRC to determine the basis for a ceasefire.[22]

The Indian Delegation seized upon this opportunity with alacrity. Within days it had convinced all 13 Arab-Asian members to co-sponsor a draft resolution incorporating Acheson's proposal for a ceasefire committee. The Heads of the Commonwealth delegations wholeheartedly supported this conciliatory first step,[23] while the US government, in light of the united Commonwealth position and the fact that Acheson had originated the resolution's provisions, was willing to give it priority over the Six-Power draft resolution.[24] The Arab-Asian proposal was thus adopted with only the Soviet bloc voting in opposition.[25] Furthermore, in fulfilment of the resolution's provisions President of the General Assembly, Nasrollah Entezam of Iran, asked two Commonwealth representatives, Rau of India and Pearson of Canada to join him on the Ceasefire Committee.[26] The Commonwealth thus had a special interest in the work of this newly formed body.

In the confusion following massive Chinese intervention, the Commonwealth had united against any attempt to push the UN into hasty action. Its unity, which was to prove important in exerting leverage over the United States, stemmed from a variety of factors. One was the dire nature of the crisis, which convinced the Commonwealth governments that any condemnatory action taken by the UN against the PRC would inevitably lead to an escalation of the conflict. Another was the role of key Commonwealth personalities, who took it upon themselves to defuse the situation. For the first time during the Korean conflict, therefore, the Commonwealth had coordinated its policy and achieved its goals at the UN.

---

[22]H[arry] S. T[ruman] L[ibrary, Independence, MO] Truman Papers, Personal Secretary's File, Subject File 1940–1953, Box 187, Memoranda for the President: Meeting Discussions: 1950, Memorandum for the President, Executive Secretary of the National Security Council (James Lay), Washington DC, 12 Dec. 1950.

[23][Ottawa, Canada,] L[ibrary and] A[rchives] C[anada], RG 25/6444/5475-DW-4-40 [Pt 5], Record of Meeting of Heads of Commonwealth Delegations, New York, 13 Dec. 1950.

[24]HSTL, [Dean] Acheson Papers, Memoranda of Conversations File, Box 67, Dec. 1951, Memorandum of Conversation with the President, 11 Dec. 1950.

[25]U[nited] N[ations] G[eneral] A[ssembly] Official Records, *Fifth Session Supplements*, No.20 (A/1775) Resolution 384 (V) adopted 14 Dec. 1950.

[26]Pearson, *Memoirs 1948–1957*, 280.

The Ceasefire Committee

By the second week of December 1950, with the UNC's reports clearly indicating that the Chinese offensive had halted north of the 38th Parallel, the Commonwealth members optimistically hoped that Bejing had achieved its war aims and that a ceasefire could be arranged. But even with the battlefield situation apparently improving, the work of the Ceasefire Committee got off to an unpromising start.

Taking advantage of India's favourable relations with the PRC, Rau was able to communicate with Wu on several occasions. But again to little effect. The Chinese representative unequivocally stated that his government did not recognise the 'illegal' Ceasefire Committee formed without China's consent and would not negotiate until it was agreed that all foreign forces would be withdrawn from Korea; that PRC sovereignty extended over Taiwan; and that the PRC would be admitted to the UN. Wu also revealed that he would be returning to China in a matter of days. In response, the Ceasefire Committee sent Wu a letter urging him to stay and talk, but even this approach was ignored.[27]

The US government, acting through the Unified Command, had cooperated with the Ceasefire Committee inasmuch as it had revealed its willingness to agree to a ceasefire at the 38th Parallel.[28] But the domestic pressure on Truman to adopt a tough stance was mounting. In the middle of December, the President declared a state of national emergency paving the way for a massive increase in US military production.[29] This action only served to heighten tension and further jeopardised the work of the Committee. And, to make matters worse, in New York the American UN Delegation also snubbed Pearson and Rau, who were trying to push for the adoption of a second Arab-Asian draft resolution recommending that the representatives of several unnamed governments meet to make recommendations for the peaceful settlement of all outstanding Far Eastern issues.[30] The Ceasefire Committee hoped that such a resolution would convince the Chinese that the UN was serious about discussing other Far Eastern issues following a ceasefire.

---

[27]Ibid., 282.

[28]NA, Microfilm C0042 Reel 1, Acheson-Austin, Washington, 15 Dec. 1950.

[29]HSTL, Truman Papers, Korean War File 1947–1952, Box 7, Massive Chinese Communist intervention and allied reactions, Press Release, Washington DC, 15 Dec. 1950.

[30]*UNGA Fifth Session First Committee* 415th Meeting, New York, 12 Dec. 1950 (A/C.1/641 and A/ C.1/642).

In spite of the toughening American stance, the Ceasefire Committee sent a cable to Beijing stating that as soon as a ceasefire had been arranged it still planned to proceed with the 12-Power draft resolution.[31] But the UN was again caught between the two belligerents. And it was not just Washington that was reluctant to negotiate. After much delay, Zhou En-lai firmly rejected the Arab–Asian Resolution arguing that it was meaningless without the 12-Power draft resolution.[32] With the bargaining position of the two main belligerents as far apart as ever, the Committee's two Commonwealth representatives realised there was little hope of brokering a deal through the UN.[33] The Ceasefire Committee's report, therefore, made no recommendations.[34]

During the Ceasefire Committee's brief efforts to communicate with both sides, the Commonwealth governments remained quiet. With the lull in fighting the US government did not press for any drastic proposals risking escalation and so the Commonwealth members saw little need to coordinate their views. Moreover, although they disapproved of Truman's decision to declare a state of national emergency, the Commonwealth members appreciated that the Unified Command had shown flexibility and had cooperated with the Ceasefire Committee, which was in marked contrast to the PRC's intransigence.

Nonetheless, the Commonwealth remained united behind the work of the Ceasefire Committee and gave much encouragement to Canada and India to persevere in their efforts. On a more personal level, Rau and Pearson showed great determination and used their connections with both the PRC and United States in their attempts to find an acceptable ceasefire. Yet their efforts were not enough to bring the positions of the belligerents any closer and the threat to international peace continued to ensure that the Commonwealth did not disunite.

The Commonwealth Prime Ministers' Conference

Despite disappointment with the failure of the Ceasefire Committee's efforts, battlefield events led to the Commonwealth's most serious challenge yet to US hegemony at the UN. On New Year's Eve 1950 Chinese forces launched a massive offensive south of the 38th Parallel. The UNC offered little resistance to the Communist advance and

---

[31]NA, RG 84/350/82/4/2 E.1030-F, Box 29, Delga 384–471 (6–30 Dec. 1950), Austin to Acheson, New York, 20 Dec. 1950.
[32]UK NA, RG 84/350/82/4/2 E.1030-F, Box 29, Delga 384–471 (6–30 Dec. 1950), Austin to Acheson, New York, 24 Dec. 1950.
[33]Pearson, *Memoirs 1948–1957*, 287–8.
[34]*UNGA Fifth Session Annexes Volume 1* A/C.1/643, 2 Jan. 1951

MacArthur recommended that the UN forces should be withdrawn from the peninsula.[35] The Truman administration, reacting to the public outcry at these developments, demanded that the PRC be branded an aggressor or else the UN would lose all credibility. The Commonwealth members were equally disturbed by the radical change in nature of the crisis, but they believed that the American proposal risked escalating the conflict and alienating the Arab-Asian members. The Commonwealth, therefore, called for another intermediary step in the hope of convincing the Chinese to accept to a ceasefire. Crucially, the US Government again agreed to put its own desires to one side, largely because Acheson believed that Beijing would inevitably reject all UN calls for a settlement, giving the Commonwealth members time to 'return to comparative sanity'.[36] The Secretary of State was therefore willing to accept a limited delay if this proved necessary to have an aggressor resolution adopted by an overwhelming majority.

The Truman administration, however, underestimated the unity of purpose of the Commonwealth in searching for an acceptable intermediary step. Pearson and Rau remained at the forefront, using the continued existence of the Ceasefire Committee to formulate a statement of ceasefire principles to propose to the PRC. These principles were an immediate ceasefire followed by the staged withdrawal of all armed forces from Korea; the creation by the UN of machinery whereby the Korean people could express themselves freely; interim arrangements for the administration of Korea and the maintenance of peace pending the establishment of the new government; and affirmation that the United States, Britain, USSR, and PRC would seek a peaceful settlement of all outstanding Far Eastern issues after the cessation of hostilities.

More vitally to Commonwealth unity, the Commonwealth Prime Ministers' Conference, called by Attlee when the crisis had just begun, coincidently opened in London on 4 January 1951. For the first time at such a conference the government leaders sought to formulate a united policy, and thereby take the initiative in the Korean debate. Bevin summed up the sentiment of the Commonwealth when he stated in the opening meeting that the nature of the organisation's membership – spanning the globe and various races as well as representing both the Western and neutral camps – meant that it could exert great moral influence at the UN and over US policy.[37] The Foreign Secretary then tabled a memorandum suggesting that a ceasefire occur simultaneously

---

[35] *FRUS 1951*, 7: 56.
[36] Dean Acheson, *The Korean War* (New York: W.W. Norton 1969), 94.
[37] LAC, MG 26 N1/22/Commonwealth – Prime Minister's Meeting 1951, P.M.M.(51)3rd Meeting, London, 5 Jan. 1951.

with settlement of the Korean question, the admission of the PRC to the UN and for Taiwan to come under Beijing's sovereignty.[38] Nonetheless, this proposal met a mixed response. Nehru predictably supported the idea of settling all Far Eastern issues, arguing that the PRC would accept no other course. Saint Laurent, Menzies and Holland, however, warned that the US government would only accept political negotiations after a ceasefire had begun.[39]

As a result, Saint Laurent, after receiving some strongly worded telegrams from Pearson, urged his colleagues to support the Ceasefire Committee's principles arguing that they might be acceptable to Washington and Beijing but that, if not, their adoption would at least postpone the submission of an aggressor resolution. This course won favour with the Australian, New Zealand and South African representatives. Nehru nevertheless stated that Panikkar had informed him that the principles were unacceptable to the PRC and suggested a simplified version of Bevin's plan merely mentioning the resolution of outstanding issues.[40] Interestingly, Nehru's rival Liaquat Ali Khan made a similar proposal.[41] After this muddled meeting Attlee took it upon himself to send a message to Truman stressing that the Commonwealth was principally concerned with Washington's intentions at the UN after the PRC was branded an aggressor.[42] But the President's reply was evasive, only stating that the UN should not shrink from stating the truth.[43] In response, Bevin suggested a resolution disapproving of Chinese intervention and calling for Chinese forces to be withdrawn and for the Great Powers to meet in order to deal with issues threatening world peace. The Commonwealth Prime Ministers tentatively agreed to this new proposal[44] but Acheson was non-committal.[45]

Meanwhile, events beyond the Commonwealth Conference worked to unify the Prime Ministers. In New York, at the behest of Rau under instruction from Nehru, the Ceasefire Committee sought to revise its

---

[38]UK NA, PREM 8/1405 Part 4, P.M.M(51)7 Memorandum by the UK Government, London, 5 Jan. 1951.
[39]LAC, MG 26 N1/22/Commonwealth – Prime Ministers' Meeting 1951, P.M.M.(51)4th Meeting, London, 5 Jan. 1951.
[40]UK NA, PREM 8/1405 Part 4, P.M.M.(51)8, Memorandum by the Prime Minister of India, London, 5 Jan. 1951.
[41]UK NA, PREM 8/1405 Part 4, P.M.M.(51)5th Meeting, Minute 2, London, 8 Jan. 1951.
[42]*FRUS 1951*, 7: 37.
[43]Ibid., 39.
[44]UK NA, PREM 8/1405 Part 4, P.M.M.(51)7th Meeting, Minute 1, London, 9 Jan. 1951.
[45]UK NA, PREM 8/1405 Part 4, Franks to Bevin, Washington DC, 10 Jan. 1951.

ceasefire principles in an effort to make them more acceptable to the Chinese. Pearson, wary of Rau's zealous efforts to appease the Chinese and his willingness to overlook the Truman administration's difficult domestic position, took it upon himself to amend the principles. After close consultation with the US Delegation, and taking into account the reports he had received from Saint Laurent regarding the Commonwealth Prime Ministers' Conference, Pearson revised the principles so that negotiations on other Far Eastern issues would take place 'as soon as a ceasefire had been agreed on', while also including specific reference to the settlement of the questions of Taiwan and Chinese representation.[46]

The Truman administration once more proved willing to compromise, despite domestic uproar, and instructed the US Delegation to vote for the ceasefire principles.[47] In light of this development the Commonwealth Prime Ministers agreed there was no longer any need to consider an alternative policy since the Americans had accepted the moderate ceasefire principles.[48] With US-Commonwealth unity intact, the General Assembly approved the Ceasefire Committee's supplementary report in spite of Soviet warnings that its principles were unacceptable.[49]

The Chinese New Year Offensive had heightened the crisis and led to the resumption of the Truman administration's demand for the PRC to be branded an aggressor. This reaction effectively united the Commonwealth in opposition to Washington's position. Furthermore, the Commonwealth Prime Ministers Conference in London used this opportunity to try to formulate an alternative UN policy. The Commonwealth members realised that the very nature of their organisation made it difficult to ignore. The fact that the Truman Administration remained silent at the UN for over a week while the Commonwealth leaders discussed this matter in isolation dramatically highlights this point, especially as the military situation worsened during this time and the American public increasingly turned against its government.

The Commonwealth Prime Ministers' Conference had, however, also demonstrated that its members were not as united as they had hoped. Attlee and Bevin were preoccupied with trying to appease Nehru who,

---

[46]UK NA, PREM 8/1405 Part 4, P.M.M/(51)9, Note by the Secretariat, London, 11 Jan. 1951.

[47]Acheson Papers, Memoranda of Conversations File, Box 67, Memorandum Conversation with President, 11 Jan. 1950.

[48]UK NA, PREM 8/1405 Part 4, P.M.M.(51)10th Meeting, London, 11 Jan. 1951.

[49]*UNGA Fifth Session First Committee* 425th Meeting, New York, 13 Jan. 1951 (A/C.1/650 and A/C.1/651).

in turn, was most concerned with placating China. In contrast, Saint Laurent, Menzies and Holland were more sensitive to the Truman administration's desperate domestic position. These fissures within the Commonwealth were soon to open into a gaping chasm. Yet for the meantime, the Commonwealth was united by the clear-sightedness displayed by Pearson and Rau on the ceasefire Committee and the US government's continued willingness to meet the Commonwealth's viewpoint.

The 'Aggressor' Resolution

The Prime Ministers' Conference represented the pinnacle of Commonwealth coordination. After this point in time, the conditions for unity were removed one by one during the second half of January 1951.

To begin with, the US government's willingness to compromise evaporated. On the same day as the ceasefire principles were adopted, Acheson, predicting that Beijing would reject the peace overture, formulated a draft resolution branding the PRC an aggressor and calling for the UN Collective Measures Committee to make recommendations accordingly.[50] After 17 January, when Zhou En-lai rejected the ceasefire principles, the Truman administration's patience finally snapped. Although the Chinese Premier did make a counter-proposal for a conference to be held in China composed of the PRC, USSR, US, Britain, France, India and Egypt to negotiate all outstanding Far Eastern issues before a ceasefire, Truman immediately told the press that the US government would seek to brand the PRC an aggressor 'with everything that we could bring to bear'.[51] In the General Assembly Austin stressed that the UN had explored every possibility for a peaceful settlement; now the time had come to take firm action or face ruin.[52] In addition, Acheson told the British that the US government's support for the ceasefire principles had brought it 'to the verge of destruction domestically' and was unwilling to make any further compromises.[53] In New York, the US Delegation was instructed to search for sponsors for the aggressor resolution, starting with the

---

[50]*FRUS 1951*, 7: 74.

[51]*UNGA Fifth Session Annexes Volume 1* A/C.1/653, 17 Jan. 1951; Truman Papers, Korean War File 1947–1952, Box 8, 26. US efforts to obtain UN action re: Chinese intervention, White House Press and Radio Conference, Washington DC, 18 Jan. 1951.

[52]*UNGA Fifth Session First Committee* 426th Meeting, New York, 18 Jan. 1951.

[53]NA, [State Department Records] RG 59/250/46/3/5, Entry 394B, Box 1, Memoranda from S and U 1951, Memorandum of Telephone Conversation, Special Assistant to the Secretary of State (Lucius Battle), Washington DC, 18 Jan. 1951.

Commonwealth members, but if none could be found then it should table the proposal alone.[54]

Under this pressure the Commonwealth alliance began to splinter. The New Zealand and South African governments were the first to support the US draft resolution as it stood. The Australian Foreign Minister Percy Spender also accepted the American proposal, but suggested that its condemnation paragraph be rephrased. And he proposed the establishment of an ad hoc body to use its good offices to bring about the cessation of hostilities.[55] In contrast, the British Cabinet called for the US draft resolution to be divided into two stages, the first would condemn the PRC for rejecting a ceasefire; the second would deal with the question of additional measures only if the first did not bring about a cessation of hostilities.[56] The Canadian government held similar views.[57] Nehru, meanwhile, was encouraged by the Chinese response and sought further elucidation of Beijing's position before committing to any UN policy.[58]

Yet, despite his aggressive posturing, Acheson remained sensitive to Commonwealth pressure. And he soon agreed to revise the US draft resolution by incorporating the Australian phrasing regarding the condemnation of the PRC, as well as adding a provision for the establishment of a Good Offices Committee, which would be composed of the President of the General Assembly and two persons he would designate to seek a peaceful solution to the conflict. The US government hoped that the addition of these clauses would allow the Common-wealth governments to co-sponsor the proposal and avoid the embarrassment of tabling its draft resolution alone. But Acheson's ploy was only partially successful. Although Australia was a willing co-sponsor, Britain and Canada continued to insist that the paragraph referring to additional measures be deleted. Under intense pressure from both Houses of Congress, the Truman administration decided to table the revised draft resolution alone.

Washington's determination to demonstrate the strength of its convictions was not shaken by the arrival of a communication from the Indian government containing a set of 'clarifications' to the earlier PRC's counter-proposal. Zhou En-lai now suggested certain conces-sions, including the removal of all conditions before negotiations and

---

[54]*FRUS 1951*, 7: 108.

[55][Canberra, Australia,] N[ational] A[rchives of] A[ustralia] A1838, 88/1/10 PART 5, Spender to Australian Delegation UN (K. Shann), New York, 17 Jan. 1951.

[56]UK NA, CAB 128/19, C.M.(51)4th Conclusions, London, 18 Jan. 1951.

[57]LAC, RG 25/4741/50069-A-40 Pt.18, Canadian Representative to the UN (David Riddell) to Pearson, New York, 18 Jan. 1951.

[58]UK NA, PREM 8/1405 Part 4, Menon to Attlee, London, 18 Jan. 1951.

that the Seven-Power conference would first agree to a ceasefire before other Far Eastern issues were resolved.[59] But the Truman administration dismissed them as nothing more than Chinese propaganda that would delay the work of the UN.

The US action thoroughly divided the Commonwealth, but not along the familiar 'old'–'new' cleavage. On one hand, Bevin and Pearson joined with Nehru in concluding that the Chinese proposals were sincere and that a window of opportunity had been opened. Australia, New Zealand and South Africa, on the other hand, were against opposing the Americans, especially now that Washington had clearly signalled that it would stop at nothing less than an aggressor resolution. On 22 January Commonwealth disunity was made public when the Indian, British, Canadian and Pakistani delegations supported a motion tabled by Rau to have the Korean debate adjourned for 48 hours so that the clarifications could be examined. The Australian, New Zealand and South African delegations abstained. Notably, in spite of a negative American vote, the motion was narrowly adopted by 27 votes to 23 with six abstentions.[60]

During the 48-hours adjournment Commonwealth unity disintegrated completely. The vote on the Indian motion had exposed the rift within the Western alliance and finally brought home to the Commonwealth members that they might find themselves voting against a US resolution. In addition, it had become increasingly clear to the Commonwealth governments by this time that the severity of the crisis had lessened in the preceding weeks. Under the operational command of Lieutenant General Matthew B. Ridgway the UN forces had halted the Chinese offensive and restored confidence that a line could be held across the peninsula. In this situation the Truman administration, with a slight easing of public pressure, felt there was no need for the UN to immediately impose additional measures upon the PRC while the Commonwealth members no longer feared that the conflict would necessarily escalate if China was branded an aggressor.

As a result, the key personalities within each Commonwealth government reassessed their positions in light of their long-term relations vis-à-vis Washington. With a possible Pacific security pact uppermost in his mind, Spender gave the Australian Delegation final instructions to vote in favour of the US draft resolution, despite Menzies' desire not to diverge from Britain.[61] Doidge, equally desirous

---

[59]NA, RG 59/250/49/5/3 E.1459, Box 3, India 1951–1952, Clarification of certain points included in the counter-proposal made by the Chinese government to Political Committee of the United Nations General Assembly.

[60]*UNGA Fifth Session First Committee* 429th Meeting, New York, 22 Jan. 1951.

[61]NAA, A1838, TS88/1/10, Spender to Shann, Canberra, 24 Jan. 1951.

of a US security guarantee for New Zealand, convinced his own Prime Minister to fully support the US draft resolution.[62] More significantly, Britain and Canada started to gravitate back towards the Americans. Pearson recognised that if Ottawa wished to maintain its special relationship with Washington it would have to vote for the draft resolution. What's more, even the British government showed the first signs of breaking. With Bevin gravely ill in hospital his more cautious deputy, Minister of State Kenneth Younger, warned the Cabinet that if it did not support the US draft resolution Britain would become isolated from her key allies. Even so, the majority of the Labour Cabinet remained firmly opposed to branding the PRC an aggressor and Attlee reluctantly agreed to vote against the draft resolution unless the provision concerning additional measures was deleted.[63] Britain thus found itself standing alone with India against the United States.

Nehru's convictions, however, were little affected by concerns of voting against the US proposal. In fact, the Indian Prime Minister had become greatly disillusioned with the Commonwealth precisely because the majority of its members had folded under US pressure at the critical moment. India, therefore, turned its attention to the neutral bloc where it continued to hold much sway. Rau had consequently been able to persuade the Arab-Asian members to revise their outstanding draft resolution to incorporate the Chinese proposal for a Seven-Power conference.[64]

Yet even though the Commonwealth was thoroughly disunited and the majority of its members had endorsed the American position, at the eleventh hour the Truman administration proved willing to make a final concession to avoid a split with Britain. While Acheson was pleased to have broken up the united Commonwealth front he recognised that Britain represented Washington's closest and most influential ally and was prepared to go one step further to maintain this partnership. Moreover, Acheson realised that without British support the Western alliance would appear acutely divided even if the other Commonwealth members voted for the US draft resolution. The Secretary of State feared the domestic response to this act of apparent British insubordination and how Communist propaganda would take advantage of the situation.

Taking all this into account Acheson unwillingly agreed to amend the US draft resolution so that the committee for additional measures would defer its report if the Good Offices Committee reported

---

[62]LAC, RG 25/4741/50069-A-40 Pt.19, Canadian High Commissioner New Zealand (Alfred Rive) to Pearson, Wellington, 25 Jan. 1951.

[63]UK NA, CAB 128/19, C.M.(51)8th Conclusions, London, 25 Jan. 1951.

[64]*UNGA Fifth Session Annexes Volume 1* A/C.1/642/Rev.1, 24 Jan. 1951.

satisfactory progress in its work.[65] The British Cabinet, content that they had forced Washington to make significant concessions and realising that they could wring no more now the Commonwealth was disunited, finally agreed to vote in favour of the aggressor resolution to avoid being alienated at the UN.[66]

Meanwhile, India continued to oppose any attempts to condemn the Chinese intervention in Korea and in a final effort to win support revised the 12-Power draft resolution so that the first action of the proposed Seven-Power conference would be to arrange a ceasefire.[67] Additionally, Rau informed the General Assembly that the Indian government had received information from the 'highest sources in Peking' that the Chinese government regarded the revised 12-Power draft resolution as 'providing a genuine basis for a peaceful settlement'.[68] In the circumstances, these efforts did not prove enough to reunite the Commonwealth or convince the majority of the UN members. When the Arab-Asian proposal was put to the vote it was rejected with a large number of members abstaining, including all of the Old Commonwealth. In comparison, the US draft resolution was overwhelmingly adopted with all the Old Commonwealth members voting in its favour, Pakistan abstaining, and India finding itself in opposition with the Soviet bloc.[69]

Over the following 18 months of the Korean conflict US leadership at the UN prevailed while the Commonwealth remained quiet. The Commonwealth accepted this passive role because of the relative stability of the conflict, once a military stalemate had been established at the 38th Parallel and the PRC failed to take any retaliatory action. Moreover, the Truman administration waited patiently for the efforts of the Good Offices Committee to peter out and then only pressed for an economic embargo on the export of strategic goods to China. When armistice talks started between the UNC and Communist High Command in July 1951 all of the Commonwealth members were content that the risk of escalation was minimal and supported the US Delegation's motion to have the Korean debate postponed until a ceasefire had been arranged. While this was a practical measure it also demonstrated Washington's concern that it could no longer expect to dominate discussions in New York with the unquestioned support of the Commonwealth. These concerns proved well judged since when the debate finally resumed in October 1952 in response to the breakdown

---

[65]*FRUS 1951*, 7: 137.

[66]UK NA, CAB 128/19, C.M.(51)10th Conclusions, London, 29 Jan. 1951.

[67]*UNGA Fifth Session Annexes Volume 1* A/C.1/642/Rev.2, 29 Jan. 1951.

[68]*UNGA Fifth Session First Committee* 437th Meeting, New York, 30 Jan. 1951.

[69]*UNGA Fifth Session Plenary Meetings* 327th Meeting, New York, 1 Feb. 1951.

THE KOREAN WAR AT SIXTY

of the armistice talks the Commonwealth, fearing a prolongation of the conflict and the American military response to such an eventuality, once again united in opposition to US policy at the UN. In this instance the Commonwealth forced the lame duck Truman administration to back down.

Nonetheless, in the crisis following Chinese intervention in the Korean War the Commonwealth by remaining united had been able to force the US government to make a number of significant concessions. These created the delay necessary to expose China's insincerity and bring about the overwhelming support of the UN members for the aggressor resolution.[70] As William Stueck points out, this delay came at a crucial time: had the United States been able to push through an aggressor resolution during January, when the battlefield situation was so bleak that a UN defeat seemed distinctly possible, then it was possible that such a resolution might have been used to give legitimacy to some of the escalatory measures the US government briefly considered. But by February the military situation on the ground was already starting to improve. The Commonwealth had thus bought some valuable time.[71]

Meanwhile, the Old Commonwealth members were generally pleased that their challenge to US hegemony at the UN had brought them closer together than they had been since World War II, and this helped to ensure that the Commonwealth remained a significant aspect of their foreign policies for the foreseeable future. More importantly, however, the Commonwealth members were relieved that this act of resistance, though serious in the short-term, had not jeopardised their long-term relations with the Western superpower. In fact, the Australian and New Zealand governments believed that the signing of the ANZUS defence treaty later that year vindicated their flexible policies during this period. For these two countries the heightened state of the Cold War over the previous months had only served to highlight that the Commonwealth, particularly Britain, could no longer guarantee their security. As a result, efforts to court Washington had been seriously stepped up and Australia and New Zealand had been willing to sign a Pacific pact excluding Britain.

On the debit side, however, for India the adoption of the aggressor resolution dented its belief in the Commonwealth as a counterweight to US influence. Nehru, therefore, placed his long-term allegiance with the neutral bloc. It was a paradoxical consequence of the high-water mark of the Commonwealth's influence on international politics.

---

[70]UK NA, CAB 128/19, C.M.(51)10th Conclusions, London, 29 Jan. 1951.
[71]Stueck, *Korean War*, 152, 163–4.

In terms of broader importance this episode demonstrated that the Commonwealth was more than a symbolic group of states bound by a common history. When certain conditions were met the Commonwealth could coordinate a united position and wield influence over the United States, especially in the multilateral environment of the UN. When these conditions were absent and the Commonwealth members acted independently none of them, not even Britain, could have hoped to constrain US policy to the extent witnessed during the crisis following Chinese intervention in the Korean War. The events that took place at the UN over the winter of 1950–51 thus suggest that in the deeply polarised world at the height of the Cold War the Commonwealth mattered and its role in international affairs warrants further academic study.

Bibliography

Acheson, Dean, *The Korean War* (New York: W.W. Norton 1969).

Blair, Clay, *The Forgotten War: America in Korea, 1950–1953* (New York: Times Books 1987).

Casey, Steven, *Selling the Korean War: Propaganda, Politics, and Public Opinion in the United States, 1950–1953* (Oxford: OUP 2008).

Dayal, Shiv, *India's Role in the Korean Question: A Study of the Settlement of International Disputes Under the United Nations* (Delhi: S. Chand & Co. 1959).

Farrar-Hockley, Anthony, *The British Part in the Korean War, Volume I: A Distant Obligation* (London: HMSO 1990).

Farrar-Hockley, Anthony, *The British Part in the Korean War, Volume II: An Honourable Discharge* (London: HMSO 1995).

Foot, Rosemary, *The Wrong War: American Policy and the Dimensions of the Korean Conflict, 1950–1953* (New York: Cornell UP 1985).

Gordon Walker, Patrick, *The Commonwealth* (London: Secker & Warburg 1962).

Hall, Hessel, *The Commonwealth: A History of the British Commonwealth of Nations* (London: Van Nostrand Reinhold 1971).

Halliday, John and Bruce Cumings, *Korea: The Unknown War* (New York: Pantheon Books 1988).

Hastings, Max, *The Korean War* (London: Michael Joseph 1987).

Leckie, Robert, *The Korean War* (London: Barrie & Rockliff with Pall Mall Press 1963).

Lowe, Peter, *The Korean War* (Basingstoke, UK: Macmillan 2000).

MacDonald, Callum, *Britain and the Korean War* (Oxford: Blackwell 1990).

Martin, Allan, 'Sir Robert Gordon Menzies', in Michelle Grattan (ed.), *Australian Prime Ministers* (Sydney: New Holland Publishers 2000).

McGibbon, Ian, *New Zealand and the Korean War – Volume 1: Politics and Diplomacy* (Auckland: OUP 1992).

Mount, Graeme, *The Diplomacy of War: The Case of Korea* (Montreal: Black Rose Books 2004).

O'Neill, Robert, *Australia in the Korean War, 1950–53. Volume 1: Strategy and Diplomacy* (Canberra: The Australian War Memorial and the Australian Government Publishing Service 1981).

Paren, Liz, *The Commonwealth: A Family of Nations* (London: Commonwealth Secretariat 2003).

Pearson, Lester, *Memoirs – Volume 2: The International Years, 1948–1957* (London: Gollancz 1974).

Rees, David, *Korea: The Limited War* (London: Macmillan 1964).

Stueck, William, *The Korean War: An International History* (Princeton, NJ: Princeton UP 1995).

Stueck, William, *Rethinking the Korean War: A New Diplomatic and Strategic History* (Princeton: Princeton UP 2002).

Whelan, Richard, *Drawing the Line: The Korean War, 1950–1953* (London: Faber 1990).

Lost Chance or Lost Horizon? Strategic Opportunity and Escalation Risk in the Korean War, April–July 1951

COLIN F. JACKSON

US Naval War College, Newport, Rhode Island, USA

ABSTRACT This article examines three questions surrounding American attempts at war termination in 1951. Was there a militarily feasible 'lost chance' for UN forces to advance to the narrow neck of the Korean peninsula? If so, why did American decisionmakers decline to pursue it? What effect might such operations have had on the course of the war and subsequent American thinking on limited war? It concludes that the US missed a critical opportunity to conclude the war on more favorable terms; that the American decision to forgo amphibious operations in June 1951 had less to do with military calculations than with the domestic political firestorm that followed MacArthur's relief; and that the 'lost chance' not only increased the cost and duration of the Korean War, but encouraged subsequent decision makers to overstate the risks of intra-war escalation and understate the risks of premature, de-escalation.

A Critical Case Misread

For the first three decades of the Cold War, the American theory of limited war rested on a single historical case: Korea. The core decisions of that war, from the initial intervention through its conduct and ultimate termination, were the raw material of the limited war doctrine that animated American decisionmaking from the 1950s through the Vietnam War. For a majority of policymakers and academics, the Korean War appeared to offer a set of 'lessons' relevant to the conduct of future limited wars. Chief among these was the notion that prompt intervention and subsequent operational restraint were the key components of success in limited war.[1] In this context, President Harry S. Truman's decision to oppose Communist aggression was hailed as far sighted, while General Douglas MacArthur's calls for an expansion in the scope of the war were portrayed as reckless.

The Korean War was seen as a success insofar as the US had blocked a Communist land grab and avoided an 'explosion' of the 'local' war into total war between the US and the USSR.[2] That the war had been exceedingly costly and had dragged on for two years after the start of armistice talks was seen as the necessary price of prudent restraint. This orthodox interpretation of the war was shared not only by the civilian architects of the Truman policy – Truman, Dean Acheson, Dean Rusk – but also by much of a large segment of the military high command including Generals Matthew B. Ridgway, Omar N. Bradley, and Joseph L. Collins.

These accepted 'lessons' of Korea rely heavily on a specific reading of the historical record of the war. The 'lessons' of intra-war restraint,[3] in particular, rest on assumptions of high escalation risk and limited US military opportunity. An alternative reading of the events of the spring and summer of 1951 suggests that policymakers overestimated the risk of Soviet escalation and that the US forfeited an opportunity to secure additional bargaining power in the wake of the collapse of the Chinese offensives.[4] Seen in this light, the American decision to suspend offensive operations in June 1951 was not a product of mutual exhaustion as some military and civilian leaders maintained; rather, it was a choice that was at once unnecessary and costly. According to proponents of this view, among them the senior American field commander at the time, Lieutenant General James A. Van Fleet, the US had a decisive military advantage in June 1951 and chose to relinquish it in the hopes of securing a rapid and equitable armistice at the 38th Parallel.[5] That decision

---

[1]Yuen Foong Khong, *Analogies at War: Korea, Munich, and the Vietnam Decisions of 1965* (Princeton UP 1992), 99–102.
[2]Morton H. Halperin, *Limited War in the Nuclear Age* (New York: John Wiley 1963), 3.
[3]Ibid., 9, 32.
[4]Bernard Brodie, *War and Politics* (New York: Macmillan 1973), 92–7.
[5]Gen. Van Fleet's views were largely shared at the time by Adm. Forrest P. Sherman, the Chief of Naval Operations, Maj. Gen. Edward M. Almond, Commander of US X Corps, Maj. Gen. Gerald C. Thomas, Commander of US 1st Marine Division, and Vice Adm. Turner Joy, the lead US negotiator at Panmunjom. The arguments first proposed by these military leaders were subsequently expanded upon by Bernard Brodie and Henry Kissinger, among others.

deprived the US of leverage in the ensuing armistice negotiations and locked the United Nations (UN) Command into a pattern of positional warfare that was as costly as it was inconclusive.

This paper re-examines the historical dispute surrounding the decisions to suspend offensive operations in 1951. The American historical record and the new archival evidence on Chinese and Soviet intentions strongly suggest that the orthodox historiography of the period distorts the 'lessons' of Korea and overstates the utility of restraint in limited war. Specifically, the record suggests that Van Fleet's proposals for an intensification of UN pursuit operations in June 1951 were militarily feasible and strategically sound; his proposal to continue the pursuit of the Chinese north to the narrow neck of the Korean peninsula was consistent with a geographically limited view of the war, and was ultimately rejected by his superior, General Ridgway, on mixed political-military grounds.

Recently released records of the cable traffic between Mao and Stalin during April and May 1951 paint a picture of acute Communist weakness and specific vulnerability to the amphibious options that General Van Fleet proposed. Taken together, the historical record and archival evidence suggest that Van Fleet's plans for intensified pursuit fell victim not to military constraints but to domestic political ones. In particular, the charged political atmosphere that followed the relief of General MacArthur in April 1951, made it awkward for General Ridgway to endorse a plan that would capitalize on Chinese and Korean vulnerabilities. Just as the military window of opportunity began to open, the domestic political window slammed shut.

The decisions of May and June 1951 had a profound impact not only on the course of the Korean War but also on subsequent theorizing on limited war. The dominant influence of the memoirs of the chief proponents of US policy, chief among them the theater commander General Ridgway, US Army Chief of Staff Collins and Secretary of State Acheson,[6] presented the Korean War as a model of prudent strategic behavior. In contrast, this paper argues that the US squandered an opportunity to shape the terms and timing of armistice. Reflexive restraint, far from safeguarding America's interests, may have cost the

---

[6]Matthew B. Ridgway, *The Korean War* (Garden City, NY: Doubleday 1967); Matthew B. Ridgway, *Soldier: The Memoirs of Matthew B. Ridgway* (New York: Harper & Brothers 1956); J. Lawton Collins, *War in Peacetime: The History and Lessons of Korea* (New York: Houghton Mifflin 1969); Dean Acheson, *Present at the Creation: My Years in the State Department* (New York: W.W. Norton 1969); Dean Acheson, *The Korean War* (New York: W.W. Norton 1969).

nation dearly. The broad acceptance of the wisdom of intra-war restraint in Korea was, in turn, to have a significant impact on the shape of US decisions in the early years of the Vietnam conflict.

A Turbulent Spring, February–May 1951

Over the course of the past decade, the release of Soviet and Chinese archival materials has revolutionized the historiography of the Korean War. Longstanding and heated debates over the origins of the war, Soviet complicity, and the motives behind Chinese intervention have been laid to rest by the documentary record. This new evidence has transformed the academic discourse and contributed to a growing historical consensus on the opening stages of the war.[7]

What has been notably absent from this surge in scholarship is an equivalent level of scrutiny on the middle portion of the war, specifically the critical period between February and July 1951.[8] In those six months, a series of American decisions set the course of the remainder of the war and the basic terms of the armistice. A period that opened with the UN in full retreat closed with the end of the war of maneuver and the false dawn of the July 1951 armistice talks.

During that spring, at least three different dramas were being played out on the Korean stage. First, a battered UN Command that had fallen back in disarray from the Yalu River in the winter of 1950 gradually regained its footing and confidence. In the face of three Chinese general offensives, the UN Command managed to resist the enemy's attacks and repulse them at ever increasing cost to the Chinese Volunteer Forces (CVF) and North Korean People's Army (NKPA) forces engaged.

Second, the great Chinese offensives coincided with the growing tension between the UN Commander, General Douglas MacArthur, and the Truman administration. MacArthur's public and private statements demonstrated his conviction that the circumstances in Korea warranted a general escalation and widening of the war. Under

---

[7]Allan R. Millett, *The War for Korea, 1945–1950: A House Burning* (Lawrence: Univ. of Kansas Press 2005); Sergei Goncharov, John Lewis, Xue Litai, *Uncertain Partners: Stalin, Mao, and the Korean War* (Stanford, CA: Stanford UP 1993); Chen Jian, 'The Sino-Soviet Alliance and China's Entry into the Korean War', *Cold War International History Project*, Working Paper, 31 Oct. 1991; Kathryn Weathersby, 'Soviet Aims in Korea and the Origins of the Korean War, 1945–1950: New Evidence from Russian Archives', *Cold War International History Project*, Working Paper No. 8, Nov. 1993; Thomas J. Christensen, *Useful Adversaries: Grand Strategy, Domestic Mobilization, and Sino-American Conflict, 1947–1958* (Princeton, NJ: Princeton UP 1996).
[8]Allan R. Millett, *The Korean War* (Washington, DC: Potomac Books 2007), 160–1.

MacArthur's plans, the UN forces would take the fight to China proper; a combination of close naval blockade, strategic bombing of Manchurian production centers and Chinese airfields, and the introduction of Kuomintang (KMT) forces on the mainland or in Korea would force the Chinese to abandon an unsupportable venture in Korea and effectively 'cripple their offensive capabilities for a generation'.[9]

The Truman administration, with Secretary of State Acheson in the lead, advocated a much narrower strategy focused on the restoration of the status quo ante bellum: an independent South Korea with a border along the 38th Parallel. The break between MacArthur and the Truman administration culminated in the general's relief on 11 April 1951. The shock of his removal and the political firestorm that followed consumed the attentions of the US senior civilian and military leadership for much of the next three months.

The third major theme of that spring was the advent of ceasefire discussions between the combatant parties. Elements of the American foreign policy establishment had long hoped that the disasters of late 1950 could be righted by a ceasefire that restored the status quo ante bellum.[10] The slipping fortunes of the UN Command made this goal seem unattainable throughout much of the winter of 1950–51; to open a channel of communications with the Soviets or Chinese during this period would have telegraphed US desperation.[11] Seen in this light, the Chinese reverses in the Fifth and Sixth Offensives (22–29 April and 16–20 May) were a welcome change in the bargaining context; the Chinese losses made possible a settlement negotiated from a position of rough parity. This desire to capitalize on the changing fortunes of the UN led to the Kennan–Malik exchanges of that year and the first steps towards armistice talks.

As these three themes played out between February and July 1951, the ground commanders and the military authorities in Washington were engaged in debates over the shape of future combat operations in the Far East. While MacArthur's arguments relating to a widening of the war with China are relatively familiar, the concurrent disputes over the objectives and constraints on operations within Korea have been largely ignored. Most commentators and historians have treated the UN limit of advance 20 miles north of the 38th Parallel as a product of mutual military exhaustion. For the Eighth Army commander, General James Van Fleet, and many of his primary subordinates, however, the last weeks of May were a period of unprecedented military opportunity

---

[9]Ridgway, *The Korean War*, 143.
[10]*F[oreign] R[elations of the] U[nited] S[tates]*, 1951, Vol.7, Part I, 166.
[11]George F. Kennan, *Memoirs: 1950–1963* (Boston: Little, Brown 1972), 28–9.

made possible by the resounding defeat of the Chinese Fifth and Sixth Offensives. Van Fleet and others urged General Ridgway, who had been promoted from Eighth Army Commander to Theater Commander in the wake of MacArthur's relief, to take advantage of this narrow window of opportunity and authorize amphibious landings on the east coast of North Korea in the general vicinity of Wonsan. Such landings, in conjunction with a ground drive north by the US I, IX, and X Corps, would enable the UN forces to encircle the retreating Chinese armies and establish a new defensive front at the narrow neck of the peninsula (Wonsan–Pyongyang).

General Ridgway did not, however, endorse Van Fleet's plans for the amphibious operations; instead he instructed him to restrict his operations to the seizure of Lines 'Wyoming' and 'Kansas' 20 miles north of the 38th Parallel.

Ridgway's seemingly minor decision to curtail amphibious operations in the eastern X Corps sector gave rise to a heated postwar debate between Van Fleet on the one hand, and the assembled Joint Chiefs of Staff (JCS), Ridgway, and Truman administration on the other. After relinquishing command of the Eighth Army in February 1953, Van Fleet made a series of public charges, first in Senate hearings[12] and later in two *Life Magazine* articles,[13] that the US needlessly conceded opportunities to achieve breakthroughs in the Korean War. Specifically, he argued that Ridgway's decision not to authorize aggressive offensive actions in late May and early June 1951 had cost the UN Command an opportunity to inflict a decisive and perhaps final defeat on the CVF and NKPA.

Van Fleet's charge provoked a storm of rebuttals. Generals Collins[14] and Ridgway[15] both argued that Van Fleet's opinions were at odds with his contemporaneous appraisals and recommendations. Dean Acheson for his part accused Van Fleet and his later superior General Mark W. Clark of engaging in post hoc myth making.[16] This mutual recrimination continued well into the 1960s with both sides claiming that their opponents had manipulated the historical record.

---

[12]US Senate, Committee on Armed Services, *Hearings*, 83rd Congress, 1st Session, General James A. Van Fleet, Testimony, 5, 6, 10 March 1953.

[13]Gen. James A. Van Fleet, 'The Truth About Korea: Part I: From a Man Now Free to Speak', *Life Magazine*, 11 May 1953, 127–42; Gen. James A. Van Fleet, 'The Truth About Korea: Part II: How We Can Win with What We Have', *Life Magazine*, 18 May 1953, 157–72.

[14]Collins, *War in Peacetime*, 306–8.

[15]Ridgway, *Korean War*, 181–2.

[16]Acheson, *Korean War*, 116.

Lost Chance or Lost Horizon?

Largely overshadowed by the arguments over MacArthur's plans for a wider war with China, this controversy over the mid-war strategy on the Korean peninsula has remained in the historical background. The purpose of this essay is to examine three central questions surrounding this controversy. First, was Van Fleet's 'lost chance' a militarily viable course of action in late May and early June 1951? Second, if this option existed, what drove the decisions to curtail military operations in the wake of the Chinese Sixth Offensive? And third, if the 'lost chance' was viable, what would the success or failure of the Wonsan operations have meant for the course of the war and the peace settlement that followed?

The answers to these questions are far from straightforward. Despite the deterministic tone of many historical works on the period, the atmosphere of mid-1951 was chaotic and the contemporary records indicate divergences of opinion and dramatic personal shifts of position over time. The united administration front presented at the Senate hearings on MacArthur's relief[17] belied the tumult within the military and the administration on relevant considerations from escalation risk and Allied sentiment to the situation on the ground. The exculpatory biases of the memoirs of the relevant participants further cloud the picture, and an attempt has been made here to rely as much as possible on contemporary, primary sources.

The Realm of the Possible: The Military Situation in Korea, January–June 1951

From the Chinese Second Phase Offensive in late November 1950 through the close of the year, the UN Command was engaged in an almost continuous retreat from its initial positions close to the Yalu river to the 38th Parallel. The Chinese Third Phase Offensive launched on 31 December 1950 succeeded in driving the Eighth Army back across the Han river and recapturing Seoul. From the American vantage point, the hasty retreat and heavy losses had raised fears of impending collapse of the UN position as a whole. Discussions both in theater and in Washington shifted from questions of victory to simple preservation of forces; the survival of the Eighth Army, the only sizeable US force in the Far East, was considered more important than the retention of the UN position in Korea.[18]

---

[17]United States Senate, *Military Situation in the Far East* (Washington DC: GPO 1951).
[18]Billy C. Mossman, *Ebb and Flow (November 1950–July 1951): The United States Army in the Korean War* (Washington DC: Center of Military History/US Government Printing Office 2000), 158.

The accidental road-death of Lieutenant General Walton H. Walker, the commander of the US Eighth Army, marked a turning point in the fortunes of the UN Command. His replacement, Lieutenant General Matthew Ridgway, made his presence felt almost immediately. Eager to rebuild the fighting spirit of his command, and accorded true freedom of maneuver by a despondent MacArthur, Ridgway made clear that the retreat and the defeatism it had engendered would end.[19] Though compelled to surrender Seoul in the face of the Third Phase Offensive, Ridgway managed to control the withdrawal and lay the groundwork for the coming UN counteroffensives.

While the first three Chinese offensives had succeeded in expelling the UN from North Korea, these drives had come at great cost to the Chinese Volunteer Forces (CVF). On 7 December 1950, two weeks before the launch of the Third Phase Offensive, Marshal Peng Teh-huai, the Chinese commander, estimated that he would need close to 150,000 troops and three months rest to restore the effectiveness of the armies in Korea.[20] Pressed by Mao to follow up the successes of December, Peng managed to seize Seoul and establish a hasty defensive line south of the 38th Parallel. Ridgway's counterattacks in late January, however, caused great concern; the Chinese losses in the preceding four months had not been made good and the firepower mismatch between the Chinese and UN forces was beginning to tell. On 27 January 1950, Peng went so far as to suggest a Chinese acceptance of a ceasefire, arguing that the Chinese forces needed several months to regroup and resupply before resuming offensive operations. Peng was increasingly leery of renewing offensive action against UNC forces whose material superiority in firepower and logistics was increasingly clear.[21]

Mao, impatient to push the Americans 60 miles farther south, largely ignored Peng's warnings and ordered the Fourth Phase Offensive in February 1951. Initial CVF successes at Hoengsong were followed by a bloody repulse at the Battle of Chipyong-ni; there a hasty attack by CVF troops met with unexpectedly strong UN resistance. A combination of renewed spirit, vast quantities of artillery and air support, and armored reserves enabled a UN regiment to hold Chipyong-ni in the face of 18,000 attacking CVF troops,[22] which in turn validated Peng's

---

[19]Clay Blair, *The Forgotten War: America in Korea 1950–1953* (New York: Doubleday Books 1987), 570.

[20]Shu Guang Zhang, *Mao's Military Romanticism: China and the Korean War 1950–1953* (Lawrence: UP of Kansas 1995), 123.

[21]Ibid., 136–7, 138, 142.

[22]Col. John F. Antal, 'Busting Through', *Military Review*, Jan.–Feb. 2000, 4; Blair, *Forgotten War*, 697–8.

earlier concerns about the sustainability of Chinese attacks in the face of superior US firepower.[23]

The Fourth Phase Offensive and the Battle of Chipyong-ni in particular demonstrated the fundamental shift in advantage from the CVF to the UN Command. By February 1951, Peng's CVF and NKPA forces were extracting diminishing returns from a strategy based on mass and sustained attack. Logistical strains and firepower deficits meant that the CVF forces engaged in the Third and Fourth Phase Offensives secured far less territory and inflicted fewer casualties than the initial surge of the fall. The weakness of the Chinese logistical services became more pronounced as the advance pushed south. As early as the Third Offensive, some CVF units entered the attack with a mere three days rations on hand.[24] The effects of expanding American air interdiction of supplies and the tripling of the number of Chinese forces deployed in theater placed additional burdens on an already strained logistical network.[25]

At the same time, the UN Command's advantages were on the rise. The learning effects of the first four months of combat with the CVF had been significant. Increased use of air and artillery support and careful coordination of advances and withdrawals had greatly diminished the effectiveness of Chinese human-wave attacks and encirclements. New leadership and recent battle successes made the UN forces far more confident of their chances in offensive and defensive operations.

The patterns foreshadowed in the Fourth Phase Offensive were played out on a larger scale in April and May 1951. The Chinese strategy of massed attack reached its zenith in these two offensives that pitted 530,000 CVF forces against a UN Command of roughly equal size.[26] On 21 April, the eve of the attack, Ridgway's successor, General Van Fleet, made the first mention of the possibility of using US amphibious landings at Wonsan (on the east coast) as part of a future counter-attack. Ridgway, quick to compare these plans with the disastrous X Corps operations at Wonsan in 1950, emphasized the

---

[23]Shu Guang Zhang, *Mao's Military Romanticism*, 142.

[24]Ibid., 130.

[25]Gen. (Ret.) Hong Xuezhi, 'The CPVF's Combat and Logistics', in Xiaobing Li, Allan R. Millett, and Bin Yu, *Mao's Generals Remember Korea* (Lawrence: UP of Kansas 2001), 131–2.

[26]These figures are drawn from Blair, *Forgotten War*. One Chinese source, Gen. Hong Xuezhi, puts the CVF total strength in Korea in mid-April 1951 much higher – close to 950,000; see Hong Xuezhi, 'The CPVF's Combat and Logistics', 131–2. The discrepancy may be the difference between the number of troops engaged and the number available in theater.

importance of focusing on the defensive phase of the battle. Ridgway made this guidance explicit in a command directive the next day. In it, he required Van Fleet to clear any advances north of line Wyoming.[27]

The Fifth Phase Offensive opened on 22 April 1951, a mere ten days after the relief of General MacArthur. Van Fleet welcomed the opportunity to meet the anticipated enemy spring offensive aimed at Seoul. Among his earliest instructions was guidance to increase the use of artillery by a factor of five; instead of consuming the standard 40 rounds per gun per day, Van Fleet set a target of 200 rounds per gun per day.[28] His instructions, combined with the increasing flexibility and scale of the UN air support, brought success in the opening days of the campaign.[29] While forced to concede some territory north of the newly recaptured capital, Van Fleet was confident of his ability to hold Seoul. The 12 CVF Armies (an estimated 360,000 men) thrown into the attack on the UN western flank and center pushed the UN back roughly 35 miles before the offensive petered out. Estimates of Chinese losses in the seven-day offensive range from 70,000 to 80,000,[30] while the UN Command lost a total of 7,000 casualties, of whom a mere 1,900 were American (314 killed in action, 2,011 wounded in action).[31]

Undeterred by the staggering losses in the Fifth Offensive, Peng launched the Sixth Phase Offensive aimed at unhinging the eastern flank of the UN line on 16 May. Here again the UN line bent but did not break. In spite of an intelligence failure that predicted a second Chinese attack on Seoul, Van Fleet managed to redeploy sufficient forces east to first block and later rout the 170,000 CVF and NKPA forces engaged. Not only did the Chinese fail to turn the UN line in the east, but the estimated 90,000 CVF/NKPA losses also prompted Peng to order a full withdrawal to the vicinity of the Hwachon reservoir.[32] The rapid American counterthrust led by armored and airborne units surprised the Chinese and led to panic in some units. Local surrenders and unit disintegration, unheard of in the first six months of the CVF intervention, followed swiftly.[33] The commander of the US X Corps,

---

[27]Blair, *Forgotten War*, 819–20.

[28]Ibid., 841.

[29]W.L. Archer, 'Observations of Close Air Support in Korea', Technical Memorandum, Operations Research Office, ORO-S-18 (FEC), 1 June 1951.

[30]Blair, *Forgotten War*, 854–5; Mossman, *Ebb and Flow*, 437.

[31]Korea Institute of Military History, *The Korean War* (Lincoln: Univ. of Nebraska Press 1998), 2: 733.

[32]Ibid., 2: 717–18.

[33]Shu Guang Zhang, *Mao's Military Romanticism*, 152.

Lieutenant General Edward M. Almond, would later recount the shattering effect of the UN counterattack in the east:

> The Chinese still defended from roadblocks in opposition to this thrust along the rear areas ... [but] the main body of the Chinese Army was soon in full retreat ... By the 1st of June, the X Corps was in complete control of this entire front line. The enemy was dispersed to the hills and we were prepared and so recommended that the pursuit be continued to achieve the destruction of this massive CCF force which was the best the Chinese had south of the Yalu River .... I repeatedly flew in a small plane up and down the roads being utilized by the retreating Chinese and I made a report to the effect that the enemy was dispersed, disorganized, disheartened, and they were being killed by every effort our forces made. 'They are dying like flies' were my exact words I think.[34]

In the wake of the losses in April and May 1951, a chastened Chinese high command would never again mount a major offensive in Korea.

The Fourth through the Sixth Chinese offensives highlighted the shifting fortunes of the CVF in Korea. Three critical relative weaknesses, in firepower, mobility, and logistics, combined to limit the effectiveness of the later Chinese thrusts. On the firepower front, changes in UN tactics and absolute changes in the scale of air support and artillery made the Chinese mass tactics hideously costly.[35] Similarly, the ability of UN forces to use tanks, airborne infantry, and air support in combined operations revealed the significant advantage they enjoyed over similar Chinese units. The mobility advantage of the UN forces cost the CVF in two ways. On the offense, the Chinese attempts to encircle and destroy large US units failed because the UN forces retained the ability to break contact and withdraw at greater speed than the attackers. This stood in sharp contrast to the successful Chinese offensives against the KMT during the Chinese Civil War. On the defense, the CVF were hard pressed to maintain an orderly withdrawal in the face of concerted pushes by their more mobile opponents. This mobility mismatch explains much of the chaos described by General Almond in his account of the X Corps counteroffensive.

In addition to these shortfalls in firepower and mobility, the Chinese labored under the weight of a pre-modern logistical system. By the

---

[34]Lt. Gen. (Ret.) Edward M. Almond, *Conversations between Lieutenant General (Ret.) Edward M. Almond and Captain Thomas Fergusson: Senior Officers' Debriefing Program* (Carlisle Barracks, PA: US Army Military History Institute 1979), 51–3.
[35]Archer, 'Observations of Close Air Support in Korea'.

Fourth and Fifth Offensives, the Chinese logistical network was only capable of replacing one half of the daily expenditures of the engaged units.[36] This inability to sustain prolonged offensive operations was increasingly understood by a UN Command eager to exploit this critical weakness. General Van Fleet, writing in 1953, summarized his impressions of threadbare Chinese approach to logistics:

> At the start of a drive, the Red soldier is more or less just pointed in the right direction and told to keep going as far and as long as he can. Unlike our soldiers, he has no armored vest, no helmet. He simply has a uniform, his cap, and a fairly good pair of canvas shoes. His rifle is loaded and in a belt around his waist he carries 200 more shells ... How long can he keep it up? At the end of five or six days he has shot his bolt ... The logistics of prolonged attack are beyond the capacities of the Red soldier.[37]

In short, by the spring and summer of 1951 the combined advantages of firepower, mobility, and logistics gave the UN Command a decisive edge in the prosecution of high intensity operations. Though the Chinese had repeatedly demonstrated the ability to mount very large-scale attacks, those attacks were strictly limited in duration and depth. The growing UN skill in applying concentrated firepower against exposed Chinese formations had translated into rapid increases in Chinese casualty rates, and the Chinese high command had begun to accept the prospect of indecisive, protracted war.

Van Fleet's Plans for Exploitation

Van Fleet's proposed landings at Tongchon were the centerpiece of his larger plans to inflict a decisive defeat on the overextended Chinese and North Korean forces. While he anticipated significant progress by I Corps north of Seoul, Van Fleet considered the encirclement of the Chinese armies on the eastern flank to be the greatest immediate prize. Whereas the Chinese forces north of Seoul had had three weeks to recover from the collapse of the Fifth CVF Offensive, the CVF and NKPA forces facing X Corps in the east were at the point of maximum vulnerability. The ill-fated Sixth Offensive had consumed most of the forward stockpiles of ammunition and food leaving the remaining

---

[36]Hong Xuezhi, 'The CPVF's Combat and Logistics', 132.

[37]Van Fleet, 'Truth about Korea: Part I', 137. Chinese generals largely agreed that Chinese élan was insufficient to overcome the massive UNC advantages in firepower, logistics and air support; see Hong Xuezhi, 'The CPVF's Combat and Logistics', 132–3.

forces far from their bases and with scant supplies to oppose a UN counterthrust.

The simplest way to exploit the collapse of the Chinese offensive was to drive north with all three UN Corps. Operation 'Detonate', as it was called, was to open with on 20 May with attacks by I Corps in the west and IX Corps in the center. Once the Chinese offensive in the east was completely spent, X Corps would join the counterattack driving north and east through Inje towards Kansong in order to cut off the retreat of the CVF lead elements.[38] The X Corps advance that opened on 23 May netted impressive early gains. In the first three days of the counterattack, Almond's X Corps advanced against light opposition and captured large numbers of Chinese and Korean prisoners. The early effort to close the pocket by driving on Kansong was stymied by a combination of UN exhaustion and enemy roadblocks in the vicinity of Inje.

With the ground encirclement beginning to falter, General Van Fleet shifted his focus to a possible amphibious landing at Tongchon. This approach would enable Van Fleet to establish a blocking position astride the enemy line of retreat without having to smash through the existing blocking positions near Inje. The revised scheme of maneuver for the remainder of the Eighth Army would be as follows. In the west, the three divisions of the US I Corps would continue to attack north into the 'Iron Triangle' to seize the enemy logistics hub there. The IX Corps would attack from the Hwachon reservoir in a northeasterly direction to link up with the Marine landings at Tongchon (60 air miles north of the 38th Parallel). On the eastern flank, X Corps, less 1st Marine Division, would attack north to Tongchon along the coast road. If successful, the Marine landings and the combined IX Corps/X Corps drive would cut off the retreat of the CVF forces located near the 38th Parallel, and open the way for an advance to the Pyongyang–Wonsan line. Van Fleet did not envision the use of out of theater reinforcements; the plan was to use available assets to cut off a broken enemy by blocking his line of retreat in the east.

The consequences of success in the Tongchon landings were potentially vast. The landing itself would force the enemy forces south of Tongchon to fight their way through 1st Marine Division to escape the pocket. With the remainder of X Corps advancing steadily north, the Chinese would face formidable enemies to the north and south. At the same time, Peng could not have afforded to ignore a potential threat to the capital at Pyongyang; if Van Fleet had chosen to reinforce the landings and drive west rather than south, then the Chinese forces in the west would be forced to withdraw, in contact, in order to avoid

---

[38]Blair, *Forgotten War*, 884–6.

becoming part of a larger encirclement. This strategic dilemma that a landing in the greater Wonsan region would create was perhaps its greatest selling point; the simple act of introducing combat forces that far north would be likely to precipitate a strategic withdrawal across the peninsula.

Success at Tongchon could have yielded any of several outcomes. At a local level, it could have entrapped the remnants of the five Chinese armies in the east. On a broader level, it might well have unhinged the CVF/NKPA line and forced a strategic withdrawal of 60 miles or more. Had such a withdrawal been forced, the UN Command might have secured a new line at the narrow neck of the peninsula running from Wonsan to Pyongyang. This would have afforded Ridgway an opportunity to consolidate along an eminently defensible, short line while in possession of the enemy's capital.

What would failure at Tongchon have meant? Given the logistical situation facing the Chinese at the end of May, it is unlikely that they would have been able to mount a full counterattack in the time to block the landings. In the unlikely event that they had been able to put overwhelming pressure on the 1st Marine Division, the UN Command had sufficient offshore naval fire support and close air support to break contact and pull the Marines off the beach. A more likely 'failure' might have been an incomplete encirclement of the Chinese forces, though even a failure of this type would have left the US forward line much farther north than the Inje/Kansong front.

In short, from a purely military point of view, the proposed operation had great merit. Success might have forced anything from the loss of large numbers of CVF/NKPA troops in the east, to a general enemy withdrawal north of the 39th Parallel. Against a broken and overextended enemy, local success at the very least seemed likely. Moreover, the potential downside of the operation was limited. Failure in the form of incomplete encirclement would still have left the UN line farther north than Lines 'Kansas and Wyoming'.

The Contemporary Debate, 28 May 1951

The contemporary debate took place within the Eighth Army and at the theater level. For Van Fleet, the Tongchon operation was a more tangible expression of his earlier musings on the advantages of an amphibious landing near Wonsan. When Van Fleet first broached the issue with his senior subordinates on 28 May, General Almond (X Corps commander) and Major General Gerald C. Thomas (Commander, 1st Marine Division) registered their enthusiastic support.[39]

---

[39]Ibid., 898.

Following that meeting, General Van Fleet wired General Ridgway in Tokyo requesting permission to execute the Tongchon plans, arguing that the 'potentiality of enemy defeat should override any objections'.[40]

General Ridgway was unconvinced. For Ridgway, the operation appeared a revival of the Wonsan plan he had earlier quashed as reckless. In face to face discussions with Van Fleet later that night, Ridgway emphasized several objections to the Tongchon element of the plan.

First, as Tongchon was well north of the 'Kansas/Wyoming' limit of advance laid out in the latest JCS guidance of 1 May, the landings would require the express permission of the JCS. This process, involving not only military commanders but likely the full panoply of the National Security Council, State Department, and Allied representatives, would have required significant effort and lead time.

Second, the recent murmurings on the terms of a possible ceasefire seemed to make seizure of 'real estate' north of the 38th Parallel meaningless; what was won on the battlefield today might well be given back at the peace table tomorrow. Within this strategic context, a steady advance by I Corps and IX Corps in the west and center, and a defensive halt by X Corps would help establish a defensible line sufficient to meet the needs of UN armistice negotiations.

On a narrower military level, Ridgway objected to the thinning of the X Corps line; the simultaneous commitment of 187th Airborne Regimental Combat Team and 1st Marine Division would leave X Corps vulnerable to enemy counterattack. Similarly, Ridgway argued that the strain of the past two weeks of combat had left 2nd Division, Almond's primary fighting force, in need of rest and reorganization. As Ridgway chose not to initiate a request for JCS permission to execute the landings, the issue was laid to rest on the night of 28 May.[41]

In an ironic twist, the general issue of the appropriate limit of advance and the abstract question of amphibious landings were discussed at some length at a State-JCS meeting the next day.[42] The meeting opened with a question by Dean Rusk as to whether recent military developments in Korea warranted a revision of the JCS recommendations of 27 March 1951 on armistice terms. Rusk specifically asked whether the shift from a 'war of maneuvers' along the 38th Parallel to a war in which the Chinese armies might be destroyed had taken place.[43] The minutes indicate that

---

[40]Radio message, GX-5-5099 KGOP, CG 8th Army to CINCFE, 28 May 1951.

[41]Ridgway recorded his objections in a memorandum on 31 May 1951. Gen. Matthew B. Ridgway, 'Memorandum for record: conference between General Ridgway and General Van Fleet, 31 May 1951', The Matthew B. Ridgway Papers, US Military History Institute, Carlisle Barracks, PA, Box 21.

[42]*FRUS, 1951*, 7: 470–2.

[43]Ibid., 470.

Generals Bradley (Chairman of the JCS) and Wade H. Haislip (Army Vice Chief of Staff) responded to the effect that the general situation had not changed dramatically:

> General Bradley indicated that the Joint Chiefs have not changed their minds. They would like to get a settlement along the lines previously discussed [March 1951]. General Haislip said there were no signs of a Chinese collapse. They are getting out of the way of our weapons. Only on the eastern front have they been hurt; on the west they are sitting tight. General Bradley said we don't have a condition under which there are wholesale surrenders. They are now back to their depots. He said he believed the opposition would be stiff from here on and that the present situation was as good as we were going to get for some time. Mr [Paul] Nitze asked whether there was any possibility of a large scale amphibious envelopment operation. General Bradley said this was out of the question, although small landings as threats or harassments were being and would continue to be carried out.[44]

But later in the meeting, Admiral Sherman, the Chief of Naval Operations, challenged Bradley and Haislip on this characterization of the enemy situation, stating that:

> in his view a line further north, perhaps as far north as Chinnampo, Pyongyang, Wonsan might be better. One could then dictate terms in exchange for drawing back to the 38th Parallel. Otherwise one would nothing to give up in exchange for what we were demanding ... Admiral Sherman said that there were plenty of indications that the Chinese had taken punishment.[45]

What is striking about the tenor of this meeting is the degree of uncertainty about the current situation, strategic goals, and desired end state. Indeed, Bradley's characterization of the enemy situation and his curt dismissal of the possibility of amphibious operations stand in direct contradiction to the appraisals of the Eighth Army commander, Van Fleet. Sherman and Paul Nitze unwittingly supported roughly the same line as Van Fleet in arguing for the possibility of moving well north of the 38th Parallel to the Wonsan–Pyongyang line. As will be seen in later sections, the broad disagreement on the nature of the enemy, his intentions, and the realm of strategic maneuver belied the

---

[44]Ibid., 470–1.
[45]Ibid., 471.

unified front that the JCS presented in Senate testimony in the two weeks before and two weeks after the 29 May meeting.

'Conceived in Tranquility': Retrospective Arguments on the Lost Chance

While the outlines of the contemporary debate are relatively clear, the arguments that the principals exchanged in later years are far less so. Both the proponents and opponents of vigorous pursuit north of the 38th Parallel tended to be liberal in their presentation of arguments and timelines. Acheson, who dismissed Van Fleet's arguments as having been 'conceived in tranquility', was guilty along with Generals Ridgway and Collins of carefully worded and not entirely consistent arguments on the subject in the years that followed.

The details of Van Fleet's plans did not emerge until 1953, and it was only then that the vitriolic exchanges among the principals began. First in a series of US Senate hearings on ammunition shortages in Korea,[46] and later in a two-part article for *Life Magazine*, Van Fleet argued that the UN Command had surrendered a golden opportunity in 1951. In his opinion, the window between 22 May and 10 June afforded the UN Command an opportunity to inflict a decisive defeat on the CVF. Thereafter, he argued, the enemy had managed to recover sufficiently to make a renewal of the offensive far more costly:

> The enemy recovered quickly from the beating we gave him in May and was entrenched again by June 10. This is the reason I concurred with General Ridgway – as has been reported in rebuttal against my belief that the enemy was on the run – that a 20 mile advance which was being considered at the time would 'cost us too many casualties'. There was no similarity between the conditions on June 26 and the opportunities that had existed 30 days earlier – or between the value of the final defeat of the enemy and a limited 20 mile advance.[47]

Van Fleet's argument that a window was open in late May and closed by mid June is the crux of the matter. In their respective memoirs, neither Ridgway nor Collins addresses the point head on. Ridgway highlights Van Fleet's agreement to hold at the 'Kansas/Wyoming' line in late June, and cites this as proof that Van Fleet's statements about the ease of advance in late May were baseless. Invoking Van Fleet's analysis of the costs and benefits of advance in late June, Ridgway suggests that

---

[46]US Senate, Committee on Armed Services, Hearings, Van Fleet, Testimony.

[47]Van Fleet, 'The Truth About Korea: Part 1', 132.

THE KOREAN WAR AT SIXTY

an advance against an entrenched opponent would be pointless if such gains were to be given back at the bargaining table.[48] More curious still, Ridgway lays out the generic arguments against an advance – including one on the logistical difficulties of sustaining an advance north of the 38th Parallel – but does not even mention the Tongchon operation. Also absent in the memoir is any mention of the political and bureaucratic challenges of clearing operations through the JCS, though this is generally cited as his primary contemporary argument against the operation.

Collins' post hoc treatment is roughly similar. As justification for the 38th Parallel restrictions imposed by the JCS in their 1 May 1951 directive to Ridgway, Collins cites a 5 April 1951 JCS meeting in which it was agreed that 'the Korean problem cannot be solved in a manner satisfactory to the US by military action alone'.[49] He goes on to cite Van Fleet's recommendations on 9 June to hold at the 'Kansas/ Wyoming' line. As in Ridgway's argument, the timeline is crucial. The 5 April JCS meeting predated the Chinese Fifth and Sixth Offensives and the fundamental shift they brought in the military situation; even if the JCS had been correct in their appraisal of 5 April, they remained open to the charge of insufficient attention to subsequent developments as revealed in the 29 May State-JCS arguments. In much the same fashion, Collins invokes Van Fleet's assessment at the end of what Van Fleet identified as the operational window as proof of the absence of opportunity weeks earlier.

Van Fleet was not without his supporters. Admiral Joy, the lead US negotiator at Panmunjom, later wrote that the US might have been overly hasty in its drive to get to the armistice table. I n his own account of the armistice negotiations, Joy argued: 'The armistice effort taught this: never weaken your pressure when the enemy sues for armistice. Increase it. In June 1951, the Communist forces were falling back steadily suffering grievously ... As soon as armistice discussions began, the UN Command ground forces slackened their offensive opera- tions.'[50] This basic argument, that unilateral cessation of offensive operations crippled the UN bargaining position just as it approached the armistice table, has been echoed by foreign policy observers from Bernard Brodie[51] to Henry Kissinger.[52]

The post hoc arguments against the Van Fleet plan share certain common flaws. First, they tend to manipulate the timing and context of

---

[48]Ridgway, *Korean War*, 181–2.
[49]*FRUS, 1951*, 7: 295, cited in Collins, *War in Peacetime*, 304.
[50]C. Turner Joy, *How Communists Negotiate* (New York: Macmillan 1955), 166.
[51]Brodie, *War and Politics*, 91–112.
[52]Henry Kissinger, *Diplomacy* (New York: Simon & Schuster 1994), 488–9.

Van Fleet's remarks later in 1951 to prove the speciousness of the general's claims about the May–June window. As Van Fleet himself aptly noted, the situations in late May and late June were entirely different; the first featured a broken and overextended enemy, the second, a partially recovered enemy in entrenched positions. In addition, once Ridgway had established strict limits on the scope of Eighth Army operations, Van Fleet focused his energies on developing strategies that operated within that box.[53] Second, they neglect the re-emergence of similar amphibious operations plans as early as 1 July 1951. As Ridgway notes in his memoirs, he asked Van Fleet to initiate plans for Operation 'Overwhelming', a multi-corps offensive nearly identical to Van Fleet's plans of May. Though this plan envisioned larger landing forces and other reinforcements, it was essentially a larger scale version of the Tongchon plan. The increased size of all forces involved reflected the increased challenge of initiating such an operation from a standing start. If Van Fleet's ideas in May 1951 were so outlandish, why did they resurface only a month later, in July, at Ridgway's behest?

Perhaps the most important evidence in favor of Van Fleet's characterization of the situation in late May has come from the Russian and Chinese archival record. Recent publications by Chinese authors have revealed the extremity of the Chinese situation in late May 1951. Peng's plan for a phased withdrawal to the Yonchon–Chorwon–Kumwha line was upset by the unanticipated speed of the UN counterpunch. This counterattack caught a number of Chinese formations in mid stride, inducing large scale panic and surrenders.[54] The chaos in theater found its way into the cable traffic between Mao and Stalin. Writing on 13 June 1951, the normally ebullient Mao outlined Peng's plan for a defense in depth and provided his own frank appraisal of the local situation:

> ... I gave an order to Comrade Peng Dehuai that our troops firmly hold the line of defense at the second and third defensive lines. The position at the front in June will be such that our forces will be comparatively weaker than those of the enemy. In July we will be stronger than in June and in August we will be even stronger. We will be ready in August to make a stronger blow to the enemy.[55]

---

[53]Mossman, *Ebb and Flow*, 497.

[54]Shu Guang Zhang, *Mao's Military Romanticism*, 152.

[55]Kathryn Weathersby, 'New Russian Documents on the Korean War', *Cold War International History Project*, Bulletins 6–7, (Winter 1995/1996), Doc. 70, 13 June 1951 ciphered telegram, Mao Zedong to Filippov (Stalin) via Roschin, 52–3.

In light of Mao's consistent optimism on military opportunities in Korea, this admission of the need for a two-month pause is an indication of the severity of the reverse the CVF had suffered in the Fifth and Sixth Phase offensives. In a message to Kim Il Sung dated the same day, Mao again emphasized the need for a two month pause.[56] In that document, his fears of an accelerating UN push centered on the possibility of major US amphibious landing:

> We have ordered Deng Hua and the commander of the armies of the 13th Army Group immediately to return to the front and firmly hold the present line of the front. In June and July preparations will be carried out intensively. In August we will carry out a larger operation. *If the enemy does not make large-scale amphibious landings in our rear, then our goal can be achieved. If the enemy does not send new reinforcements and does not make an amphibious landing, then in August we will be significantly stronger than now.*[57]

The Chinese command's emphasis on the threat of amphibious landings was not new. Indeed, in his analysis of Peng and Mao's planning of the Fifth and Sixth Phase Offensives, historian Shu Guang Zhang highlights Chinese fears of impending US reinforcement of the Korean theater. In early April, Peng even characterized the upcoming Chinese offensives as a means to force a decision in advance of US reinforcement and ensuing amphibious attack:

> Peng believed that 'it is most likely that the enemy will launch a frontal attack in the east coordinated by an amphibious landing on Wonsan or Tongchon, which would aim at controlling north of the 39th Parallel so as to prevent us from attacking its forces from the eastern mountainous areas'.[58]

What emerges then from the Russian and Chinese sources is a sense of the enormity of the collapse of the Chinese spring offensives and the acute fears of US amphibious action. It is particularly striking that Mao identified amphibious landings in the rear areas as the critical variable in his estimates of the Chinese regrouping effort. Taken together, Mao and Stalin's cables suggest that their freedom of maneuver in practical,

---

[56]Ibid., Doc. 71, 14 June 1951, handwritten letter from Gao Gang and Kim Il Sung, with 13 June 1951, handwritten letter from Mao Zedong to Gao Gang and Kim Il Sung, 53–54.

[57]Ibid., Doc. 71, 54.

[58]Shu Guang Zhang, *Mao's Military Romanticism*, 146.

military terms was highly limited and that the greatest UN threat was prompt amphibious landings.

Lost Chance?

Based on the available evidence, it seems clear that the Chinese spring offensives ended in a failure severe enough to push Soviet and Chinese leaders first to assume a defensive strategic posture and later to seek armistice negotiations. Even the US decisions to suspend large-scale offensive operations in July 1951 did not encourage the Communist command to attempt further large-scale offensives against the UN forces. This abrupt shift from the mass offensives to 'piecemeal' strategy is perhaps the best evidence of the blow the Chinese had absorbed in April and May 1951.[59]

Similarly, the collapse of the spring offensives appears to have opened a window of opportunity for the UN Command. Chinese records indicate that, contrary to General Bradley's characterization in the 29 May State/JCS meeting, the CVF were recoiling in disarray and did not, in the opinion of their own commanders, possess the resources to renew the offensive before August 1951. On balance, Van Fleet's intuitive feel for the military situation, its risks and opportunities, was superior to that of Ridgway and the JCS. In this sense, the lost chance appears to have been just that: a missed opportunity to shift the line 60 miles north and fundamentally alter the pre-armistice strategic setting.

Worse still, the Tongchon decision, reinforced by the subsequent decision to suspend all large-scale offensive operations, redefined the war in a way that surrendered all of the UN's major advantages. The firepower advantage that had shattered the last three Chinese offensives could be nullified by primitive fortification once the war settled into an immobile phase. Similarly, mobility – armored, airborne, or amphibious – had no meaning in a war in which movement had been suspended on political grounds. And finally, the cessation of UN offensive operations released the CVF from the logistics trap of high intensity war. With sufficient time and a protected sanctuary, the Chinese were able to construct a logistical structure sufficient to support low level, selective operations. As Van Fleet put it in 1953, 'This kind of war gives the enemy all the initiative. He can save up his ammunition and his strength and strike when and where he feels like it. We can only sit tight ...'.[60]

---

[59]Gen. Paik Sun Yup, *From Pusan to Panmunjom* (McLean, VA: Brassey's 1992), 155–6.

[60]Van Fleet, 'Truth about Korea: Part II', 164.

Strategy and Domestic Politics

If the military situation on the ground was ripe for Van Fleet's plan, why was the lost chance not taken? In a literal sense, the 28 May 1951 rejection of the Tongchon landings was General Ridgway's decision; presumably his decision rested on his appraisal of the relative merits of the plan. Yet, as most historical accounts indicate, his decision appeared to have been a product of his political as well as military appraisal of the situation. A commander who had assumed command from MacArthur only 90 days earlier was acutely aware of the importance of following the JCS/Administration guidance on Korean operations. For this reason, his decision must be viewed through the lens of contemporary American grand strategy, a strategy shaped in Washington and dominated by its concerns.

Competing Demands: The Primacy of Europe and Rearmament

While the military situation in Korea was undergoing a steady shift in favor of the UN Command, the civilian policy apparatus had long been focused on three primary problems: the defense buildup in Europe, the problem of allied unity, and the design of an exit strategy from Korea. The Korean War marked an inflection point in American perceptions of the Cold War. As the first major ground engagement of the conflict, it revealed the depth of Western and particularly American military weakness born of the World War II drawdown. From the vantage point of most American strategists, the Korean War's importance was as a prelude to a more significant and perhaps imminent clash with the Soviet Union. Europe, still recovering from the devastation of World War II, was in no condition to resist a Soviet push in Europe. Thus, in keeping with the notion of strongpoint defense, the administration and JCS were firmly focused on the threat of general war with the USSR.[61]

In the opinion of Bradley and Secretary of Defense General George C. Marshall in particular, Korea represented at once a diversion of scarce resources and a potential strategic feint by the USSR. Given time, the US rearmament triggered by the Korean conflict would enable the US to provide credible deterrents to future action in Europe and Japan. In the very short term, however, America was compelled to choose: reinforce a conflict on the periphery or pour resources into the areas of greatest national strategic value.

This view was even more closely held in the capitals of Western Europe. The British Cabinet had from the early stages of the Chinese intervention sought to prevent a diversion of resources from Europe to

---

[61]*FRUS, 1951*, 7: 295; *Military Situation in the Far East*, 2: 731–2.

Korea.[62] US Secretary of State Acheson was receptive to this line of argument. For while he saw the Korean War as a useful spur to American rearmament,[63] he shared Attlee's conviction that Korea was a distraction and Europe was the theater of decision.[64] More important, Acheson was also convinced that time was on the Western side if rearmament could continue for some time before the start of a general conflict with the USSR.[65]

In this context, and in light of the reverses of the fall and winter of 1950, American policy makers increasingly saw the Korea operation as a salvage case.[66] With the Chinese now in the war, the objective of military unification of Korea was no longer feasible. The best that could be hoped for was a negotiated settlement based on the restoration of the status quo ante bellum, and much of the State Department and National Security Council (NSC) planning in early 1951 flowed from this assumption. The dilemma, according to policy analysts inside and outside government,[67] was that such a deal could not be struck from a position of obvious weakness. Such a move would be a clear signal of desperation, and would make an acceptable deal based on the status quo ante bellum unattainable. The key was to wait for an improvement in the UN position to execute the cease-fire solution.

These three influences – the importance of rearmament, the problem of allied sentiment, and the perception of Korea as a peripheral conflict – drove American policymakers away from any options that smacked of a reinforcement of Korea. While this did not necessarily rule out aggressive action on the Korean peninsula, the anti-expansion mood in Washington reduced the attractiveness of options not squarely aimed at a prompt cessation of hostilities. In this sense, the Van Fleet's proposals may have suffered from conflation with MacArthur's more grandiose plans.

Guilt by Association: MacArthur's and Van Fleet's Plans Contrasted

This confusion was unfortunate in the sense that there had emerged two distinct categories of strategic options, one regional and resource intensive and the other local and largely self-reliant. MacArthur's

---

[62]William Stueck, *Rethinking the Korean War: A New Diplomatic and Strategic History* (Princeton UP 2002), 124–5; *FRUS, 1951*, 7: 36.

[63]Christensen, *Useful Adversaries*, 186.

[64]John Lewis Gaddis, *Strategies of Containment: A Critical Appraisal of Postwar American National Security Policy* (Oxford: OUP 1982), 115.

[65]*Military Situation in the Far East*, 3: 1720.

[66]*FRUS, 1951*, 7: 41–3, 165–6.

[67]Kennan, *Memoirs*, 28–9.

views, expressed repeatedly in private and by March 1951 in public, were expressly regional in nature. He argued that the Chinese Communist regime could be driven to abandon the Korean venture by applying broad economic and military pressure on it outside the Korean theater of operations.[68]

MacArthur's specific plans to place pressure on China included increased support to KMT forces inside China and in Korea as well, a naval blockade of China, and UN attacks on the productive capacity of China in the sanctuary areas of Manchuria.[69] MacArthur further argued that an attack by Chinese or Soviet air forces on the UN Command would demand a full retaliatory strike on those air bases. In short, MacArthur's plan was to increase the pressure on China in China. By bringing the war to the young regime's front door, MacArthur was confident he could extract a settlement favorable to the US and UN.[70]

As his critics were quick to point out, MacArthur's plans were far from costless. The diversion of US naval[71] and air[72] assets to the Far East would limit both the scope of operations in Korea proper and the range of military options elsewhere, particularly in Europe. At a time when World War III was considered to be close at hand, the notion of dramatically increasing US commitments in a peripheral area would, in the words of General Omar Bradley, 'involve us in the wrong war, at the wrong place, at the wrong time, and with the wrong enemy'.[73]

What is more, MacArthur's arguments first emerged during the panicky winter of 1950–51. In his own opinion, the UN Command faced a choice between a wider war with China and the inevitable abandonment of Korea. Though his arguments were to continue through the early spring of 1951, they remained rooted in the strategic calculations of the winter of 1950.

Van Fleet's proposals of late May and early June 1951 were entirely different in intent, origin, and resource intensity. Whereas MacArthur had seen a widened war with China as a means of staving off

---

[68]*Military Situation in the Far East*, 1: 42–3.

[69]MacArthur's requests came in the form of a 30 Dec. 1950 message to the JCS; see Blair, *Forgotten War*, 590. It is well worth noting that MacArthur's recommendations were largely adopted by the JCS as a whole in their 12 Jan. 1951 memorandum to MacArthur; see *FRUS 1951*, 7: 71–2. While the JCS position soon shifted against broad expansion of the war, the 12 Jan. 1951 memorandum is evidence of the frequent and significant changes in military opinion among the JCS.

[70]*Military Situation in the Far East*, 1: 43.

[71]Ibid., 2: 1541–2.

[72]Ibid., 2: 1379.

[73]Ibid., 2: 732.

impending defeat, Van Fleet hoped to capitalize on the catastrophic failure of the Chinese spring offensives. Unlike MacArthur's plans to attack China's productive capacity, Van Fleet's proposed amphibious operations were limited to the Korean theater of operations. Moreover, Van Fleet's proposed attacks did not envision any substantial reinforcement of the forces in theater; MacArthur's own plans would have required dramatic increases in aid to the KMT and the redeployment of substantial US fleet and air assets.

Yet in the political and bureaucratic context of May 1951, all options that smacked of expansion were suspect. That Van Fleet's operation would not have required additional forces was beside the point; the JCS guidance that led Ridgway to dismiss the landings assumed that any move north of the 38th Parallel would demand reinforcement and hence resource diversion.

Escalation Risk

During the MacArthur hearings, the administration argument against MacArthur's plans came in two parts. The first, as described above, dealt with the primacy of Europe and the scarcity of military resources. The second argument dealt with escalation risk. The administration, from the President through the JCS were adamant that they did not seek to widen the war; indeed they framed MacArthur's relief as a repudiation of a risk-laden policy of deliberate expansion. In front of the Senate Committee at least, the leaders of American diplomatic and military policy were unanimous in their judgment that MacArthur's plans posed grave escalatory risks.[74]

This public unanimity belied a more wide-ranging internal debate on escalation. As MacArthur had noted in his own defense, the JCS had supported more vigorous action against the Chinese in a 12 January 1951 memorandum to the Secretary of Defense.[75] In that document, the JCS supported all the major elements of MacArthur's plan: a naval blockade of China, reconnaissance flights over Manchuria, logistical and training support for KMT guerrilla activities on the mainland of China, and retaliatory naval and air strikes against the mainland in the event of enemy attack. The pendulum swings on military action against mainland China were an expression of underlying differences of opinion on escalation risk.

By the start of 1951, senior policy circles were split on the likely effects of more aggressive US action against China. One group composed of Acheson, Nitze, Edmund Chubb (Director of the Office

---

[74]Ibid., 1: 324–5, 621; 3: 1719.
[75]*FRUS, 1951*, 7: 71–2.

of Chinese Affairs) and the bulk of the intelligence community feared that bombing of Chinese targets would trigger the Sino-Soviet Treaty and direct Soviet entry into the war. The other group, which included Kennan, Rusk, Philip C. Jessup, and MacArthur, contended that any Soviet decision to enter the war would be based on Moscow's calculations rather than reactions to US actions against China.[76] In light of these fundamental disagreements on expected Soviet reactions, the administration opted for the safer course of avoiding direct action against China.[77]

While administration caution on the MacArthur options may have been warranted, the simple extension of these arguments to the discussion of the appropriate limit of advance in Korea was more problematic. Whereas MacArthur's plans held the plausible risk of Soviet intervention, it was unclear that an advance that stopped short of the Yalu posed any similar escalation risk. A draft memorandum sent by Acheson to Secretary of Defense Marshall on 23 February 1951 laid out the case against an advance north of the 38th Parallel. While acknowledging the potential advantages of such a move – increased costs to the enemy, reduced Chinese adventurism elsewhere, and increased Sino-Soviet tension – the memorandum argued against such an advance on multiple grounds:

> The principal factors militating against a general advance across the 38th Parallel are: (a) the capability of the Moscow-Peiping [Beijing] axis to inflict a decisive defeat upon United Nations forces if they make the decision to do so, (b) the risk of extending the Korean conflict to other areas and even into general war at a time when we are not ready to risk general war, (c) the heavy additional drain on American manpower and resources without a clearly seen outcome of the effort, (d) the loss of unity among our allies and in the United Nations in support of the Korean effort, and (e) the diversion of additional United States effort from other vital requirements.[78]

The reaction of Secretary Marshall and the JCS was swift and negative; the JCS argued that the memorandum's conclusions were premature and counter-productive.[79] The JCS were particularly sensitive to the

---

[76]Rosemary Foot, *The Wrong War: American Policy and the Dimensions of the Korean Conflict, 1950–1953* (Ithaca, NY: Cornell UP 1985), 124–6; *Military Situation in the Far East*, 1: 9.

[77]*FRUS, 1951*, 7: 177.

[78]Ibid., 7: 192–3.

[79]Ibid., 7: 205.

possibility that such a limit of advance would create a sanctuary for the numerically superior enemy. In addition, they argued that the ground commander should be afforded sufficient freedom of maneuver to maintain the security of his own forces.

Though the memorandum was never forwarded to the President, the draft and the JCS response captured the unresolved debate on the merits and risks of advance north of the 38th Parallel. What remained unexpressed on the State Department side were the grounds for these fears of escalation. Arguably, the Chinese capability to escalate pressure had reached its high watermark in the winter of 1950; while Mao could theoretically push more troops into Korea, his ability to arm and support additional forces was questionable. In addition, the fledgling Chinese Air Force was not yet ready to meet the US air forces on anything approaching equal terms.

If escalation risk existed, then, it was risk of Soviet not Chinese action. Why the Soviets would choose to enter a general war with the US over a UN ground advance north of the 38th Parallel when they had refrained from any such action in 1950 remains unclear or unexpressed. This debate over escalation risk and Soviet intentions resurfaced in the 29 May 1951 State/JCS meeting with an emphasis on the distinction between an advance north of the 39th Parallel and a halt at the Pyongyang–Wonsan line.[80] Navy Secretary Francis P. Matthews and presidential advisor Averell Harriman both emphasized the increased risk of general war associated with a move north of Wonsan, but appeared to accept Admiral Sherman's contention that a limit of advance around the 39th Parallel would be tenable in political terms.[81] This then was the ironic climax of the 'lost chance'. One day after Ridgway rejected the Tongchon operation on the grounds that it conflicted with JCS guidance, that same body, unaware of the Tongchon plan, was moving in the direction of agreement on a Wonsan–Pyongyang limit of advance.

On the question of escalation, the Russian and Chinese archival records suggest a significant American overestimation of the risks. First, while Mao's cables to Stalin and Kim Il-sung repeatedly refer to the risk of American amphibious landings, at no point does Mao mention or request plans for dramatic escalation or Soviet entry into the war.

---

[80]Ibid., 7: 471.

[81]Since the record of this critical meeting is in the form of loosely compiled minutes, Matthews' and Harriman's views on the escalation risks of an advance on Wonsan are not explicitly stated. The record does state that both emphasized the danger of moving north of that line; the author infers from this statement that they did not object to Admiral Sherman's statements earlier in the meeting advocating a Wonsan limit of advance.

Second, Stalin's own correspondence, particularly with his own advisors in Korea, suggests quite the opposite. Stalin appears to have been eager to maintain a situation in which the Chinese armies bore the brunt of the fighting, while the Soviets provided materiel, training, and limited defensive air support. On this last point, Stalin was particularly anxious to complete the training of the Chinese air forces so that they, rather than the Soviets, could assume all air operations at the front.[82] All of Stalin's correspondence and actions in the Korean conflict point to a desire to avoid direct confrontation with the US. This aversion to conflict stands in sharp contrast to the aggressive and calculating motives attributed to him by various American policy-makers at the time.

The Machinery of Government: NSC-48/5 and the MacArthur Hearings

The debates on all these issues found expression in the redrafting of the US policy document on Asia by the National Security Council, NSC-48/5. The redrafting effort began in January 1951, in the depths of the UN military crisis, and went through a series of revisions that culminated in Truman's signature to NSC 48/5 on 17 May 1951. From the outset, NSC-48/5 identified the US objective in Korea as the restoration of peace on the basis of the pre-war borders.[83] While the US maintained a political interest in the reunification of Korea, such an objective was strictly political. The basis for an armistice agreement was a restoration of the status quo, and the interim strategy of the US forces was to resist aggression against South Korea while inflicting maximum casualties on the enemy. In this sense, NSC 48/5 was entirely consonant with recent Presidential statements on the desire to limit the war, and the sentiments of America's closest allies.

The policy articulated in NSC-48/5 and trumpeted by every government witness in the MacArthur hearings (3 May–25 June 1951), formed the core of the administration case against MacArthur and against escalation. The public testimony by a series of military and civilian witnesses demonstrated near unanimity on the importance of restraint and the proximate risks of general war with the Soviets. While the cohesion of the government witnesses did much to strengthen the apparent case for MacArthur's relief, the public simplification of the strategic options had the effect of limiting the administration and the JCS' subsequent room for maneuver. A government that had

---

[82]Weathersby, 'New Russian Documents', Doc. 68, 13 June 1951, ciphered telegram, Filippov (Stalin) to Soviet military advisor in Beijing, Krasovsky, 51.
[83]*FRUS, 1951*, 7: 439–42.

decried MacArthur's proposals as dangerous and short sighted would have difficulty justifying a near simultaneous intensification of the war in Korea without appearing grossly hypocritical.

Thus, just as the administration confronted the post-MacArthur shifts in the military situation, it was fully engaged in a process of political and strategic retrenchment. Not only had every one of the Chiefs of Staff testified publicly against escalation, but vast amounts of their time during this critical period were consumed in that preparation and delivery of that testimony. As a review of that timeline reveals, the Secretaries of Defense and State, and the full complement of the JCS were summoned to testify just as the pivotal events of the Fifth and Sixth Chinese Offensives were unfolding. Under these circumstances, it seems hardly surprising that the administration and the JCS in particular were less responsive to events in Korea than they might otherwise have been.

Thus, the inaction on the part of Ridgway and the Truman cabinet in May 1951 was the product of the exceptionally charged policy environment of Washington in the months following MacArthur's relief. Longstanding beliefs about Chinese military advantage and Soviet escalation risk were advanced as part of an administration rebuttal of General MacArthur's positions on regional escalation. The public display of the MacArthur hearings forced the administration to present a stylized and increasingly dated version of a conflict that was shifting during their three weeks of testimony. Had Ridgway chosen to bring the Van Fleet proposals to the JCS on 28 May, his proposal would have placed an already taxed JCS in the awkward position of reversing their previous guidance, and opening the administration to new charges of hypocrisy. It is hard to imagine a less inviting atmosphere for the delivery of Van Fleet's plans, whatever their military merits. Van Fleet's plans were in this sense the final casualties of the MacArthur controversy.

Why Does it Matter?

Even if we accept the feasibility of Van Fleet's plans, why should this particular counterfactual loom large in the record of the Korean War? If Van Fleet had continued the pursuit of the Chinese armies as he wished and Mao feared, what difference might it have made?

On a local level, the impact of a successful landing at Tongchon might have had a decisive impact on the local military balance and by extension the terms and timing of the armistice. If Mao's cable of 14 June 1951 is an accurate indicator of the capabilities of the Chinese armies, then they would have been hard pressed to mount a significant counterattack against the UN until August and perhaps much later. The

THE KOREAN WAR AT SIXTY

weakness of the Chinese forces would have made a rapid, 60-mile exploitation to the Wonsan–Pyongyang line fully feasible. Seizure of this line would have been significant in and of itself; the line was one third shorter than the 'Kansas/Wyoming' line and eminently defensible against later Chinese efforts to dislodge the UN.[84] In addition, the capture of Pyongyang would have been an important tangible sign of the changed fortunes of the combatants and one likely to loom large in any armistice negotiations.

As Admiral Sherman had suggested in the 29 May 1951 JCS/State meeting, possession of the northern line would have given the Americans a potent card in the armistice talks. The US could opt to hold the new defensive line and demand a political and military settlement based on the facts on the ground, or trade the new found gains for a rapid settlement. A settlement at the 39th Parallel would have left a large portion of the North Korean population in South Korean control and would have pushed the NKPA/CVF forces well out of range of the South Korean capital.[85] Some abbreviation of the conflict would have been highly significant in terms of UN losses, as the last two years of positional warfare in Korea (1951–53) cost as many UN casualties as the first year.

Furthermore, a successful push to the Wonsan–Pyongyang line would probably have cost the Chinese forces dearly. Short on ammunition and unable to bring fresh forces forward in time, any Chinese withdrawal would likely have resembled the debacle of the last week of May. If the Chinese losses in the Fifth and Sixth Phase Offensives are a guide, two more weeks of high intensity combat would have cost the Chinese upwards of 70,000 to 90,000 casualties. While the Chinese were capable of replacing these losses in the long term, cable traffic between Beijing and Moscow suggests that the Soviet ability to provide materiel support was neither infinite nor immediate. Mao's 24 June 1951 objection to the slow speed of Soviet equipment transfers (only 16 division sets in 1951)[86] elicited a testy response from Stalin:

> As concerns arms for 60 divisions then I must say to you directly that to fulfill this application in the course of a single year is physically impossible and altogether unthinkable. Our production

---

[84]Stueck, *Rethinking*, 310.

[85]This point looms particularly large in the post-Cold War era as North Korea's nuclear extortion rests in large part on its credible threat to use its artillery arrayed along the DMZ to inflict great damage on Seoul. Had the armistice line been drawn north of Pyongyang, the South Korean capital would be well outside the range of anything save ballistic or cruise missiles.

[86]Weathersby, 'New Russian Documents', Doc. 72, 21 June 1951, ciphered telegram, Mao Zedong to Filippov (Stalin), 54.

THE KOREAN WAR AT SIXTY

and military specialists consider it completely impossible to give arms for more than 10 divisions in the course of 1951.[87]

This exchange between Mao and Stalin in June reveals one of the critical weaknesses in the conventional wisdom on the strategic calculus of the Korean War. If the CVF and NKPA forces sustained somewhere on the order of 200,000 casualties in the April to June timeframe,[88] this amounted to up to 20 lost division sets of equipment. Had Van Fleet executed the Tongchon operation in tandem with I Corps operations in the west, the additional 70,000 to 90,000 (7–9 division sets) expected casualties would have put the equipment losses at close to three years worth of Soviet production capacity – arguably well beyond the means of the Chinese or their Soviet sponsors. No matter how many Chinese soldiers were theoretically within the theater, the binding constraint on Chinese field capabilities was always logistical, and the losses incurred in high intensity operations far outstripped Soviet replacement capabilities. In short, by spring 1951, high intensity war was not a sustainable strategic option for the CVF.

On an international level, the possible consequences of success in June 1951 are harder to judge. How might China and the Soviet Union have reacted to such a dramatic shift in fortunes? The pattern of Mao's behavior in the Chinese Civil War, all phases of the Korean conflict, and the later Indochina wars, suggests that his appetite for risk was immense; a sharp rebuff in Korea would not necessarily have led to a more conservative stance on the use of force elsewhere.[89] Stalin, on the other hand, had only endorsed the 1950 invasion under the assumption that the US would not enter, and had consistently avoided direct combat with American forces.[90] Indeed, his specific limits on Soviet air combat strongly indicated that he wanted to minimize the chance of accidental escalation.[91] Stalin's greater conservatism suggests that he would have been unlikely to intervene in the case of a UN advance that stopped at the Wonsan line. It is reasonable to assume

---

[87]Ibid., Doc. 73, 21 June 1951, ciphered telegram, Filippov (Stalin) to Mao Zedong, 55.

[88]Mossman, *Ebb and Flow*, 504.

[89]Shu Guang Zhang cites a chilling discussion between Mao and Soviet Foreign Minister Andrei Gromyko in Aug. 1958 in which Mao stated that, 'if the USA attacks China with nuclear weapons, the Chinese armies must retreat from the border regions into the depths of the country. They must draw the enemy deep in deep so as to grip US forces in a pincer inside China ... Only when the Americans are right in the central provinces should you give them everything you've got.' Shu Guang Zhang, *Mao's Military Romanticism*, 258.

[90]Weathersby, 'Soviet Aims in Korea', 24.

[91]Ibid., 28.

that Stalin would have been more receptive to the lessons of such a military rebuff than either Mao or Kim Il-sung.

Perhaps most intriguing is the notion that severe reverses in Korea might have accelerated the Sino–Soviet split. As the exchanges between Mao and Stalin show, the tensions in the relationship were at their greatest in May and June 1951 as the Communist position began to deteriorate. Ever increasing Chinese demands for support, and increasing Chinese resentment of what they perceived to be stingy Soviet responses, might well have pulled forward the time at which the two sides broke off substantive contact.

For the US, a speedy end to the war or a conclusion that left the West in control of Pyongyang could have turned a bloody draw into what Henry Kissinger has termed a 'limited victory'.[92] The lessons of Korea, chief among them the notion that limited force could be used to secure agreements at the bargaining table, formed the basis of many American calculations of the Vietnam era. A Korean War that had ended with a limited and less costly victory might have led US policymakers to adopt a more aggressive policy in the crucial 1965–68 period. Whether this alternative 'theory of victory' would have been sufficient to change the outcome of the Vietnam War is impossible to tell. What is clear is that the 'lessons' of Korea as internalized by many American policymakers represented powerful brakes on offensive action in that war. The American way of limited war that emerged from Korea saw the containment of aggression as the goal and strictly limited force as the means to reach the bargaining table. Had other plans prevailed in May 1951, it is reasonable to assume that different 'lessons', appropriate or not, would have governed the course of future American conflicts.

Acknowledgements

The author would like to thank colleagues who reviewed this article and provided invaluable feedback. They include Thomas Christensen, Owen Cote, Brendan Green, Llewelyn Hughes, Karl Jackson, Bradford Lee, Jon Lindsay, Austin Long, William Norris, Barry Posen, and Josh Rovner.

Bibliography

Acheson, Dean, *Present at the Creation: My Years in the State Department* (New York: W.W. Norton 1969).
Acheson, Dean, *The Korean War* (New York: W.W. Norton 1969).
Almond, Edward M., *Conversations between Lieutenant General (Ret.) Edward M. Almond and Captain Thomas Fergusson: Senior Officers' Debriefing Program* (Carlisle Barracks, PA: US Army Military History Institute 1979).

---

[92]Kissinger, *Diplomacy*, 487.

Antal, Col. John F., 'Busting Through', *Military Review* (Ft Leavenworth, KS: Command and General Staff College) Jan.–Feb. 2000.

Archer, W.L., 'Observations of Close Air Support in Korea', Technical Memorandum, Operations Research Office, ORO-S-18 (FEC), 1 June 1951.

Blair, Clay, *The Forgotten War: America in Korea 1950–1953* (New York: Doubleday Books 1987).

Brodie, Bernard, *War and Politics* (New York: Macmillan 1973).

Chen Jian, 'The Sino-Soviet Alliance and China's Entry into the Korean War', *Cold War International History Project*, Working Paper, Woodrow Wilson International Center for Scholars, 31 Oct. 1991.

Christensen, Thomas J., *Useful Adversaries: Grand Strategy, Domestic Mobilization, and Sino-American Conflict, 1947–1958* (Princeton UP 1996).

Collins, Gen. J. Lawton, *War in Peacetime: The History and Lessons of Korea* (New York: Houghton Mifflin 1969).

Foot, Rosemary, *The Wrong War: American Policy and the Dimensions of the Korean Conflict, 1950–1953* (Ithaca, NY: Cornell UP 1985).

Gaddis, John Lewis, *Strategies of Containment: A Critical Appraisal of Postwar American National Security Policy* (Oxford: OUP 1982).

Goncharov, Sergei, John Lewis and Xue Litai, *Uncertain Partners: Stalin, Mao, and the Korean War* (Stanford, CA: Stanford UP 1993).

Halperin, Morton H., *Limited War in the Nuclear Age* (New York: John Wiley 1963).

Gen. (Ret.) Hong Xuezhi, 'The CPVF's Combat and Logistics', in Xiaobing Li, Allan R. Millett, and Bin Yu, *Mao's Generals Remember Korea* (Lawrence: UP of Kansas 2001).

Joy, C. Turner, *How Communists Negotiate* (New York: Macmillan 1955).

Kennan, George F., *Memoirs: 1950–1963* (Boston: Little, Brown 1972).

Khong, Yuen Foong, *Analogies at War: Korea, Munich, and the Vietnam Decisions of 1965* (Princeton UP 1992).

Kissinger, Henry, *Diplomacy* (New York: Simon & Schuster 1994).

Korea Institute of Military History, *The Korean War, Volume 2* (Lincoln: Univ. of Nebraska Press 1998).

Millett, Allan R., *The War for Korea, 1945–1950: A House Burning* (Lawrence: UP of Kansas 2005).

Millett, Allan R., *The Korean War* (Washington DC: Potomac Books 2007).

Mossman, Billy C., *Ebb and Flow (November 1950 – July 1951): The United States Army in the Korean War* (Washington DC: Center of Military History 2000).

Paik Sun Yup, Gen., *From Pusan to Panmunjom* (McLean, VA: Brassey's 1992).

Ridgway, Matthew B., *Soldier: The Memoirs of Matthew B. Ridgway* (New York: Harper & Brothers 1956).

Ridgway, Matthew B., *The Korean War* (Garden City, NY: Doubleday 1967).

Shu Guang Zhang, *Mao's Military Romanticism: China and the Korean War 1950–1953* (Lawrence: UP of Kansas 1995).

Stueck, William, *Rethinking the Korean War: A New Diplomatic and Strategic History* (Princeton UP 2002).

United States Senate, *Military Situation in the Far East* (Washington DC: GPO 1951).

Van Fleet, Gen. James A., 'The Truth About Korea: Part I: From a Man Now Free to Speak', *Life Magazine*, 11 May 1953.

Van Fleet, Gen. James A., 'The Truth About Korea: Part II: How We Can Win with What We Have', *Life Magazine*, 18 May 1953.

Weathersby, Kathryn, 'Soviet Aims in Korea and the Origins of the Korean War, 1945–1950: New Evidence from Russian Archives', *Cold War International History Project*, Working Paper No. 8, Woodrow Wilson International Center for Scholars, Nov. 1993.

Weathersby, Kathryn, 'New Russian Documents on the Korean War', *Cold War International History Project*, Bulletins (USSR) 6–7 *Cold War in Asia* (Washington DC: Woodrow Wilson Center 1996).

Appendix Table 1. US Escalation Options (1951).

Strategic Option	Date Introduced	Main Effort	Objective (Limit of Advance)	Scheme of Maneuver	Reinforcements required	Escalation Risk
MacArthur Option	Feb. 1951	Regional (Mainland China and Manchuria)	Yalu	1. Naval blockade PRC 2. Support KMT operations on mainland 3. Reconnaissance flights in Manchuria 4. Retaliatory strikes against PRC cities and airfields on call	1. Naval assets 2. Air assets 3. Logistical support	China: Medium Russia: Medium
Tongchon (Van Fleet)	28 May 1951	Korea	Wonsan–Pyongyang (NB: Original plan did not include subsequent objectives north of Tongchon)	1. 1st Marine Div lands at Tongchon 2. IX and X Corps attack northeast and north to trap CVF south of Tongchon 3. I Corps attacks north into Iron Triangle	None	China: Low Russia: Low

(*continued*)

Appendix Table 1. (*Continued*).

Strategic Option	Date Introduced	Main Effort	Objective (Limit of Advance)	Scheme of Maneuver	Reinforcements required	Escalation Risk
Operation 'Overwhelming' (Van Fleet)	1 July 1951	Korea	Wonsan–Pyongyang	1. XVI Corps at Kojo (2 US Army divs) 2. IX and X Corps attack northeast and north to trap CVF south of Tongchon 3. I Corps attacks north into Iron Triangle	2 US divs in Japan (XVI Corps)	China: Medium Russia: Low

Casualty Reporting and Domestic Support for War: The US Experience during the Korean War

STEVEN CASEY

International History Department, London School of Economics and Political Science, UK

ABSTRACT The common argument that public support for war is casualty sensitive ignores the fact that casualty figures are not revealed automatically. While the military decides when, and to whom, to release such information, political elites can question, even condemn, how the government goes about this business. After briefly exploring how the US military operated during the two world wars, this article focuses on American casualty reporting during the Korean War, arguing that the way the figures were revealed often sparked enormous political controversy, which at two crucial moments helped to undermine domestic support for this distant war.

According to John Mueller's famous formulation, the American public's support for war can be explained by a 'simple association: as casualties mount, support decreases'.[1] In the years since the end of the Vietnam War, this simple and powerful argument has become accepted conventional wisdom, cited frequently by analysts, commentators and politicians alike. According to one account, it is even enshrined in current US Army doctrine.[2]

Yet, despite its enormous influence, Mueller's thesis is not without its detractors. Numerous political scientists have refined, questioned and

---

[1] John Mueller, *Wars, Presidents, and Public Opinion* (New York: Wiley 1973); and 'The Iraq Syndrome', *Foreign Affairs* 84/6 (Nov.–Dec. 2005), 44.

[2] For a summary of recent literature, and its impact on conventional wisdom, see Christopher Gelpi, Peter Feaver and Jason Reifler, *Paying the Human Costs of War: American Public Opinion and Casualties in Military Conflicts* (Princeton UP 2009), 1–2, although the book itself is a sustained challenge to the Mueller thesis.

challenged its central components, undertaking research, for instance, into whether some groups in American society are less casualty averse than others or whether the public is more likely to accept high casualties in certain types of conflict.[3] Detailed historical studies of big wars also suggest that the government does not stand idly by while domestic support wanes, but tries instead to 'remobilize' the home front, devising more eye-catching goals that turn the war into some sort of crusade for basic American values.[4]

Moreover, as this article demonstrates, even on its own terms Mueller's thesis neglects an important dimension of the casualty problem: namely that, in the short term at least, the public is often unaware of the true cost of the war. This is partly because the government has considerable power over casualty reporting. The military decides what to release, when and to whom. Officials also have ways of softening the blow – of keeping certain types of casualty out of the overall figures so that the totals are not as high as they might appear; of closely regulating photographic images of American dead so as to avoid excessive anguish; and of releasing details of losses in conjunction with news of victories in order to demonstrate that the sacrifice was worthwhile. True, the government must always handle such efforts at sugarcoating with care. Great controversies can easily be sparked by allegations that the administration is trying to massage the figures and thereby mask the extent of defeat from the American public. But even these controversies reveal an important point that has often been lost in all the debate about how many losses the American public will tolerate: casualties do not enter the political discourse automatically; like so many other aspects of war, they are subject to debate, confusion and manipulation.[5]

---

[3]See, for instance, Bruce W. Jentleson, 'The Pretty Prudent Public: Post-Vietnam Opinion on the Use of Military Force', *International Studies Quarterly* 36/1 (March 1992), 49–73; Peter D. Feaver and Christopher Gelpi, *Choosing Your Battles: American-Civil Relations and the Use of Force* (Princeton UP 2004).

[4]This is one of the arguments in my recent book, *Selling the Korean War: Propaganda, Politics and Public Opinion* (New York: Oxford UP 2008), esp. 279–89. The concept of 'remobilization' is developed by John Horne, 'Remobilizing for "Total War": France and Britain, 1917–1918', in John Horne (ed.), *State, Society, and Mobilization in Europe during the First World War* (Cambridge: CUP 1997), 195–211.

[5]Adam J. Berinsky, 'Assuming the Costs of War: Events, Elites, and American Public Support for Military Conflict', *Journal of Politics* 69 (2007), 975–97 emphasizes the importance of 'patterns of elite discourse', especially partisan clashes over the meaning of key wartime events, in shaping public attitudes.

The aim of this article is to explore the importance of casualty reporting in the American home front's reaction to the Korean War. It begins by looking briefly at how the US military grappled with publicizing casualty figures during the two world wars. This surprisingly neglected subject is extremely significant in its own right, for it reveals the existence of problems and patterns that have continued to plague the military. But, for the purposes of this essay, its primary importance stems from the fact that these earlier wars created precedents and procedures that the military would utilize between 1950 and 1953.

The bulk of this article then focuses on the United States' Korean War experience. Korea is an extremely useful case study because it marks a major transition between the past and present, not just as the United States' first modern 'limited war' but also because in this conflict the military developed several techniques for handling battle dead that have endured.[6] Over the last decade, historians have explored some of these techniques, such as how the US military commemorated its battlefield casualties after 1953, while also examining other related issues, such as American cultural attitudes towards death during this early phase of the Cold War.[7] But the focus of this paper is quite different. It will look first at how the military publicized casualties in the midst of ongoing battles, uncovering not just the huge practical problems that emerged at the outset but also the evolution of more premeditated efforts to influence how the public perceived the figures as the fighting dragged on. The article then examines when and why this casualty reporting generated controversy among elites, especially in the media and Congress, who were in a position to mute or magnify how the home front perceived the human cost of war. And the article ends with an assessment of whether the government's casualty reporting, or the resulting elite controversy, had any impact on the mass public's support for the war.

---

[6]For an analysis of the casualty figures, see Frank A. Reister, *Battle Casualties and Medical Statistics: US Army Experience in the Korean War* (Washington DC: Dept. of the Army 1973).

[7]Michael Sledge, *Soldier Dead: How We Recover, Identify, Bury, and Honor Our Military Fallen* (New York: Columbia UP 2005), 222; Shuji Otsuka and Peter N. Stearns, 'Perceptions of Death and the Korean War', *War in History* 6/1 (Jan. 1999), 72–87; Bradley Lynn Coleman, 'Recovering the Korean War Dead: 1950–58: Graves Registration, Forensic Anthropology and Wartime Memorialization', Virginia Military Institute Archives, <www.vmi.edu/uploadedFiles/Archives/Adams_Center/EssayContest/20052006/ColemanBL.pdf>

Such an analysis is timely. In recent years the George W. Bush administration's news embargo on images of returning dead GIs has sparked enormous controversy. In the wake of this experience, the following pages not only seek to add an extra dimension to our knowledge of the Korean War experience. They also try to deepen our knowledge of how casualties were debated inside the United States during wartime.

Casualty Reporting before Korea

Modern casualty reporting dates back to the world war era. Before then, the American state did not accept much responsibility for undertaking this grisly task. During the Civil War, for example, individual generals kept careful lists of active soldiers, together with the numbers of dead and wounded in each engagement, but only to ascertain the strength of their units for the battles ahead. Neither they nor the military establishment in Washington deemed they had a duty to notify the next of kin, let alone the press and public.[8]

By 1917, however, the state's attitude had changed. After the Civil War, it began to accept an obligation towards those who had fallen fighting in its defence, as demonstrated by its massive programme to rebury the dead in national cemeteries.[9] Then, with the development of the General Staff at the turn of the twentieth century, the War Department created the capability to plan, regulate and systematize a whole range of military tasks. In terms of casualty reporting, the General Staff's most important innovation was to introduce ID (identity) tags (or dog tags) in 1913, which now made it possible to identify more accurately those soldiers who had fallen on the battlefield.[10]

Having assumed the obligation, the US military faced numerous practical problems once it finally went to war in 1917. Many of these stemmed from the simple fact that the officers given the job faced three competing audiences: their own superiors, who were determined to deny sensitive information to the enemy; the relatives of the fallen soldier, who ought to hear the grim news first through official channels; and the media, who naturally wanted to publish as much as it could as quickly as possible.[11]

---

[8]Sledge, *Soldier Dead*, 33, 37, 97; Drew Gilpin Faust, *This Republic of Suffering: Death and the American Civil War* (New York: Knopf 2008), 14, 102–5, 118–22, 252–3.

[9]Faust, *Republic of Suffering*, 230–41.

[10]'History of the Dog Tag', <www.173rdairborne.com/dogtag.htm>.

[11]N[ational] A[rchives, College Park, MD], [AEF Records] RG 120, Entry 222, box 6110, Dennis Nolan, Memorandum for the Commander-in-Chief, 3 March 1918; RG

Navigating slowly around all these problems, the military's journey towards an effective system was far from smooth. Sometimes it lurched uneasily from openness to a complete clampdown, as in March 1918 when the War Department suddenly (and briefly) decided to halt the release of all lists after an internal disagreement over whether or not to include names and addresses in public announcements. On other occasions civilian agencies accused the military of excessive censorship.[12] And almost always the media was a critical observer, ready and willing to depict any problems in the most sinister light – as, at best, a mindless act of suppression that would harm morale, and, at worst, a plot to hide the true scale of the war's cost.[13]

Over time, though, the War Department did establish a satisfactory system. It depended, first and foremost, on ensuring that no names were published until the next of kin had been notified. But it tried to build in sufficient flexibility so that reporters could get the names of heroic soldiers and write them in their dispatches, although the battlefield censor would hold these stories for 24 hours until after the telegram had been dispatched to the family.[14] Inside the War Department, meanwhile, officers also worked hard to confront other practical problems, such as whether or not to include the slightly wounded in lists, and what, for that matter, was the difference between a slight and severe wound.[15] It also ensured that the huge number of media organizations received the information in a timely and efficient manner, so that no one was scooped – something that the media itself came to appreciate, looking back later on the 1918 system as 'a tremendous task' that 'received the expert handling that it required'.[16]

This positive assessment came just after the United States formally entered World War II. Inevitably, teething problems plagued the early months of this new war, in large part because any positive experience gleaned from the earlier conflict was initially outweighed by the immense problems associated with waging a truly global war: the fact that the military was now strung out across various theatres, which

---

120, Entry 239, box 6195, Dennis Nolan, Memorandum for the Commander-in-Chief, 20 March 1918.

[12]'Publication of Casualty Lists', *Army and Navy Journal*, 16 March 1918; 'Casualty Lists Placed Under Ban', *New York Times*, 3 April 1918.

[13]See, for instance, editorial, 'An Inexplicable Order', *New York Times*, 4 April 1918.

[14]RG 120, Entry 240, box 6207, Francis C. Wickes to Memorandum for Lt Morgan, 24 March 1918; RG 120, Entry 222, box 6112, Mark S. Watson to Dengler, 15 May 1918.

[15]RG 120, Entry 222, box 6110, E.R. Warner McCabe, Memorandum to Press Officers, 3 July 1918.

[16]'Casualty Lists', *Editor and Publisher*, 24 Jan. 1942.

made compiling figures much more difficult; that the Army had to liaise with the Navy, which had a notoriously restrictive attitude towards releasing any information to the press; and that the United States was now a leading player in the Grand Alliance, which made coordination with the British and Dominion governments essential.

Because of these pressures, delay was the hallmark of the World War II system. Indeed, it took almost eight months before the media 'at last prized loose' the first complete casualty list from the government, partly because of the difficulty of getting all the branches to agree on what could be publicized.[17] And even thereafter the military placed a much longer time-frame on releases. Gone were the days of World War I when reporters could cable a story within 24 hours of the casualty details being sent to the United States. After D-Day, the Army in the European Theater decreed that names would only be passed by the censor a week and a half after the next of kin had been notified. And for much of the war, the War Department took 75 days to collect, check and release the total monthly loss figures.[18]

Although these delays occasionally resulted in predictable complaints, especially from war correspondents who suggested 'that casualty figures were withheld in order to minimize the gravity of the fighting',[19] as the war dragged on the media was generally willing to accept that any tardiness stemmed from legitimate constraints associated with waging a global, alliance war. Rather than criticize the basic structures the military had established, increasingly the central controversy revolved around the highly sensitive matter of whether or not the government should use casualty reporting as a conscious part of its overall propaganda campaign.

In both world wars senior officials, fretting that domestic support was fragile, sometimes looked for ways to soften the blow. Towards the end of 1944, for example, worried about mounting congressional opposition to using 18-year-olds in combat, the War Department first revised how it calculated the overall casualty figure, reducing it by including only specific combat-related categories, and then, in March 1945, stopped publishing total monthly lists altogether.[20]

---

[17]'Casualties: Just as Bloody', *Time*, 3 Aug. 1942.

[18]NA, [SHAEF Records] RG 331, Entry 86, Press Censor Guidance, No.158, 'Casualties', 30 June 1944.

[19]M[ilitary] H[istory] I[nstitute, Carlisle, Pennsylvania], Richard H. Merrick Papers, box 1, 'History of US and SHAEF Press Censorship in the ETO, 1942–45', July 1945.

[20]D.M. Giangreco, '"Spinning the Casualties": Media Strategies during the Roosevelt administration', *Passport: The Newsletter of the Society for Historians of American Foreign Relations* 35 (Dec. 2004), 22–9. For an earlier example, see Edward M.

Significantly, however, the greatest domestic furore surrounding a conscious government effort to manipulate casualty releases centred not on an act of suppression. It came, rather, from the Roosevelt administration's attempt to be more realistic about the human cost of war. In late 1943, with many officials fearing that the public was too confident about an imminent victory, the Office of War Information (OWI) released a number of 'horror' photographs for publication that revealed for the first time the gruesome nature of battlefield death in a modern campaign.[21] To prime the public for the need for continued sacrifice, a few weeks later James F. Byrnes, Roosevelt's principal domestic policy advisor, went even further, predicting the likelihood of 'heavy war casualties in the next 90 days'. Yet, rather than spark a new determination to defeat the Axis, this effort at candour immediately backfired. The press, in particular, recoiled at the idea that casualties were being used by the government for a propaganda purpose. As one OWI media survey pointed out, Byrnes's gloomy prediction 'evoked strongly emotional, antagonistic editorial comment. It was viewed as untactful, brutal, unnecessary, stupid, in execrable taste and as a shocking blunder, contributing to general confusion and domestic wrangling.'[22]

About the best that could be said for this episode was that at least most of the practical problems had now been ironed out. In particular, although total monthly figures were not always published, the War Department worked hard to ensure that regional and local lists went to the large numbers of newspapers scattered across the country, giving each plenty of time to prepare the names for publication so that no one could steal a march on its rivals.

Korean War Casualty Reporting: The Theory

The world war experience, then, was instructive. It vividly demonstrated the sensitivity of the casualty issue, even during wars in which popular support for total victory remained relatively robust until the very end. It also revealed the enormous dangers inherent in government efforts to link casualty reporting to its broader propaganda campaign.

Coffman, *The War to End All Wars: The American Military Experience in World War I* (Madison: Univ. of Wisconsin Press 1986), 67–8.

[21]'Lifts Picture Ban on War's Realism', *New York Times*, 5 Sept. 1943; George H. Roeder, *The Censored War: American Visual Experience during World War II* (New Haven, CT: Yale UP 1993), 13–14.

[22]NA, [OWI Records] RG 44, Entry 149, box 1712, Bureau of Special Services, 'Prediction of War Casualties, 23–31 December 1943', Analysis of Public Opinion, No. 30.

But the record was not all negative. Importantly, these earlier experiences also gave the US military a massive headstart in the summer of 1950, which was fortunate because Korea was an unexpected war.

Indeed, although the Cold War was at its height in 1950, before the North Korean invasion no one in the American government seriously anticipated that US troops would soon be fighting on the faraway Korean peninsula. In the last week of June, the brazen nature of the North Korean attack suddenly changed this calculation, swiftly uniting both the American public and a broad United Nations (UN) coalition behind the need to defend South Korea. But the first American units who were sent into action were green, ill-equipped and more used to the charms of occupation in Japan than the rigors of combat in Korea.[23] With these troops almost immediately pushed back down the peninsula, the summer of 1950 was not a time for leisurely trial and error. It was a major crisis in which the US military inevitably turned to the procedures and precedents it had developed during the two world wars.

On 4 July, even before the first American units went into action, General of the Army Douglas MacArthur, the US Far Eastern Commander, began making preparations, instructing qualified personnel 'to assist local commands in improving [their] reporting technique'.[24] In the next few weeks, as MacArthur's under-prepared units were forced to retreat by the North Korean Army, these qualified men were often overworked. At each layer of the military command – from individual regiments all the way up to MacArthur's own headquarters in Tokyo – they had to ensure that every one of the growing number of casualty figures was 'checked, rechecked and double checked to guarantee its authenticity'. In the Pentagon, the Casualty Section of the Adjutant General's Office then took enormous care to ensure that the notification of relatives was handled sensitively. As well as the customary condolence letter confirming the death, which was sent out by airmail, the Casualty Section used Western Union to dispatch telegrams, instructing the telegraph company to inform it as soon as each delivery had been made to the next of kin. Only then was the Pentagon prepared to release the name to the press.[25]

---

[23]Roy E. Appleman, *South to the Naktong, North to the Yalu* (Washington DC: Office of the Chief of Military History 1961), 179–81.

[24][Douglas] MacArthur Papers [Norfolk, VA], RG 9, box 26, Douglas MacArthur to Dept. of Army, 10 July 1950.

[25]NA, [Office of Secretary Defense Records] RG 330, Entry 149A, box 1, Press Branch, 'Casualty Releases', 10 Aug. 1950; OPI, Memorandum for the Press, 'Summary of Casualty Reporting Procedure', 11 Aug. 1950.

Acutely aware of the media complaints in previous wars, the US military was at pains to ensure that this publication process was swift and orderly. During the first month of the war, when total figures were still quite small, the Pentagon grouped all the casualties into one list, arranged alphabetically, which newspapers could publish the minute they received it. Then from 1 August, as the numbers mounted, the Casualty Section broke the list down by states, 'for the convenience of newspapers and radio stations' who invariably catered to a small local market. Working with the Office of Public Information (OPI), it then mailed out these about 60 hours ahead of their release time, to ensure that all newspapers could publish at the same time. The OPI also made sure that each list was numbered, 'so that recipients may have a quick check to determine that none is lost in transit or mislaid', while facilitating the answering of inquiries 'concerning any listed casualty'.[26]

This system, the Pentagon was quick to point out, was similar to the tried and tested methods devised during the two world wars, but with some significant improvements that promised to reduce the delays that had scarred earlier efforts. One change was related to the simple fact that the three services had been unified in 1947, which meant that the military was able to swiftly release just one list, including the Army, Navy, Marines and Air Force. Another stemmed from the existence of new technologies. Whereas in World War II the Army sent machine record cards from the theatre headquarters back to the War Department, now MacArthur's command was able to relay back the same information using electrical messaging, which cut down the transmission time dramatically. As the Adjutant General was quick to point out, this service was 'a far cry from the days of the Civil War' when relatives and the public had received the information in haphazard fashion from newspapers, town square message boards, or letters from chaplains and officers. Now the Pentagon planned to notify both the families and the media in as sensitive and speedy a fashion as possible.[27]

Korean War Casualty Reporting: The Practice

This, at least, was the theory. But, as past wars demonstrated, even the most efficient of systems could easily run into trouble, and Korea soon proved no different, largely because the early fighting was extremely fluid.

---

[26]Ibid. See also RG 330, Entry 134, box 152, OPI, 'Activity Reports', 6 July 1950.

[27]Edward F. Witsell, 'The Casualty Report Tells the Story', *Army Information Digest* 11 (Nov. 1950), 7–10; 'Army Tells How Casualty Report is Speeded Up', *Editor and Publisher*, 9 Dec. 1950.

In the first battles, under-prepared and outnumbered GIs were often encircled by North Korean forces in short and vicious encounters; suddenly cut off, they had to make long, dispiriting marches through hostile territory before they renewed contact with their unit command.[28] Then, during the bitter winter of 1950–51, a big chunk of the US Army was swiftly surrounded by the massive Chinese intervention. In northeast Korea the situation was particularly grim, with a large contingent of the X Corps cut off almost 80 miles from the safety of the port at Hungnam, facing fierce Chinese attacks and only one escape route that ran through frigid mountain passes up to 2,500 feet high.[29]

In such situations, casualty reporting was extremely difficult. For one thing, during these periods of defeat the enemy invariably controlled the battlefield, making it hard to recover bodies. For another, because many troops did ultimately make it back to American lines, the first estimates of losses were often inflated by large numbers of MIA (missing in action), who could, within days or weeks, be accounted for. With early figures so unpredictable, the military faced a problem. Its new improvements pointed in the direction of speed. But the practical matter of fighting the war often entailed countless delays.

During the summer, the Pentagon's first instinct was to try to explain this difficult situation to potential critics. At the end of July, with US forces still retreating back to what would soon become their defensive Pusan perimeter, Army officials met with senior media figures. 'The front is too confused now to make any real estimate', they informed a senior *Time* magazine correspondent. *Time*, which wanted to revive its World War II format of publishing weekly 'box scores' of casualties, was told that any figures it 'went to press with would be meaningless, and certainly inaccurate. Therefore, the Army refuses to release any.' *Time* thus deferred its box scores for a few weeks until the US front line was 'considerably shorter, tighter and better organized'.[30] In the meantime, the Army followed its own World War II precedent by being as candid as possible to senior legislators on key congressional committees, providing them with 'unconfirmed flash figures' in closed-door sessions so that they at least had some sense of what was happening at the front.[31]

---

[28]Appleman, *South to the Naktong*, 82–6, 94, 146–80.

[29]Roy E. Appleman, *Escaping the Trap: The US Army X Corps in Northeast Korea, 1950* (College Station: Texas A&M UP 1990), 11, 29.

[30][Houghton Library, Harvard Univ., Cambridge, MA] Time Dispatches, Folder 589, Clay Blair to Don Bermingham, 'Box Scores', 28 July 1950.

[31]RG 330, Entry 149A, box 1, OPI, Memorandum for the Press, 'Summary of Casualty Reporting Procedure', 11 Aug. 1950.

Yet, as we shall see, these initiatives soon created real problems, especially as they became inextricably intertwined with a final element in the government's casualty reporting: the efforts by some senior officers to try to influence how the home front perceived the war's cost. Here, MacArthur was the main driving force. Despite his enormous experience during the two world wars, first as chief censor in 1917 and then as a highly public relations-conscious commander between 1941 and 1945, MacArthur was strangely naive about the prospects of managing the press during the early months of the Korean War.[32]

For the first six months of the fighting, the US Far Eastern Commander permitted the 200 or so correspondents who flocked to the front to operate in a censor-free environment. His hope was that reporters would use this freedom responsibly, which, to him, meant basing stories on his command's daily communiqués and press briefings.[33] But MacArthur's public statements were rarely neutral. Most contained a clear slant, invariably stressing successes and downplaying disasters. Casualties were a case in point. Although precise figures were given out by the Pentagon, MacArthur was rarely content to let these stand on their own. Sometimes he announced American losses alongside a bigger enemy toll, in an effort to stress that US sacrifices had not been in vain.[34] On other occasions he simply minimized the number of American casualties in big battles, even disastrous ones. On 19 July, for instance, as the Kum River line crumbled and the fall of the key city of Taejon loomed, MacArthur's communiqué was relentlessly upbeat. 'Our hold upon the southern part of Korea represents a secure base', he told reporters. 'Our casualties, despite overwhelming odds, have been relatively light. Our strength will continue to increase while that of the enemy will relatively decrease.'[35]

As the military hastened to add, casualties had been so light largely because of the sterling work of the US medical teams. Indeed, this was one of the few success stories of the first weeks of the war, and the military was naturally anxious to encourage correspondents to follow

---

[32]On MacArthur's pre-Korean War publicity activities, see Clayton D. James, *The Years of MacArthur* (Boston: Houghton Mifflin 1970–75) 1: 130–5 and 2: 89, 164–5, 277–8, 708–9.

[33]On MacArthur's Korean War press system and the reasoning behind it, see MacArthur Papers, RG 6, box 4, Marion P. Echols to Correspondents, 2 July 1950; MHI, Marion P. Echols Papers, box 2, Official Correspondence Folder, Marion P. Echols to Virginius Dabney, 31 July 1950; Ray Erwin, 'Voluntary Censorship Asked in Korean War', *Editor & Publisher*, 8 July 1950.

[34]NA, [Allied Operational and Occupation HQ Records] RG 332, Entry 1102, box 27, SCAP, GHQ, PIO, Press Releases, 11, 13 and 20 July 1950.

[35]Ibid., SCAP, GHQ, PIO, Communiqué No.99, 20 July 1950. For the battle itself, see Appleman, *South to the Naktong*, 146–80.

these medical units around in Korea – and delighted when reporters like Marguerite Higgins of the *New York Herald Tribune* duly reported that 'the speed with which the wounded were tended and evacuated was one of the most remarkable performances this correspondent has seen in the Korean War'.[36] Back in the United States, Defense Department officials also worked hard to shift the media's attention in this direction. Because of air evacuation, exemplary cooperation between the services and the very latest treatments, Pentagon spokesmen repeatedly stressed, 'the death rate in military hospitals from battle wounds has been the lowest of any similar military campaign in our nation's history'.[37]

Domestic Controversy over Casualties

The MASH (Mobile Army Surgical Hospital) image of the Korean War, which remains the dominant one in American popular culture, was thus born at a very early stage, the product of a particular propaganda urge to mute the public's response to casualties. But this, along with the other efforts to minimize the costs, did not really work. On the contrary, rather than accept the military's efforts to soften the blow, other opinion makers in the American polity challenged official figures, and in the process often served to magnify the sense that Korea was a particularly bloody war.

This challenge was scarcely surprising, and not just because it had already happened in both world wars. Korea came at a time when Congress was increasingly scarred by partisanship. Republicans, desperate to win back the White House after five straight election defeats and increasingly convinced that the Democrats had fatally prioritized Europe over Asia, seized on the war to attack the administration.[38] This Republican offensive came in many guises, but the military's informal use of unconfirmed 'flash' figures provided the first opening to exploit the casualty issue. During the summer of 1950

---

[36]Marguerite Higgins, 'Newswoman Tells Harrowing Tale of Night Infiltration Raid on US Command Post', *Washington Post*, 4 Aug. 1950. See also, 'Medics in Arms', *Time*, 7 Aug. 1950.

[37]'Death of Wounded Reduced in Korea', *New York Times*, 10 Nov. 1950. See also NA, [Army Dept., Adjutant General Records] RG 407, Entry 429, box 362, Far East Command, PIO, 'Amazingly Low Death Rate in Korea', 23 Oct. 1950. The Pentagon placed a complete block on all press interviews with the wounded who returned home; see RG 330, Entry 148, box 755, 'Return of War Wounded Personnel', 14 July 1950.

[38]Ronald J. Caridi, *The Korean War and American Politics: The Republican Party as a Case Study* (Philadelphia: Univ. of Pennsylvania Press 1968); David R. Kepley, *The Collapse of the Middle Way: Senate Republicans and the Bipartisan Foreign Policy, 1948–1952* (New York: Greenwood Press 1988).

senators on the Appropriations Committee soon spotted the large discrepancy between the data the Pentagon had furnished them in a secret session and the official numbers found in newspapers across the country, and they hastened to tell the public. According to the Committee's ranking Republican, Styles Bridges, this difference indicated that the appalling cost of the war was 'being concealed', and Americans were going to be shocked when 'the whole truth' about the real losses was finally divulged.[39]

The media, for its part, was keen to fan these flames. Drew Pearson, the highly influential and 'flamboyant muckraker' who reached millions of Americans through his syndicated column and radio show, quickly latched on to Bridges' allegations, claiming that 'the Army is holding back the true casualty lists in Korea', which he believed were in fact 75 percent higher than what had been announced. Bert Andrews of the *New York Herald Tribune* then amplified this charge, pointing to a paragraph that had been 'buried in a dispatch from Tokyo' by the war correspondent, Keyes Beech. 'The greatest source of anger and frustration here is Washington's apparent refusal to recognize the Korean War as a first-class war', Beech had written. 'It may not be a first-class war in any conventional sense. But Americans are going to be in for a rude shock when they see the casualty figures.' If this was a hint by Beech that the military had been glossing over the true state of affairs, then Andrews had absolutely no doubt who he would believe. 'Newspaper reporters who know Mr Beach's [*sic*] reputation as an accurate reporter', Andrews declared, 'are aware that he was saying between the lines that he knew what the casualties were, and that the shock when the true number was announced would be "rude" indeed.'[40]

In Washington, the Pentagon moved swiftly to counter the congressional allegations of a cover-up, pointing out that it had given the Appropriations Committee unconfirmed figures as a courtesy to keep it informed but had always stressed that these totals could easily change and were not accurate enough for general release.[41]

In Tokyo, MacArthur was equally quick to retaliate. Just weeks into the war his whole attempt to dominate media coverage without censorship seemed to be in tatters, as correspondents roamed freely around the front – and then, equally freely, sent back stories of their

---

[39]'Unproved Casualties Handed to Congress', *New York Times*, 12 Aug. 1950.

[40]'100 Seek War Beat Despite Privations'; 'Communications Snag for War Reporters'; both in *Editor & Publisher*, 12 and 26 Aug. 1950. RG 330, Entry 134, box 152, OPI, 'Activity Reports', 8 Aug. 1950.

[41]'US Army Confirms 2,616 Casualties'; 'Casualty Gap Denied'; both in *New York Times*, 8 and 11 Aug. 1951.

experiences that were published to great acclaim. Particularly galling to MacArthur was the correspondents' emphasis on the enormous human cost of the war. 'Losses sustained by American forces in Korea have been greatly exaggerated in press reports at the front', the General announced in a July communiqué. 'Reports of warfare are, at any time, grisly and repulsive and reflect the emotional strain normal to those unaccustomed to the sights and sounds of battle. Exaggerated stories obtained from individuals wounded or mentally shocked have given a completely distorted and misrepresentative picture to the public.' To back up his claims, MacArthur mentioned the case of a so-called Lost Battalion, which war correspondents had reported as 'close to annihilation', though 'its actual losses amounted to only two killed, seven wounded and 12 missing'.[42]

Yet, rather than beat reporters into submission, MacArthur's riposte simply fanned the embers of controversy still further. Indeed, war correspondents who had witnessed battles at first hand, increasingly accused MacArthur of trying to sugarcoat the news – of covering up snafus, obscuring defeats and burying losses. And when China massively intervened in the war in October–November, their instinct was to expose what they saw as the growing credibility gap between Tokyo's rose-tinted communiqués and the grim reality on the ground.[43]

MacArthur, for his part, now moved from slanting casualty reports to suppressing the figures altogether. His motives were partly personal: he was desperate blunt the home front impact of this massive defeat, especially as he was increasingly getting the blame.[44] But the US Far East Commander was also driven by familiar practical problems: the simple fact that it took time to account for American losses, especially in the enormous turmoil generated by the long retreat from North Korea, not to mention the very real concern not to give any sensitive information to the Chinese enemy at such a pivotal moment in the fighting.[45]

In the wake of China's massive intervention, then, the scene was set for the major controversy about the real cost of the war. The starting point was the lack of hard figures. Although the Pentagon continued to release monthly numbers, these, it admitted, were roughly six weeks

---

[42]MacArthur Papers, Box 149, CINCFE to Dept. of Army, 12 July 12 1950; RG 331, Entry 1102, box 27, Far East Command, PIO, Communiqué No.72, 13 July 1950; 'Needed: A Rule Book', *Time*, 24 July 1950.

[43]Casey, *Selling the Korean War*, 146–54.

[44]'MacArthur's Own Story', *US News & World Report*, 8 Dec. 1950; AP Report, 2 Dec. 1950, copy in H[arry] S. T[ruman] L[ibrary, Independence, MO,] Harry S. Truman Papers, OF 584, box 1397.

[45]MacArthur Papers, RG 9, box 53, Douglas MacArthur to Army Commanders, 10 Dec. 1950.

behind events on the battlefield, and so during December 1950 and January 1951 they did not contain any indication of the casualties caused by the Chinese victory.

With no recent and relevant data coming from official sources, the media worked hard to fill the information vacuum. War correspondents on the ground were particularly active, especially since most were now deeply suspicious of MacArthur's command. Moreover, caught up in the cold and chaotic march back down the Korean peninsula, and witnessing horrific battles when whole units appeared to be wiped out, they were in a position to relay back vivid eyewitness accounts, as yet uncensored, that totally undermined any official efforts to dampen the cost. In western Korea, Homer Bigart of the *New York Herald Tribune*, who was with the imperilled US 2nd Infantry Division as it fought a bitter and murderous engagement to cover the Eighth Army's retreat, described the result as 'slaughter. Many wounded had to be left behind. It was as ghastly a night as the veteran troops had ever spent.'[46] In northeast Korea, Fred Sparks of the *Chicago Daily News*, who was with X Corps during its retreat in the eastern part of the peninsula, believed this gruesome episode would be 'irrevocably etched in the mind – and the conscience – of the American people. The etching will have frostbitten boys slipping, falling, and dying – but fighting, though facing a vastly greater foe, dragging out their dead and wounded, by hand, by jeep, by oxcart.'[47]

As well as providing these dramatic firsthand accounts, many reporters tried to piece together the exact cost of defeat. One obvious problem was the large number of surrounded troops, which meant the MIA figure was initially very high. MacArthur's command clearly expected that many would return, and this was one reason for its sluggishness in providing totals. Some war correspondents effectively challenged this assumption, however, sending home grim eyewitness accounts that suggested that many MIAs would be lost forever. As Charles Moore reported in early December 1950, the few survivors from the 7th Infantry Division who had made it back to US lines after the harrowing battle at the Chosin Reservoir were telling gruesome stories 'that fanatical Chinese burned wounded prisoners alive and danced around the flames "like wild Indians" while the GIs scream in pain.'[48]

Other units appeared to have suffered even more. In mid-December, the *Washington Post* ran a banner headline stating 'Marine Losses

---

[46]Homer Bigart, 'Ghastly Night Put in by Yanks', *Washington Post*, 28 Nov. 1950.
[47]Fred Sparks, 'Nightmare Valley Ahead of Yanks', *Chicago Daily News*, 6 Dec. 1950.
[48]Charles Moore, 'Wounded GIs Burned Alive, Survivors Say', *Washington Post*, 3 Dec. 1950.

"Heavier Than Tarawa"'. According to an Associated Press report, although the military had yet to release figures of confirmed dead, it had announced that more than 4,000 wounded men had already been flown out of the Chinese trap, which was almost double the number of wounded at Tarawa, 'the costliest single Marine action in World War II.' And overall casualties were bound to be higher than this notorious 1943 battle.[49]

Desperate to confirm such sizable figures, Washington correspondents probed their sources. On 8 December, one Pentagon official told a *Time* reporter – off the record – that the Chinese intervention had probably inflicted about 50,000 casualties on US forces in Korea. The Marines, meanwhile, initially estimated to the press that around 7,000 of their men would be lost trying to escape to the Hungnam beachhead. Determined to get harder proof, some journalists were highly innovative. As one wired his editor on 6 December:

> you might be interested in the fact that the Defense Department asked the Red Cross this week to double its blood collections during December. As of now, the Red Cross is collecting over 90,000 pints of blood a month, for the armed forces and civilian hospitals. This month, the Red Cross and other cooperating blood banks have been told to increase collections by nearly 100 percent.[50]

As a matter of fact, the actual numbers proved to be nowhere near these grandiose expectations. According to official data published in the middle of January 1951, total losses since June 1950 were only in the region of 42,700, of which 6,247 had been killed in action. But by the time that these official figures had been released, the damage had been done. The public had been bombarded by stories that suggested a far costlier fight. During December, for instance, even the more restrained reports indicated that casualty figures just from the Chinese intervention would be huge – well above the bloodiest battles in the World War II, and perhaps approaching 48,000 (excluding the '22,000 more men listed as non-battle casualties, most of them the victims of frostbite or frozen feet').[51]

---

[49]'Marine Losses "Heavier Than Tarawa"', *Washington Post*, 11 Dec. 1950; Time Dispatches, Folder 622, Robert Sherrod to Don Bermingham, 'Add Casualties', 11 Dec. 1950.

[50]Time Dispatches, Folder 620, 'The Battle', 6 Dec. 1950.

[51]'The Price'; 'U.S. War Casualties'; both in *Time*, 1 and 22 Jan. 1951. Peter Edson, 'Korea and World War I', *Washington Daily News*, 2 Jan. 1951.

THE KOREAN WAR AT SIXTY

In this frenzied atmosphere, official statements often served to heighten, rather than dampen, the impression of a full-scale disaster. Sometimes, these were simply clumsy, such as an Army announcement that thousands of National Guardsmen might soon be sent into the combat zone because casualties had been so high and Army training centers had not been able to produce sufficient men.[52]

But on other occasions, they were due to another important rivalry, this time between the Army and the Marines, which generated further controversy about the cost of the war, and helped to fix in the public mind the sense that Korea was an excessively bloody fight. Perhaps the most alarming episode occurred when Marines discovered the bodies of men from the 2nd Division, who had been killed by a Chinese attack on the night of 12 February 1951. The Marines immediately dubbed the area 'Massacre Valley'– a nickname soon picked up by an Associated Press reporter, who filed a story indicating that upwards of 2,000 men had been killed. Appalled, the Army launched an investigation, which ultimately resulted in the Associated Press publishing a detailed apology for its 'deceptively written story'. But again this retraction came too late. For as one senior officer pointed out, the idea of a 'massacre' stuck in the public mind, while 'the correction was never given the circulation the original story had gotten'.[53]

Yet, just as this casualty controversy threatened to spiral out of control, its nature changed decisively. From the spring of 1951 it suddenly became less a product of vivid firsthand reporting from the Korean battlefield and more a manifestation of intensifying partisan bickering inside Washington DC. The media's declining role stemmed partly from events on the battlefield, which settled down into a trench stalemate by the summer of 1951, with daily patrols and intermittent offensives but no major efforts to strike a knockout blow to win the war. Although such fighting remained extremely bloody – and indeed the United States sustained 45 percent of its overall battlefield casualties during the last two years of the war[54] – as the battlefield slowly stabilized the military was able to control journalists' access to the fighting front, something that had rarely been possible during the fluid battles of the war's first nine months.

---

[52]'Casualties Forcing Army to Add 50,000 Draftees', *New York Times*, 12 Jan. 1951. NA, [Army Staff Records] RG 319, Entry 206A, Unclassified Decimal File 000.7, box 54, Floyd Parks to Lawton Collins, 26 Feb. 1951.

[53]RG 319, Entry 206A, Unclassified Decimal File 000.7, box 54, Floyd Parks, Memorandum For Deputy Chief, 15 March 1951; Floyd Parks to Doyle Hickey, 21 March 1951; Doyle Hickey to Floyd Parks, 1 April 1951.

[54]Rosemary Foot, *Substitute for Victory: The Politics of Peacemaking at the Korean Armistice Talks* (Ithaca, NY: Cornell UP 1990), 208.

More importantly, after MacArthur belatedly introduced a strict censorship regime at the start of 1951, the military was finally in a position to control what correspondents actually wrote about, deleting unsubstantiated claims about overall casualty figures, or toning down reports that vividly detailed the bloodiness of particular battles.[55]

These changes were clearly evident during the flare-up of fighting between August and October 1951. Attacking a series of sophisticated North Korean and Chinese defences, US forces suffered about 22,000 casualties in battles the GIs ominously dubbed 'Bloody Ridge' and 'Heartbreak Ridge.' For the troops caught up in the carnage, conditions were just as appalling as anything that had been encountered at earlier stages of the war.[56] But little of this brutal reality was now conveyed back to the home front. Indeed, the Army began by instituting a total clampdown on news, only allowing reporters to mention the battles after the first partial victory had been won. And even then the story was carefully orchestrated. Correspondents were permitted merely to report that the United States and the UN had launched a series of 'limited objective attacks', whose aim was to wrest key areas from the enemy 'with a minimum of casualties to UN troops'. Crucially, the censors also made sure that the 'Bloody Ridge' label was used *not* to describe the awful conditions faced by UN forces but to depict the terrible suffering of enemy troops, whose 'positions had been shattered by a tremendous torrent of artillery –390,000 rounds'.[57]

By the summer of 1951, with the casualty controversy no longer being fuelled by graphic reports from Korea, the focus shifted to the partisan fight on the home front. Again, MacArthur was at the forefront, although this time in a very different role. In April Truman sacked him for persistent insubordination. Returning to the United States, MacArthur immediately began a nationwide speaking tour, in which he criticized the President and his senior advisors for denying him the power to win the war and advocated a number of escalatory measures to bring it to a successful conclusion. At the heart of MacArthur's case, which got its most extensive airing at special

---

[55]RG 407, Entry 429, boxes 1151 and 1163, Eighth Army, PIO, Command Report, Jan. and Feb. 1951.

[56]Walter G. Hermes, *Truce Tent and Fighting Front* (Washington DC: Center of Military History, US Army 1992), 80–103. For a vivid description see Clay Blair, *The Forgotten War: America in Korea, 1950–1953*, new ed. (Annapolis, MD: US Naval Institute Press 2003), 947–50.

[57]RG 319, box 5, Korean War Communiqués, Unnumbered Press Release, 5 Sept. 1951; '18-Day Fight Won!', *Chicago Daily News*, 5 Sept. 1951; 'US Troops Battle for Weeks', *Washington Post*, 5 Sept. 1951; 'US Forces Win Korea Ridge in 17-Day Battle', *New York Herald Tribune*, 6 Sept. 1951.

congressional hearings in May, was the mounting human toll. Our losses, he stressed numerous times:

> are approaching 65,000. This conflict in Korea has already lasted almost as long as General Eisenhower's decisive campaign which brought the European War to an end. And yet the only program that I have been able to hear is that we shall indecisively go on resisting aggression, whatever that may mean. And if you do, you are going to have thousands and thousands of American lives that will fall, and in my own opinion events will finally catch up with you, so that you will have to stop it in some way; and then the great question is – Where does the responsibility for that blood rest? This I am quite sure – It is not going to rest on my shoulders.[58]

Keen to use MacArthur's huge prestige and popularity to bolster their own attacks on the Truman administration, Republicans lined up to exploit the casualty issue. Many latched on to the administration's effort to exclude non-battle casualties from the overall figure, especially the large number of troops who had fallen victim to frostbite throughout the winter, knowing full well that if these were included the total figure would jump dramatically to around 140,000.[59] According to Harry Cain, this shocking figure meant that United States had suffered more casualties in the undeclared Korean 'police action' than it had in a comparable period during World War II.[60] According to Robert Taft, this huge loss of life simply confirmed that Korea was a 'useless and expensive waste'.[61]

Significantly, those on the right of the Republican Party were not the only ones to stoke the casualty controversy. In the 1952 presidential campaign, General of the Army Dwight D. Eisenhower, the Republican nominee, constantly referred to the human cost of the Korean War,

---

[58]US Senate, *Military Situation in the Far East* (Washington DC: GPO 1951), 30,44, 65–6.

[59]*Military Situation in the Far East*, 610–11, 937, 950, 1278–9, 1286–8; *Congressional Record* Vol. 97 (Washington DC: GPO 1951), 5418, 5778, 6605, 6623–8, A3122. This was a constant theme of media reports, see, for instance, Drew Pearson, 'Casualty Figures Held Faulty', *Washington Post*, 7 March 1951; 'Bradley Discloses Non-Battle Loss', *New York Times*, 25 May 1951; 'US Non-Battle Casualty Total', *New York Herald Tribune*, 7 March 1952.

[60]*Congressional Record*, 97: 12,537–39; 98: 1598–1600.

[61]CBS, 'People's Platform', 6 May 1951, copy of transcript in Virginia Military Institute, Lexington, VA, George C. Marshall Papers, box 195A, Folder 16; Library of Congress, Washington DC, Robert Taft Papers, box 968, Subject File: Foreign Policy, Robert Taft to Smith, 23 May 1951.

albeit with some subtle differences. Whereas Republican nationalists tried to inflate the figure by including non-battle figures, Eisenhower stuck closely to the official Defense Department figures, which by now were edging up to 117,000. Whereas the Republican right tended to mention big losses in the same breath as the need to get out of Korea altogether, Eisenhower generally accepted that the war was necessary, and only emphasized casualties in the context of the administration's failure to deter Communist aggression before June 1950. Nonetheless, on this issue candidate Eisenhower was well within the Republican mainstream. Although widely viewed as a man above party, he was firmly wedded to the Republican effort to emphasize the human toll of 'Truman's War'.[62]

Mass Opinion and the Casualty Controversy

What impact did all this controversy have on American popular opinion? At two crucial moments – January 1951 and October 1952 – domestic support for the Korean War suddenly dipped. Although care must be taken not to ascribe too much weight to just one variable, it is nevertheless clear that the controversy over casualties did exert some impact on mass opinion at these two points in time.

After the Chinese intervention, the most visible change in popular attitudes came on 21 January 1951, when George Gallup published a poll revealing that 66 percent of Americans now wanted to 'pull our troops out of Korea as fast as possible'. Although this single result was undoubtedly driven by numerous factors – not least the overall military setback currently being suffered by US and other UN forces – the casualty controversy undoubtedly played a role. For one thing, Gallup's interviews were conducted during the first weeks of January, at a time when inflated casualty reports were widespread in the media.[63] For another, those groups in American society who were in some way vulnerable to appearing in future casualty statistics now clearly had grave doubts about the wisdom of fighting in Korea.[64]

---

[62]D[wight] D. E[isenhower] L[ibrary, Abilene, KS], Stephen Benedict Papers, Campaign File, 1952: Speeches and Statements, boxes 2 to 7, Dwight D. Eisenhower, Campaign Speeches, 15 and 22 Sept., 23 Oct. 1952. See also David Lawrence, '6,000 US Boys Dead in Korea Called Real Issue of Campaign', *New York Herald Tribune*, 30 Sept. 1952.

[63]George Gallup, 'Public Favors Withdrawing from Korea by Nearly 3 to 1', *Washington Post*, 21 Jan. 1951.

[64]For the argument that citizens from communities who experience a higher loss of life are more likely to oppose a war, see Scott Gartner, Gary Segura and Michael

University students were one such group. During the first weeks of 1951 universities reported a wave of panic enlistments, as thousands of college students dropped out and volunteered for the military, since this gave them a chance to pick what service to enter (whereas if they waited to be drafted the military would instruct them where to go). Significantly, most students opted for the Air Force or the Navy, which seemed a far safer option given that so many Army casualties were currently being reported in Korea. And by 19 January the situation was so bad that, to end the panic, the Pentagon changed the draft law so that students could end their studies in their summer and then pick what service to apply for.[65]

But even with this hasty change, the draft still faced major problems. For most of the Korean War, to be sure, it operated in a remarkably smooth fashion. Unlike the Vietnam era, there were no protests about unfairness, let alone efforts to dodge military service or burn draft cards. In fact, selective service was widely popular both in Congress, where its extension was approved with wide bipartisan support in June 1951, and among mass opinion, with polls consistently finding that about 60 percent favoured the current system. It was also remarkably successful, delivering 5.5 percent more men than requested during the first year of the war.[66] But there was one highly significant exception. During January 1951, in the wake of exaggerated casualty reports, the Federal Bureau of Investigation suddenly faced the job of tracking down 2,200 new cases of Selective Service Act violations. According to one account, the growing number of 'draft delinquents' who failed to respond to their selective-service call-up was now much higher than compared to a similar period of World War II.[67]

As news of Korean losses continued, senior military officials also noted 'considerable restlessness for rotation of troops on the battle-front'. If some forces were brought home, however, this would mean sending two National Guard units overseas immediately. Across the country, as the Army's chief information officer conceded, there had been 'a great deal of concern on the part of individual [National] Guardsmen as to their particular status'. Many were particularly concerned that they would be sent straight to Korea without any proper

---

Wilkening, 'All Politics are Local: Local Losses and Individual Attitudes toward the Vietnam War', *Journal of Conflict Resolution* 41/5 (1997), 673–6.

[65]'Casualties Forcing Army to Add 50,000 Draftees'; 'Educators Favor Draft Proposals'; both in *New York Times*, 12 and 20 Jan. 1951.

[66]George Q. Flynn, *Lewis B. Hershey: Mr Selective Service* (Chapel Hill: Univ. of N. Carolina Press 1985), 180–7; and George Q. Flynn, *The Draft, 1940–1973* (Lawrence: UP of Kansas 1993), 114–25.

[67]Time Dispatches, Folder 629, 'Draft "Delinquents"', 26 Jan. 1951.

training, merely as cannon fodder to replace regular units. Working in tandem with their congressional delegations, they therefore lobbied the Pentagon for reassurances that they would not be put in harm's way in the near future.[68]

For senior administration officials these were all disturbing signs. Not only did they threaten to undermine their current policy in Korea but they also placed a big question mark against the United States' overall Cold War strategy, which needed draftees to fill up the new conventional Army that was being constructed. About the only saving grace was that this particular spasm of doubt and panic soon passed. By March 1951, as the battlefield stabilized, and the military moved to correct earlier misperceptions about the scale of American losses, public opinion began to revive. According to one survey, 67 percent now wanted to stay in Korea as long as necessary, while only 20 percent favoured pulling out.[69]

Support for the war then remained relatively robust for the next 18 months, in part because Republican efforts to sustain the casualty controversy now had far less traction.[70] Not until the emergence of Dwight D. Eisenhower as the Party's nominee in the 1952 presidential campaign did Republican casualty claims again start to resonate. The reasons were revealing. As a former military man (retired from active duty May 1952 and resigned from the Army in July), Eisenhower was widely viewed as much more moderate and reliable than the right-wing Republicans who had earlier taken up the issue, not to mention MacArthur, whose attempt to exploit casualties appeared decidedly hypocritical in light of his earlier attacks on any reporter who had adopted a similar stance.[71]

During October 1952 Eisenhower was also helped by sudden flare-up in the fighting, as the Chinese Communists launched an assault on White Horse Mountain, in the center of the UN line.[72] Although the military censors again worked hard to sterilize the story, the gist of what happened soon seeped back to the United States. Indeed,

---

[68]HSTL, Dean Acheson Papers, Memoranda of Conversations File, box 67, Memorandum of Telephone Conversation between Sec. of State Dean Acheson and Sec. of Defense Gen. of the Army George Marshall, 19 Feb. 1951; William M. Donnelly, *Under Army Orders: The Army National Guard during the Korean War* (College Station: Texas A&M UP 2001), 178–9.

[69]NA, [State Dept. Records] RG 59, Entry 568L, box 12, PA, Monthly Survey of American Opinion, Feb. 1951.

[70]For an analysis of these polls, see Casey, *Selling the Korean War*, 292–3.

[71]Martin Medhurst, 'Text and Context in the 1952 Presidential Campaign: Eisenhower's "I Shall Go to Korea" Speech', *Presidential Studies Quarterly* 30/3 (Sept. 2000), 469.

[72]Hermes, *Truce Tent*, 303–18; Blair, *Forgotten War*, 970.

influential organs like *Time* magazine ran with headlines like 'Bloodshed in the Hills' or 'Then He was Dead', which drove home the fact that this remained a bloody war.[73] The day before the country went to the polls on 4 November, *Time* described what was happening:

> In Korea last week there was more dogged, costly, back & forth fighting for Triangle Hill, Sniper Ridge, Iron Horse Mountain. Temperatures dipped below freezing as another wretched winter approached, and this time, with no peace in sight, warm clothing and boots had been distributed early and efficiently. US casualties were sharply up. Latest Defense Department figures listed 122,117 (an increase of 963 in one week). They include 21,377 battle deaths, 88,128 wounded, 10,793 missing, 1,819 known captured.[74]

In this context, Eisenhower's constant claims about casualties clearly helped to spark the second dip in popular support for the war. Indeed, whereas in January 1952 only 33 percent had viewed Korea as one of the gravest issues facing the country, by October this figure had shot up to 52 percent. More significantly, as Election Day neared, one poll found that 56 percent of the population had reached the conclusion that 'the war in Korea was *not* worth fighting' – a level of disillusionment not recorded since January 1951.[75]

Of course, the casualty controversy was only one reason behind such figures, but it certainly played a role. During the campaign, Samuel Lubell conducted numerous grassroots interviews with American voters, and he was in no doubt that Eisenhower's use of the casualty controversy was important. Parents whose sons have been drafted, Lubell wrote, 'were bitterly resentful of the administration'. Although Adlai Stevenson, the Democratic nominee, tried to change the basic narrative of the campaign by shifting the emphasis to the strength of the economy, even this initiative backfired. As Lubell put it, 'surprising numbers of voters came to resent the prevailing prosperity as being "bought by the lives of boys in Korea". The feeling was general that the Korean War was all that stood in the way of an economic recession.

---

[73]'Then He was Dead', *Time*, 6 Oct. 1952; 'Bloodshed in the Hills', *Time*, 27 Oct. 1952.

[74]'An Old Pattern', *Time*, 3 Nov. 1952. See also, 'Relationship of Friendly Casualties to Enemy Fire', undated, copy in DDEL, Dwight D. Eisenhower Papers, Whitman File: Administrative Series, box 40, Wilson Folder.

[75]RG 59, Entry 568L, box 12, PA, Monthly Survey of American Opinion, Jan., Oct., and Nov. 1952.

From accepting that belief, many persons moved on emotionally to where they felt something immoral and guilt-laden in the "you've never had it better" argument of the Democrats.[76] Put another way, in 1952 the controversy over the current human cost of the war for once trumped the electorate's normal focus on bread-and-butter domestic issues.

Conclusion

In the large literature on the popularity of American wars, two competing assumptions are often evident. One is that an automatic connection exists between casualties and public support, which nothing can alter. The other is that governments have enormous power to manipulate and mould public opinion, especially during periods of real crisis. Although this article has focused on the first of these assumptions, its arguments challenge both.

For a start, while the public is clearly sensitive to casualties, it does not always have a clear picture of the full cost of the war. As a practical matter, it takes time for the military to identify bodies and notify the next of kin. The military is also frequently tempted to try to integrate the publication of casualties into its overall propaganda effort to sell the war, searching for ways to deaden the impact or to make the ultimate sacrifice appear worthwhile. But, crucially, its power is often limited. Other opinion-makers are rarely willing to stand meekly aside.

The media is chary of efforts to sugarcoat the news. While correspondents in the war zone are keen to grab scoops, which often centre upon stories of human suffering, reporters in the capital are keen to establish the precise scale of a defeat, especially if official figures are not forthcoming. Moreover, opposition politicians believe that partisan advantage can be gained by questioning the government's veracity, inflating the actual totals or simply by constantly stressing the immense human toll.

In short, casualties are clearly important. But the specific impact they have on the home front depends on the complex interplay between the military's casualty reporting on the one hand and elite efforts to question the official narrative on the other. Korea vividly demonstrates this complex interplay. But it was by no means the last war in which it cast an important shadow over the American domestic debate, as the controversy over the 2001–09 Bush administration's news embargo on images of returning dead GIs so vividly demonstrates.

---

[76]Samuel Lubell, *Revolt of the Moderates* (New York: Harper & Bros. 1956), 39–40.

Acknowledgements

The author would like to thank the US Army Center of Military History and the Truman Library for the award of a travel grant that made the research for this article possible.

Bibliography

Appleman, Roy E., *South to the Naktong, North to the Yalu* (Washington DC: Office of the Chief of Military History 1961).

Appleman, Roy E., *Escaping the Trap: The US Army X Corps in Northeast Korea, 1950* (College Station: Texas A&M UP 1990).

Berinsky, Adam J., 'Assuming the Costs of War: Events, Elites, and American Public Support for Military Conflict', *Journal of Politics* 69 (2007), 975–97.

Blair, Clay, *The Forgotten War: America in Korea, 1950–1953,* new ed (Annapolis, MD: US Naval Institute Press 2003).

Caridi, Ronald J., *The Korean War and American Politics: The Republican Party as a Case Study* (Philadelphia: Univ. of Pennsylvania Press 1968).

Casey, Steven, *Selling the Korean War: Propaganda, Politics and Public Opinion* (New York: OUP 2008).

Coffman, Edward M., *The War to End All Wars: The American Military Experience in World War I* (Madison: Univ. of Wisconsin Press 1986).

Coleman, Bradley Lynn, 'Recovering the Korean War Dead: 1950–58: Graves Registration, Forensic Anthropology and Wartime Memorialization', Virginia Military Institute Archives, <www.vmi.edu/uploadedFiles/Archives/Adams_Center/EssayContest/20052006/ColemanBL. pdf>.

Donnelly, William M., *Under Army Orders: The Army National Guard during the Korean War.* (College Station: Texas A&M UP 2001).

Faust, Drew Gilpin, *This Republic of Suffering: Death and the American Civil War* (New York: Knopf 2008).

Feaver, Peter D. and Christopher Gelpi, *Choosing Your Battles: American-Civil Relations and the Use of Force* (Princeton UP 2004).

Flynn, George Q., *Lewis B. Hershey: Mr Selective Service* (Chapel Hill: U of North Carolina P, 1985).

Flynn, George Q., *The Draft, 1940–1973* (Lawrence: UP of Kansas 1993).

Foot, Rosemary, *Substitute for Victory: The Politics of Peacemaking at the Korean Armistice Talks* (Ithaca, NY: Cornell UP 1990).

Gartner, Scott, Gary Segura and Michael Wilkening, 'All Politics are Local: Local Losses and Individual Attitudes toward the Vietnam War', *Journal of Conflict Resolution* 41/5 (1997), 669–94.

Gelpi, Christopher, Peter Feaver and Jason Reifler, *Paying the Human Costs of War: American Public Opinion and Casualties in Military Conflicts* (Princeton UP 2009).

Giangreco, D.M., '"Spinning the Casualties": Media Strategies during the Roosevelt Administration', *Passport: The Newsletter of the Society for Historians of American Foreign Relations* 35 (Dec. 2004), 22–9.

Hermes, Walter G., *Truce Tent and Fighting Front* (Washington DC: Center of Military History, US Army 1992).

'History of the Dog Tag', <www.173rdairborne.com/dogtag.htm>.

Horne, John, 'Remobilizing for "Total War": France and Britain, 1917–1918', in John Horne (ed.), *State, Society, and Mobilization in Europe during the First World War* (Cambridge: Cambridge UP 1997), 195–211.

James, Clayton D., *The Years of MacArthur.* 2 vols (Boston: Houghton Mifflin 1970–75).

Jentleson, Bruce W., 'The Pretty Prudent Public: Post-Vietnam Opinion on the Use of Military Force', *International Studies Quarterly* 36/1 (March 1992), 49–73.

Kepley, David R., *The Collapse of the Middle Way: Senate Republicans and the Bipartisan Foreign Policy, 1948–1952* (New York: Greenwood Press 1988).

Lubell, Samuel, *Revolt of the Moderates* (New York: Harper & Bros. 1956).

Mueller, John, *Wars, Presidents, and Public Opinion* (New York: Wiley 1973).

Mueller, John, 'The Iraq Syndrome', *Foreign Affairs* 84/6 (Nov.–Dec. 2005), 44–54.

Medhurst, Martin, 'Text and Context in the 1952 Presidential Campaign: Eisenhower's "I Shall Go to Korea" Speech', *Presidential Studies Quarterly* 30/3 (Sept. 2000) 464–84.

Otsuka ,Shuji and Peter N. Stearns, 'Perceptions of Death and the Korean War', *War in History* 6/1 (Jan. 1999), 72–87.

Reister, Frank A., *Battle Casualties and Medical Statistics: US Army Experience in the Korean War* (Washington DC: Dept. of the Army 1973).

Roeder, George H., *The Censored War: American Visual Experience during World War II* (New Haven: Yale UP 1993).

Sledge, Michael, *Soldier Dead: How We Recover, Identify, Bury, and Honor Our Military Fallen* (New York: Columbia UP 2005).

US Congress, *Congressional Record*. Vols. 97 and 98 (Washington DC: GPO 1951).

US Senate, *Military Situation in the Far East* (Washington DC: GPO 1951).

POWs: The Hidden Reason for Forgetting Korea

CHARLES S. YOUNG

Department of History, Southern Arkansas University, Magnolia, Arkansas, USA

ABSTRACT Despite recent attention, the Korean War (1950–53) remains underappreciated and further explanation of its 'forgottenness' is needed. Korea originally faded to gray because there was no satisfying victory. National security planners had ample reason to try and rehabilitate the war in the mind of the public, but had little success. This was because a primary accomplishment of the second half of the war – forcing the enemy to accept so-called voluntary repatriation of POWs (prisoners of war) – was semi-secret and never declared as a major war aim. Since the nation was never united around securing voluntary repatriation, there was little raw material for creating a memory of success.

It is remembered as the forgotten war. A quick online search finds endless merchandise with 'forgotten' and 'Korean War' in the title, from books and documentaries to commemorative patches, coins, and video games. Scholarly articles, starting with this very one, are numerous, including 'Canada's Forgotten War' and 'Unconventional Warfare in Korea: Forgotten Aspect of the "Forgotten War"'. A *Journal of Asian Studies* article began by saying it was a 'cliché' to call it forgotten, an observation that may already be passé. The outpouring of research prompted the inevitable title: 'Korea: No Longer the Forgotten War'.[1]

---

[1]David Bercuson, 'Canada's Forgotten War', *Canadian Historical Review* 65/1 (1984), 107; Richard L. Kiper, 'Unconventional Warfare in Korea: Forgotten Aspect of the "Forgotten War"', *Special Warfare* 16 (Aug. 2003), 26; Bonnie B.C. Oh, 'The Korean War, No Longer Forgotten', *Journal of Asian Studies* 57 (1993), 156; Glen Steven Cook, 'Korea: No Longer the Forgotten War', *Journal of Military History* 56 (1992), 489.

The flush of attention makes it worthwhile to pause and recall that in the west, the Korean lacunae, was and is real. Students cannot place its decade, and the diminishing number who can know it only because of the American television series *MASH* (Mobile Army Surgical Hospital). The war's 50th anniversary inaugurated the golden age of forgotten war studies, but even among the most literate, Korea has not taken its place as the pivotal event in the militarization of containment and putting America on a permanent war footing. This is a measure of forgetfulness that is not remedied simply by a spike in new titles.

For the United States, Korea broke the pattern that armies go home at the end of a war. Many events put the US on the Cold War course, but it was the fighting from 1950 to 1953 that quadrupled the military budget, consolidated the national security state, and began the era of permanent mobilization. America has not been a peacetime society since 1950. Korea was monumentally important, yet few people on the street would answer 'Korea' if asked 'what was the most far-reaching episode of the Cold War?' Measured by the height of the event and the shortness of its shadow, Korea may proportionally still be the most forgotten war.

Explanations for misplacing Korea share a theorem: that humans do not like to dwell on unpleasant memories, especially when they go unredeemed by later triumph. Korea was a miserable war. The United Nations (UN) forces were twice in danger of being driven into the sea. Seoul changed hands six times, and distance wise, troops made the longest retreat in US history – at the hands of Chinese peasants. The most straightforward cause of a nightmare in need of repressing was the failed invasion of the North. It started out well – UN Supreme Commander General Douglas MacArthur's successful amphibious attack at Inchon with X Corps was, in basketball terms, like a full-court basket at the buzzer, a jubilant moment that erased months of distress. Imagine if President Harry S. Truman had stopped MacArthur's forces at the 38th Parallel rather than invite disaster by inciting China. The masterstroke at Inchon would have won the war in four months. Korea would have been America's finest moment in the Cold War, outshining the Berlin Blockade or the Cuban Missile Crisis.

Instead, after the frighteningly unpredictable first year, both sides concluded they could not push the other off the peninsula. As the stalemate in the trenches ground on, it faded from the headlines. It was no longer electrifying like an imminent victory or defeat.

When armistice talks began in summer 1951, most expected a ceasefire within weeks. But tiresome, interminable negotiations ended up taking two-thirds of the three–year war, wearing out civilians as well as fighters. The war lost focus. After talks began, there were no clear objectives for a war public to fervently embrace. South Korea had been saved by the US, North Korea had been saved by China, the crux of the war was settled. Yet it went on. Through two years of talking. Soldiers expressed their resentment with the catchphrase that they did not want to 'die for a tie'. The public was no more enthused. The limited nature of the conflict was a difficult sell for a nation used to evil on a global scale, where defeating Hitler and Tokyo were considered matters of literal survival. This led to Washington taking it from all points of the political spectrum – from the Right who said if it was worth fighting it was worth winning, so use the Atomic Bomb already, and from the Left who said it was not worth fighting, so pull out. Republican Party leader Senator Robert A. Taft called Truman's war a 'useless and expensive waste'. *US News* magazine even conjectured it continued as a laboratory for new weapons: 'Will Korea be used indefinitely to blood troops, test weapons, try out tactics for later big wars?' the magazine asked with jarring cynicism.[2] In the journalist David Halberstam's words, it neither united like World War II, or divided like Vietnam, 'it was simply a puzzling, gray, very distant conflict' that went on and on.[3]

With Korea, amnesia began during the conflict itself. At least by the fall of 1951, the media had already dubbed it 'the forgotten war'.[4] The US *Army Times* later editorialized that it was 'the most forgotten war', with GIs as 'lonesome symbols of a nation too busy or too economy-minded'.[5] The *Army Times* had a point. America of the 1950s was enjoying a spectacular shopping cornucopia which must have made it easier to turn away from the killing in northeast Asia. The new television channels did not yet have news networks capable of timely, gripping disaster coverage.

Possibly the strongest evidence of dissatisfaction with the war was the termination of two men's political careers: Harry Truman and Douglas MacArthur. President Truman was so unpopular he could not attempt reelection for a second term. MacArthur was eagerly testing the waters. His firing by Truman in spring 1951 was especially unpopular and guaranteed him a boisterous reception from millions when he returned to the US in civilian clothes. But his popular acclaim did not transfer into political success. His personality did not hold up

---

[2]Cited in Steven Casey, *Selling the Korean War: Propaganda, Politics and Public Opinion* (New York: OUP 2008), 363; 'Korea: The "Forgotten" War: Casualties Rise – No End to Conflict in Sight', *US News and World Report*, 5 Oct. 1952, 21.

[3]David Halberstam, *The Coldest Winter: America and the Korean War* (New York: Hyperion 2007), 2.

[4]'Korea: The "Forgotten" War: Casualties Rise – No End to Conflict in Sight', *US News and World Report*, 5 Oct. 1952, 21.

[5]Found in Richard K. Kolb, 'Korea's "Invisible Veterans"', *VFW* (Nov. 1997), 27.

well to scrutiny by a Senate committee for seven weeks in May/June 1951, and the former Supreme Commander was too closely associated with the war no one wanted to think about.

Other than damaging Truman, MacArthur's political relevance evaporated. The General's keynote address to the Republican national convention at Chicago on 7 July 1952 (where Dwight D. Eisenhower received the nomination) was calculated to be a great moment, but the audience had soured and it became his swan song. Even a celebrated hero had been kept at arm's length. It was like a Veterans Day parade, where everyone loved to cheer, but did not want to know in detail what the soldiers went through.

An armistice finally came in summer 1953 with, as one author put it, 'no victors, no vanquished'.[6] With the fighting over, forgetting could start in full. It was like a terminally ill relative whose family had lived with the loss so long that the actual moment of death was anticlimactic. The trial could now be put behind them. The turn away from it was so eager that initially the grave markers in Arlington National Cemetery were not even going to say 'Korean War'. A compromise added the Korea, but not the war.[7] South Korea built memorials to the foreign soldiers who died there before the United Nations participants themselves did. Britain's memorial was opened in 1987, the American not until 1995.

Except among specialists and military buffs, Korea remained obscure for nearly 50 years. A search of an online bookseller shows how much more attention has been paid to Vietnam. For the pre-1985 period, the key words 'Korean War' bring up 1,662 items, while 'Vietnam War' has 3,005, despite more years passing since the former. In popular culture, Korea left a tiny footprint. Few feature films were made about it, and even they often had the look and feel of World War II movies. The solitary American television series was the exception that proved the rule. The long-running *MASH* began in 1972 and was really about Vietnam. Its irreverence and pacifism were distinctly of the counter-culture era, which the producers knew they could not pull off if directed at an ongoing war, so Korea it was.

An undertow pulled Korea out of sight of both historians and the general public. However, this amnesia begs a question: governments have a talent for spin, why was Korea so little apotheosized after the fact? Memory is experienced in the present, which can be so much more inventive than the past. Political-military affairs are full of cases where

---

[6]Stanley Sandler, *The Korean War: No Victors, No Vanquished* (Lexington: UP of Kentucky 1999).

[7]G. Kurt Piehler, *Remembering War the American Way* (Washington DC: Smithsonian Institution Press 1995), 157.

remembrances traveled far from original experiences, sometimes by conspiracy, more often by group effort. Americans won no important concessions from Britain in the War of 1812, failed to conquer Canada, and saw their capital sacked, but still got 'The Star Spangled Banner' out of it and experienced a surge of patriotic feeling over the Battle of New Orleans (8 January 1815). Kennedy's brinkmanship during the 1962 Cuban Missile Crisis is seen as his finest hour, but considering what the Russians gained – the safety of Cuba and removal of missiles from Turkey – it had a crucial element of compromise. The Vietnam War was a tough one, but as H. Bruce Franklin showed, the Nixon administration deftly used the prisoners of war to salvage as much honor as it could from defeat.[8] These examples pale before Myth of the Lost Cause that dominated writing about the American South and the War Between the States.

Clever minds seemingly could have found ways to repackage Korea. Why not adjust the definition of 'win'? Hiroshima, Berlin, and Carthage provided the usual understanding of total battlefield victory. But never in Korea was the complete annihilation of the enemy – Communism – contemplated. If success is measured by the effort put forth, Korea might become a victory. The goal was containment, and that was achieved.

That the Korean experience was largely left to molder is even more curious considering how keenly national security planners worried about public morale. Even before the Korean debacle, cold warriors worried the public was a weak link. Upon completion of World War II, Americans were impatient for all the boys to come home, just as Washington was becoming more worried about the Soviet Union. Secretary of the Navy James Forrestal anguished over people 'going back to bed at a frightening rate'.[9] With the onset of the Cold War, the American people were being asked to support something new – a permanent, expensive, global projection of power. NSC-68, the Truman administration's planning document for a national security state warned in April 1950 that:

A large measure of sacrifice and discipline will be demanded of the American people. They will be asked to give up some of the benefits which they have come to associate with their freedoms.

---

[8]H. Bruce Franklin, *M.I.A. or Mythmaking in America* (New Brunswick, NJ: Rutgers UP 1993).

[9]Found in Richard J. Barnet, *The Rockets' Red Glare: War, Politics, and the American Presidency* (New York: Simon & Schuster 1990), 252. Forrestal was in the Navy Dept. 1940–47 and became the first US Secretary of Defense 1947–49.

Nothing could be more important than that they fully understand the reasons for this.[10]

Developing popular understanding was the specialty of the Department of State's Edward Barrett, who was enthused by NSC-68's ambitious plans, but warned that 'the US public would rapidly tire of such an effort' and candidly recommended 'a psychological "scare campaign"' to ensure support.[11]

Despite the intensity of McCarthyism, Washington was always anxious over support for the nuts and bolts of the Cold War project and its great costs in treasure and blood. Brooding over public interest in foreign affairs became urgent with Korea. This can be seen in President Dwight D. Eisenhower's announcement of the end of fighting in July 1953. In an address to the nation at 10pm on a Sunday night, he struck a somber tone with little sense of relief or deliverance: 'We have won an armistice on a single battleground – not peace in the world. We may not now relax our guard nor cease our quest.' The President did try to hit a high note in saying that 'the challenge of aggression' had been met and South Korea secured.[12] But it was two years too late for a declaration of victory on that. Repulsion of the North Korean invasion after Inchon was obscured by toxic mud. Washington needed a way to sanctify the Korean War.

In fact, the armistice agreement contained a significant concession from the Communists that national security leaders might have raised high on a banner. The issue was known as 'voluntary repatriation', and it was bitterly resisted by the northern alliance (North Korea, China and the USSR) for 18 months. There were 130,000 North Korean and Chinese prisoners of war held by the United Nations, some of whom were actually anti-Communists who came out of the closet during captivity and feared returning home. In late 1951, American negotiators made it clear they would not repatriate prisoners who would not go voluntarily. In reality, the limited ranks of anti-Communist prisoners had been swelled through a massive campaign of bludgeonings, spearings, hackings, and forced tattooing of rightist slogans, something many US officials, including Truman, did not

---

[10]Ernest R. May, *American Cold War Strategy: Interpreting NSC 68* (Boston: Bedford Books 1993), 54.

[11]Found in Nancy E. Bernhard, *US Television News and Cold War Propaganda, 1947–1960* (New York: Cambridge UP 1999), 83.

[12]D[wight] D. E[isenhower] L[ibrary, Abilene, KS], Carl W. McCardle Papers, Series I Conference and Trip Files, Box 1, Folder: Korean Truce Negotiations, 26 July 1953.

appreciate.[13] But whatever the cause, the Chinese and North Korean leaders faced an epic humiliation: tens-of-thousands of salt-of-the-earth peasant soldiers would be seen turning away from Marxism. For 18 months, the exchange of prisoners was the only substantive issue left to be negotiated.

How voluntary repatriation emerged to stall peace negotiations was a story in and of itself. A seemingly secondary issue arose as the battlefield faded in importance. Since neither stalemated contender could win the war outright, the belligerents competed for world opinion by other means, and the means were the POWs. American firepower could not vanquish the enemy, but the UN nations found they could top the enemy by persuading its soldiers to defect. As Rosemary Foot put it, in a phrase marvelous enough to name a book, voluntary repatriation became 'a substitute for victory'.[14] This was a play on the proclamation of General Douglas MacArthur, who first wrote his famous refrain to Congressman Joseph Martin Junior on 6 April 1951, 'In war there can be no substitute for victory.' In Foot's explanation, moral victory on repatriation became a substitute for triumph on the battlefield. Credit for winning the first Korean War – saving the South – had been washed away by losing the war for the North. Voluntary repatriation would be a humiliating political defeat for the enemy and demonstrate American commitment to individual rights and dignity. Washington would remind itself and the world that it was the twentieth century's mover and shaker. Having failed to conquer an East Asian peninsula, the substitute victory would have to do.

The desire for a substitute came from blood and frustration. The Chinese entry brought a series of disheartening headlines, like, 'Seoul Abandoned to Red Armies; City Afire', then 'Reds Now Half Way to Pusan Beachhead', which sounded like a repeat of the disastrous

---

[13]On the forcible withholding of prisoners, see Charles S. Young, *Name, Rank, and Serial Number: Korean War POWs and the Politics of Limited War* (New York: OUP forthcoming); Barton J. Bernstein, 'The Struggle Over the Korea Armistice: Prisoners of Repatriation?', in Bruce Cumings (ed.), *Child of Conflict: The Korean-American Relationship, 1943–1953* (Seattle: Univ. of Washington Press 1983); Rosemary Foot, *A Substitute for Victory: The Politics of Peacemaking at the Korean Armistice Talks* (Ithaca, NY: Cornell UP 1990); John Toland, *In Mortal Combat: Korea, 1950–1953* (New York: William Morrow 1991); Se Hee Oh, *Stalag 65: A Memoir of a Korean POW* (Portland, OR: Artwork Publications 2000); Albert D. Biderman and Samuel M. Meyers (eds.), *Mass Behavior in Battle and Captivity: The Communist Soldier in the Korean War* (Univ. of Chicago Press 1968). See also a fictionalized account based on real events: Ha Jin, *War Trash* (New York: Vintage Books 2004).
[14]Foot, *Substitute for Victory*.

beginning of the war.[15] Once Associated Press reporter Don Whitehead got back to New York, away from censors, he could write: 'The bleak, bloody story of Korea is approaching an end.' According to Whitehead, many officers and 'most war correspondents' were certain that a complete evacuation of the peninsula was 'inevitable'.[16] Secretary of State Dean Acheson said the Chinese intervention was the worst defeat of an American army since Bull Run (1861) at the beginning of the Civil War, and Chinese sources reported that the US lost 6,000 vehicles.[17]

By early February 1951, the danger of complete defeat faded, as the Chinese phalanx was ground down by superior UN firepower. Chinese troops were exhausted by months of effort, astounding casualties, and short supplies that took weeks to arrive under cover of darkness. Chinese troops began deserting in significant groups, especially those press-ganged out of Nationalist forces defeated in the just ended Chinese Civil War.

The UN troops were able to reretake Seoul and return to the general area of the 38th Parallel. A major new Chinese offensive in spring 1951 progressed for a time, even rereretaking Seoul, but was turned around by the end of May. The collapse of the spring offensive resulted in an especially large number of POWs. China lost 90,000 troops in the last week of the campaign, 10,000 to capture.[18] Chairman/President Mao Tse-Tung and his advisors concluded they could not win the war outright, although Chinese generals remember the war as a successful one because it prevented an American invasion of Manchuria.[19]

After the spring 1951 Chinese offensive failed, neither side believed it had a sensible chance of winning, and the character of the war changed for good. Expectation of a negotiated settlement meant facts on the ground would shape peace talks, so jockeying for advantage and narrow attacks to adjust an armistice line became the rule. This meant that keeping territory already won would require elaborate fortifications – networks of trenches and cement bunkers. The Chinese dug hundreds of miles of tunnels, what they called a Great Wall underground.[20] Once military stores were deep enough to withstand

---

[15]'Seoul Abandoned to Red Armies; City Afire; UN Retreat Orderly', *New York Times*, 4 Jan. 1951; 'Reds Half Way to Pusan Beachhead', *Philadelphia Inquirer*, 11 Jan. 1951.
[16]Don Whitehead, 'Withdrawal Inevitable: Observer Back From Korea Says Military Men Favor Leaving Before Army's Lost', *Newark Sunday News*, 14 Jan. 1951.
[17]Xiaobing Li and Allan R. Millett, *Mao's Generals Remember Korea* (Lawrence: UP of Kansas 2001), 34.
[18]Kaufman, Burton I., *The Korean War: Challenges in Crisis, Credibility, and Command* (Philadelphia: Temple UP 1986), 54.
[19]Li, *Mao's Generals Remember Korea*, 41.
[20]Ibid., 46.

bombardment, the UN lost part of its edge. Offensives against UN firepower had always entailed great sacrifice, but the underground Great Wall now made UN offensives exceptionally costly also.

For the United Nations, the last major attempts to shift boundary lines began in late summer, 1951. The US Army's 2nd Infantry Division suffered 3,000 casualties to take three small hills in the area known as the Iron Triangle. Nearby, an attack on the infamous Heartbreak Ridge cost 5,600 killed or wounded. After weeks of effort and thousands of casualties, the enemy simply backed up to the next line of hills. This dulled the American command's appetite for major ground offensives. UN Supreme Commander General Matthew B. Ridgway decreed that all assaults battalion size and up had to be approved by the Far East Command.

For the rest of the war, the UN relied more on the aerial bombardment of fortifications and North Korean cities than infantry offensives. The battlefield began to resemble the trench warfare of World War I. This 'sitzkrieg', as one historian called it, was grueling and demoralizing for combatants as well as their homelands.[21] With fighting largely static, sacrifice was becoming more and more pointless. Morale rotted along with leather boots and trenchfoot toes.

The military stalemate dictated the remaining course of the Korean War. Surrender terms were usually mandated by the victors in other wars, but in Korea, every last detail – including POWs – could be contested and cause paralysis. Both sides still had fight left; they had each defeated an invasion and were not so desperate for peace that they would swallow a poisonous truce. Neither had been defeated, and considered negotiations just an extension of the fight into another arena – politics and opinion. They would do their best to turn armistice negotiations to their benefit. Shifting gears into political warfare was natural for both contenders since they had so much to tell the world about their respective merits. The Americans were enamored by psychological operations (psyops), and the Chinese were experienced revolutionary agitators.

Since the Cold War was more about ideological struggle than bullets, targeting minds was a natural course to take. As a universalist creed, Communism jumped boundaries of nation, ethnicity, and religion. Meeting it was a total war, fought in culture, politics, and economics, as well as on battlefields. Everything could impact the psychological condition of the enemy or the allies, making the purview of psyops very broad. The US Joint Chiefs of Staff declared not long after the Korean War began that 'we have

---

[21]Callum A. MacDonald, *Korea: The War Before Vietnam* (New York: Free Press 1986), 220.

been engaged in full-scale psychological warfare with the Soviets since 1946 at least'.[22] The rest of the world would choose sides according to the whole package offered by a political-economic system – its prosperity, security, resplendence, and comity, as well as martial prowess. Political warfare was elevated to a strategic place alongside nuclear deterrence and securing natural resources.

In Korea, political warfare took the form of persuading prisoners to reject their homelands. Even before voluntary repatriation ensnared peace talks, US psychological warfare specialists had gone to work. Agents from Taiwan (Nationalist Chinese Formosa) and South Korea posing as prisoners took control of many compounds. Assisted by a detachment of the US 704th Counter Intelligence Corp, they set up friendly brotherhoods and secret societies in the compounds.[23] The Republic of Korea (ROK) National Police and the Kuomintang Pao Mi Chu security bureau in Taiwan helped comb through the prisoners for right-thinking individuals who could be promoted to compound leadership.

The Anti-Communist Youth League (ACYL), which had branches throughout South Korea, expanded into the massive compounds on Koje-do, the prison island several miles off the port of Pusan in the southeast of the ROK where they were confined.[24] With help from the guards, the ACYL arranged the arrest and segregation of committed Marxists and systematically promoted friendly gang leaders. In Korean Compound 83, the South Korean camp authorities chose a new police chief on the recommendation of Lieutenant Pak, an anti-Communist prisoner and influential advisor to the administration. Pak's people identified the Red 'plotters' in the compound, who were quickly segregated by the camp authorities.[25] 'It was the [inmate] guards who wielded the real power in the camp', recalled inmate Se Hee Oh. Called Section Police, they wore armbands and numbered about 100 in his compound. In C-65 they were commanded by a major from the South Korean military.

---

[22]DDEL, President's Committee on International Information Activities (Jackson Committee) Records 1950–1953, Numbered documents, Box 11, Joint Chiefs of Staff, 'Memo for Secretary Johnson: NSC 74 – A Plan for National Psychological Warfare', 1 Aug. 1950.

[23]Oh, *Stalag 65*, 169.

[24]S.N. Prasad, *History of the Custodian Force (India) in Korea 1953–54* (Delhi: Armed Forces of the Indian Union, Historical Section 1976), 69.

[25]William C. Bradbury and Samuel M. Meyers, 'The Political Behavior of Korean and Chinese Prisoners of War in the Korean Conflict: A Historical Analysis', in Meyers Biderman, *Mass Behavior*, 265.

'I never learned how he happened to become a prisoner of the US Army', said Oh.[26]

Compared with the awesome arrays of power in contention, the lives of individual prisoners barely registered. In the big picture, was repatriation an issue at all? Like a divorcing couple fighting over division of the record collection, there was much beneath the surface. Washington felt it was bleeding the enemy while strengthening itself, and the other side was sure its prowess impressed the world while dividing its enemies. Would not both sides continue the war under one pretext or another for as long as they benefited? Although many factors allowed the prisoners to become the deal breaker, it was still the axis that other issues coalesced around. In opening talks, both sides considered the conflict virtually over. They were close to agreement in spring 1952 that some POWs would not return, but could not settle on a number.[27] It is likely that if the US had not demanded or the northerners not refused incomplete repatriation, the war would have been settled much sooner. Armistice negotiations stalled when it came up, and concluded as soon as it was settled.

And while the causes of wars are endlessly complex, they still have to be explained and justified in narrative fashion. That is, in order to conduct war, the disparate parts of the government need a common goal – not an exegesis on historical causation. And the operative rationale in the Truman administration was that there could be no armistice until the enemy gave in on POWs. If the stalemated war can be explained in ten words, fighting continued over the right of POWs to refuse repatriation. This was understood by insider Charles C. Stelle, of the State Department's Policy Planning Staff. He wrote in January 1952, just as Washington was finalizing its position, 'If we want an armistice badly, and immediately, there is no question but that a concession on the POW issue would be calculated to give us the best chance.'[28]

The official US Army history of the Korean War recognized repatriation as the lynchpin of the last phase of the war. In his classic *Truce Tent and Fighting Front*, Walter G. Hermes wrote:

> [T]he UNC [United Nations Command] had kept faith with the non-repatriate prisoners and won a psychological victory.... Yet the humanitarian approach in protecting nonrepatriates had been

---

[26]Oh, *Stalag 65*, 163, 172,

[27]William Stueck, *Rethinking the Korean War: A New Diplomatic and Strategic History* (Princeton UP 2002), 166.

[28][N]ational A[rchives, College Park, MD, State Dept. Records] RG 59, PPS Files, Subject: Korea, box 20, Stelle to Paul Nitze: Alternative Courses of Action on POW Problem, 28 Jan. 1952.

expensive. To safeguard their rights had cost over 125,000 UNC casualties during the 15-month period while the enemy lost well over a quarter of a million men.... Viewed from this angle, the precedence given the 50,000 nonrepatriates and the 12,000-odd prisoners held by the enemy over the hundreds of thousands of soldiers at the front raised a complicated question. In negotiating a military truce, should the prime consideration be for the men on the line and in action or for those in captivity?[29]

Hermes' qualms aside, the eventual substitute for victory was just that: victorious. The enemy kicked and screamed for 18 months, but in the end, accepted an armistice that did not return all its prisoners, even though Mao and Kim Il-sung knew painfully well that many, if not most, of the stay-behinds had been forced to renounce their homes. Washington had prevailed. Seemingly, it finally had something to celebrate after the long interval since Inchon. But this was a victory they could not revel in.

That armistice talks halted over voluntary repatriation was not a state secret, but it was a public secret. Its centrality went unrecognized by all but a few outside observers, and Washington was not saying any different. In public discourse, peace negotiations were understood to be blocked by a bewildering snarl of petty bickering, inscrutable 'Oriental' stubbornness, and senseless desire to keep killing. The insistence on getting back anti-Communist prisoners was just part of the mix of unreasonable, wicked ways the Communists prevented peace.

The significance of voluntary repatriation was so successfully obscured that it remains unappreciated by historians and laymen to this day. The administration wanted it that way. The officials of Truman, then Eisenhower, openly said they did not want to force any prisoners who did not want to return to Communism. They did take tentative steps to garner support for it. But voluntary repatriation was never elevated to a war aim. It was not used to move the public, rejuvenate morale, or stir troops in battle. It was never 'why we fight'.

Although repatriation was the nub in negotiations, Washington calculated that if it were known that the only thing standing between American families and hugging their boys was Communist prisoners in UN hands, support for the war would collapse. Even the truncated discussion of the issue revealed this danger. Radio commentator John Vandercook, intoned, 'Isn't our first business rather to return to their homes the American and other Allied prisoners the Reds have reported

---

[29]Walter G. Hermes, *Truce Tent and Fighting Front: United States Army in the Korean War* (Washington DC: Office of the Chief of Military History, US Army 1966), 432, 500.

THE KOREAN WAR AT SIXTY

to be alive?'[30] Keeping Chinese and North Korean prisoners after the war invited retaliation. Mallory Brown of the staff of the National Security Council worried that:

> At the present time there is no widespread active concern in the US on the question of possible failure on the part of the Chinese to return all American prisoners. But articles now beginning to appear in the press raise the specter that the issue might be presented to the American public as an 'exchange of Chinese lives for American lives'. Should this develop, it is likely that the public outcry would obscure the basic moral issue and jeopardize the effectiveness of the US policy decision.[31]

Stelle in the State Department said it was a 'Probability that US domestic opinion would shift against support of general principle of "voluntary repatriation" if it became clear that the fate of Communist prisoners was the only issue preventing cessation of hostilities and return of US prisoners.'[32]

State's public relations guru Edward Barrett agreed, and suggested that 'negotiators should be instructed to take pains to avoid having negotiations break down on the single issue of forcible return of POWs'. Anticipating a public relations disaster, Barrett reasoned:

> [W]e could be accused of sacrificing the moral obligations of any government to rescue its own prisoners – in order to help some Chinese and North Koreans who are not political defectors but prisoners of war who were once shooting at us and who surrendered to save their own skins.[33]

For the remainder of the war, the whole spectrum of POW affairs was treated very carefully. For instance, in early 1953, the Secretary of Defense himself, Charles E. Wilson, complained that not enough was being said about brainwashing and mistreatment of UN prisoners by the Chinese. He proposed to Central Intelligence Agency Director Allen W. Dulles a publicity campaign accusing the Chinese of a war atrocity – the murder of minds. But even as he suggested it, Wilson realized that:

---

[30]Cited in Casey, *Selling the Korean War*, 285.

[31][Harry S. Truman Library, Independence, MO,] PSB Files, SMOF, Mallory Browne, box 32, 383.6, The Strategic Significance of Involuntary PW Repatriation in Korea, Feb. 1952.

[32]Stelle to Nitze, 'Alternative Courses of Action on POW Problem', 28 Jan. 1952.

[33]RG 59, Assistant Secretary of State for Public Affairs, Memos, Edward W. Barrett File, box 2, Barrett to Mathews, Korean Prisoners of War, 4 Feb. 1952.

To date, the ugly specter of American prisoners of war having been 'brain-washed' has received but sporadic attention. Because of feared public reaction against the UNC position on repatriation, US public information and foreign information agencies have aped the ostrich and buried their collective heads in the sands of irresolution.[34]

It was not until after the war that Washington began a very concerted, wide-ranging campaign accusing the Communists of mistreating prisoners, particularly Air Force pilots who had been forced to confess to germ warfare. POW issues could not be erased from the public record, but the administration was very careful not to fan them. Doing so could lead to a clamor to bring the boys home and forget about Red prisoners. If that happened, even a substitute victory would be denied.

On 26 July 1953, President Dwight D. Eisenhower went before the nation and told it the guns were silent. He first paid homage to the 'thousands of homes' that had lost sons. He thanked the wounded for their sacrifice, and wished a swift return to soldiers 'wearied by many months of imprisonment'. The short speech thanked the allies, praised ROK President Syngman Rhee, and promised to remain vigilant during the final steps of the armistice. The Commander-in-Chief made no mention, however, of voluntary repatriation. The principle that had been fought over for half the conflict went unremarked. Eisenhower might have had stirring words about former Communist prisoners reaching freedom in Formosa or South Korea, thanks to UN steadfastness. He could have added that one day they might be reunited with their families, if the cause of liberty could spread to their homelands. Helping former soldiers escape communism was full of rhetorical possibilities, but none were availed. Eisenhower could not proclaim victory on voluntary repatriation because no one knew that was what they were fighting for. Unlike unconditional surrender in World War II, or slavery late in the Civil War, America had not declared it as a war aim.

The Korean War had sapped public patience for a Pax Americana, but Washington was left with very little to salvage for a usable past. It did have the saving of South Korea, but that was mitigated by reversals. There were a few scattered attempts to honor the war for creating a new human right of asylum for POWs, but they never took hold as common wisdom. National security planners had run up against a basic conundrum of limited war. When a nation is moved to fight by existential threat, but the war is pursued according to expediency and

---

[34]DDEL, White House Central File, box 29, PSB 7025, Confidential File 1953–61, Charles E. Wilson, 'Proposal to Allen Dulles', 19 Feb. 1953.

empire, the memory becomes unmanageable, and it may be better to just forget.

Bibliography

Barnet, Richard J., *The Rockets' Red Glare: War, Politics, and the American Presidency* (New York: Simon & Schuster 1990).

Bercuson, David, 'Canada's Forgotten War', *Canadian Historical Review* 65/1 (1984).

Bernhard, Nancy E., *US Television News and Cold War Propaganda, 1947–1960* (New York: Cambridge UP 1999).

Bernstein, Barton J., 'The Struggle Over the Korea Armistice: Prisoners of Repatriation?' in Bruce Cummings (ed.), *Child of Conflict: The Korean–American Relationship, 1943–1953* (Seattle: Univ. of Washington Press 1983).

Biderman, Albert D. and Samuel M. Meyers (eds.), *Mass Behavior in Battle and Captivity: The Communist Soldier in the Korean War* (Univ. of Chicago Press 1968).

Bradbury, William C. and Samuel M. Meyers, 'The Political Behavior of Korean and Chinese Prisoners of War in the Korean Conflict: A Historical Analysis', in Samuel M. Meyers and Albert D. Biderman, *Mass Behavior in Battle and Captivity: The Communist Soldier in the Korean War* (Univ. of Chicago Press 1968).

Casey, Steven, *Selling the Korean War: Propaganda, Politics, and Public Opinion in the United States* (OUP 2008).

Cook, Glen Steven, 'Korea: No Longer the Forgotten War', *Journal of Military History* 56 (1992).

Cumings, Bruce (ed.), *Child of Conflict: The Korean-American Relationship, 1943–1953* (Seattle: Univ. of Washington Press 1983).

Editors, 'Korea: The "Forgotten" War: Casualties Rise–No End to Conflict in Sight', *US News and World Report*, (5 Oct. 1952).

Foot, Rosemary, *A Substitute for Victory: The Politics of Peacemaking at the Korean Armistice Talks* (Ithaca, NY: Cornell UP 1990).

Franklin, H. Bruce, *MIA or Mythmaking in America* (New Brunswick, NJ: Rutgers UP 1993).

Halberstam, David, *The Coldest Winter: America and the Korean War* (New York: Hyperion 2007).

Hermes, Walter G., *Truce Tent and Fighting Front: United States Army in the Korean War* (Washington DC: Office of the Chief of Military History, US Army 1966).

Jin, Ha, *War Trash* (New York: Vintage Books 2004).

Kaufman, Burton I., *The Korean War: Challenges in Crisis, Credibility, and Command* (Philadelphia: Temple UP 1986).

Kiper, Richard L., 'Unconventional Warfare in Korea: Forgotten Aspect of the "Forgotten War"', *Special Warfare* 16 (Aug. 2003).

Kolb, Richard K., 'Korea's "Invisible Veterans"', *Veterans of Foreign Wars* (Nov. 1997).

Li, Xiaobing and Allan R. Millett, *Mao's Generals Remember Korea* (Lawrence: UP of Kansas 2001).

MacDonald, Callum A., *Korea: The War Before Vietnam* (New York: Free Press 1986).

May, Ernest R., *American Cold War Strategy: Interpreting NSC 68* (Boston: Bedford Books 1993).

Oh, Bonnie B. C., 'The Korean War, No Longer Forgotten', *Journal of Asian Studies* 57 (1993).

Oh, Se Hee, *Stalag 65: A Memoir of a Korean POW* (Portland: Artwork Publications 2000).

Piehler, G. Kurt, *Remembering War the American Way* (Washington DC: Smithsonian Institution Press 1995).

Prasad, S.N., *History of the Custodian Force (India) in Korea 1953–54* (Delhi: Armed Forces of the Indian Union 1976).

Sandler, Stanley, *The Korean War: No Victors, No Vanquished* (Lexington: UP of Kentucky 1999).

Stueck, William, *Rethinking the Korean War: A New Diplomatic and Strategic History* (Princeton UP 2002).

Toland, John, *In Mortal Combat: Korea, 1950–1953* (New York: William Morrow 1991).

Young, Charles S., 'Missing Action: POW Films, Brainwashing and the Korean War, 1954–1968', *Historical Journal of Film, Radio and Television* 18/1 (1998), 49–74.

Young, Charles S., *Name, Rank, and Serial Number: Korean War POWs and the Politics of Limited War* (New York: OUP forthcoming).

Index

Page numbers followed by a represent appendix.
Page numbers followed by n represent endnotes.

2nd Army Division 143
2nd Infantry Division 163
7th Infantry Division 143
12-Power draft resolution 80, 88
13th Army Group 112
38th Parallel 2, 16–17, 22, 24–5, 38, 41, 51, 59–61, 63–4, 66, 73–4, 79, 94, 97, 100, 107–9, 156, 162; Chinese offensive south 80; S. Korean crossing 63; stalemate 88; UN advance 110, 117–19; UN retreat 99
39th Parallel 106, 112, 119; settlement 122
704th Counter Intelligence Corp 164

Abe, Governor-General Nobuyuki 19, 24
Acheson, D. 74–5, 77–8, 81–5, 87, 97–8, 109, 115, 118, 162
aggressor resolution 82, 84–90
Almond, General E. 103, 105–7
American Civil War: casualty reporting 132, 137
Andong 54, 65–6
Andrews, B. 141
anti-Americanism 44–5
Anti-Communist Youth League (ACYL) 164
ANZUS defence treaty 89
Appropriations Committee 141
Arlington National Cemetery 158
armistice 6, 158, 160, 165, 168; announcement (July 1953) 168; talks 7, 9, 88–9, 94–7, 107, 110, 113, 122, 156, 165–6, *see also* ceasefire
Army Times 157
Arnold, Major General A. 25
artillery 102, 103, 146, 162–3
Journal of Asian Studies 155
Associated Press 144, 145, 162

Attlee, Prime Minister C. 76, 81–3, 87, 115; government 72, 76
Austin, W. 75, 84
Australia 72, 76, 85; UN Delegation 86
Australian government 89

Barnes, R. 1–13, 69–91
Barrett, E. 160, 167
Batitskii, P. 55
Battle of New Orleans (8 Jan 1815) 159
Beech, K. 141
Beijing 3–4, 8, 49–68, 74, 81, 84–5, 122
Bevin, E. 71, 75, 81–3, 86–7
Biao, L. 61
Bigart, H. 143
Binhai border areas 62
Black Sea talks 62, 64, 66
'Bloody Ridge' 146
Boose, D. 9
Bradley, General O. 108, 113–14, 116
Bridges, S. 141
Britain 4, 8, 22, 158, 159; Cabinet 85, 88, 114; Great Power status 71; UN Delegation 74; UN influence 69–91, *see also* Commonwealth; London
British government 71, 72, 76, 87; Labour 71
Brown, M. 167
Bulganin, N. 57
Bush, President George W. 15; administration 132, 152
Byrnes, J. 135

Cain, H. 147
Cairo declaration (Nov 1943) 21, 24
Camp Hood (Texas) 29
Canada 71–3, 76, 80, 85, 87, 159
Canadian government 73, 85
Capitol Hill 36

INDEX

Casey, S. 1, 5, 6, 9, 129–54
casualty reporting 6, 129–54; American
  Civil War 132, 137; controversy 140–
  52; exaggerated perception 144; MIA
  figures 143; Pentagon improvements
  137; public opinion 148–52;
  suppression 142; war fluidity
  problems 138
cease-fire 5; negotiations 4–5, 62, 66,
  76–7, 78, 81–4, 88, 97, 156, 163;
  principles 4, 82; secret talks 63–4, *see
  also* armistice
Ceasefire Committee 78–84; principles
  82
Central Intelligence Agency (CIA) 50n,
  167
Chen, J. 8
Chiang, Kai-shek (Jiang Jieshi) 67
Chicago Daily News 143
Chicago Tribune 33
China 3–4, 7–8, 41–2; allegiances 49–68;
  archives 3, 8, 49–68, 96, 111–12, 119;
  negotiation demands 79
Chinese Civil War 67, 103, 162
Chinese Communist Party (CCP) 65;
  Central Committee 64; Politburo 60,
  62
Chinese government 52–3, 88
Chinese intervention 3–4, 6, 8, 49–68,
  74–8, 138, 142–4, 148, 162;
  deployment and planning 53–4, 58–9;
  intervention catalyst 60; October
  (1950) 50; UN diplomacy 69–90
Chinese military 51, 56, 64–5, 150; Air
  Force 119–20; amphibious landing
  fears 112–13; defences 162–3;
  deployment 58–62; losses 122;
  weaknesses 61, 100, 103–4, 121–3, 162
Chinese offensives 94, 96, 100, 103–5,
  122; Second Phase Offensive (Nov
  1950) 99; Third Phase Offensive (Dec
  1950) 99–101; Fourth Phase Offensive
  (Feb 1951) 100–1, 104; Fifth Phase
  Offensive (22–29 April) 97, 102, 104,
  110, 112, 121–2; Sixth Phase
  Offensive (16–20 May) 97, 99, 102,
  104, 110, 112, 121–2; New Years Eve
  (1950) 80, 83; Spring Offensives 5,
  112–13, 117, 162
Chinese Volunteer Forces (CVF) 60–1,
  65, 96, 101–2, 104–6, 109, 112–13,
  122–3; logistics issues 103–4; losses
  100, 104; retreat 102–3; weaknesses
  100, 103–4

Chipyong-ni Battle 100–1
Chosin Reservoir Battle 143–4
Chungking 20
Clark, General M. 98
Cold War 2–5, 7, 44, 50, 136, 156, 159–
  60; crisis 69; ideological struggle 163;
  propaganda 9; US perceptions 114;
  US strategy 150
Collins, General R. 109
Committee for the Preparation of
  Korean Independence (CPKI) 19
Commonwealth 4, 8, 69–91; before
  China's intervention 70–4;
  governments 72, 73, 85–6; 'New
  Commonwealth' nations 4, 71, 73;
  'Old Commonwealth' nations 4, 70–1,
  73, 88–9; Prime Ministers' Conference
  71, 80–4; unity disintegration 86; war
  fears 76–80
Commonwealth's US and UN influence
  69–91; aggressor resolution 84–90;
  before China's intervention 70–4;
  ceasefire committee 79–84; Chinese
  intervention's effect 74–8; Prime
  Ministers' Conference 80–4
Communist alliance formation 49–68;
  Kim's foreign air support anticipation
  55–8; Mao's eagerness to send troops
  58–62; Moscow's attitude to Chinese
  intervention 53–5; Stalin's air cover
  refusal 62–6; Stalin's Air Force
  promise 50–3
Communist Party of Soviet Union
  (CPSU): Central Committee 57;
  politb010 63
Communists 20, 40–1, 150, 159–60, 163;
  aggression 148; command 113;
  Korean Politburo 60; land grab 94;
  powers 3
Confucian culture 27
Cox, J. 44n
Cuba 159
Cuban Missile Crisis (1962) 159
Cumings, B. 24
Czechoslovakia 53

D-Day (WWII) 134
Dearborn (Michigan) 37
decision-making 93
Defense Department (US) 140, 144, 148
democracy 45
Democratic Party 140, 152
Democratic People's Republic of Korea
  (DPRK) *see* North Korea

INDEX

Doidge, F. 72, 86
domestic support (US) 129–54, 166–7
Dulles, A. 167

Eighth Army 105–6, 111; retreat 143;
  survival 99–100
Eisenhower, General D. 6, 7, 36, 147–8,
  150–1, 160; administration 7, 9, 166;
  armistice announcement (July 1953)
  168; casualty controversy use 151
'end-the-war' offensive 75
Entezam, N. 78
escalation risk 93–128; draft
  memorandum 118–19; reasoning 117–
  20; US options *126–7a*
Europe 18, 72, 114–16, 140
exile groups 21–2

Far Eastern issues 79, 81–4
Federal Bureau of Investigation (FBI)
  149
First World War *see* World War I
Foot, R. 7, 161
'forgottenness' 155–70
Forrestal, J. 159
Franklin, H. 159
frostbite 147

Gallup, G. 148
Gao, G. 64–5
Gayn, M. 33, 35
General Staff (US) 132
Germany 32, 37
Good Offices Committee 85, 87–8
Grand Alliance 134
Great Depression 38

Haislip, General W. 108
Halberstam, D. 157
Han river 99
Harriman, A. 119
'Heartbreak Ridge' 146, 163
Hermes, W. 165–6
Higgins, M. 140
historiography 96
Hodge, General J. 2, 20–6, 28–9, 35–6,
  39–40, 43; arrival 24; frustrations 26;
  troop behaviour concerns 29–34;
  troop behaviour missive 34
Hoengsong 100
Holland, Prime Minister S. 72
House Military Affairs Committee 35
Hua, D. 112
Hungnam 138; beachhead 144

Hwachon reservoir 102, 105

I Corps 104–5, 107, 123
Ili 39
Inchon 23, 39, 51, 56, 160, 166; landings
  3, 58–60, 74, 156
India 71–4, 76, 80, 86–9; PRC relations
  79; UN Delegation 78
Indian government 74, 85, 88
Inje 105; Inje/Kansong front 106
intra-war restraint lessons 94–6
Ireland 71
Iron Triangle 163
Isaacs, H. 29–30
IX Corps 105, 107

Jackson, C. 1, 5, 8, 9, 93–128
Japan 2, 7, 16–18, 27–8, 32–3, 37–40,
  42, 114, 136; colonial authorities 18–
  21, 24, 26–7, 31; surrender 22–3;
  wartime propaganda 23; WWII
  conflict 30
Jebb, G. 74, 76
Johnston, R. 23
Joint Chiefs of Staff (JCS) 5, 9, 17, 107–
  8, 110, 113–14, 117–21, 163;
  escalation risk testimonies 121
journalists 6, 29, 33, 35, 133–4, 139–41,
  144, 146, 152, 157, 162; accounts of
  US retreat 143–4; innovation 144;
  MacArthur accusations 142, *see also*
  media
Joy, Admiral T. 110

Kansas/Wyoming line 107, 109, 122
Kansong 105, 106
Kashmir 72
Kennan-Malik exchanges 97
Khan, L. 72, 82
Kim, Il-sung 16, 50, 62, 64, 119, 124,
  166; foreign air support anticipation
  55–8
Kim, K. 20, 25, 53–5, 59–61, 66–7
Kissinger, H. 124
Koje-do 164
Korea: culture 27, 31–2, 45; independent
  government 41; interaction with
  Americans 18–43; Japanese rule 19;
  natives appearance 30–1; political
  elites 40; society 2; US occupation
  (1945–8) 15–47; US occupation
  (second) 3; US zone 15–47, *see also*
  North Korea; Republic of Korea
  (ROK)

173

INDEX

Korean Compound (83) 164
Korean People's Republic (KPR) 24;
  formation 20
Korean Provisional Government (KPG)
  20–2, 25
Krasovskii, S. 55
Kum River line 139
Kunsan 37, 39
Kuomintang (KMT) forces 97, 116–17
Kuomintang Pao Mi Chu security
  bureau 164
Kwangju 27

land reform 16–17
Langdon, W. 25
left-wing politics 19–20, 25, 157
Life Magazine 98, 109
limited war 93, 95, 131, 168
Liu, S. 59
London 71, 76, 81, 83
London Declaration 71
'lost chance' 99, 109–13
Lubell, S. 151
Lushun naval base 57–8

MacArthur, UN Commander General
  D. 5, 20, 24, 27, 36, 39, 63, 74–5, 81,
  94–7, 100, 147, 150, 156–7, 161;
  casualty reports handling 139–42;
  hearings 117, 120; media handling
  136–7, 139–41, 146; political attempt
  158; relief 97–9, 102, 117, 121, 146,
  157; war plans 97, 99, 115–18
McCarthyism 160
MacDonald, D. 27
Malan, D. 72
Manchuria 116–17, 162
Mao, Chairman Zedong 3, 5, 8, 50, 52–
  6, 62, 64–7, 100, 111–12, 119, 121–4,
  162, 166; eagerness to deploy troops
  58–62
The Selected Works of Mao Zedong 55
marines 145; 1st Division 105, 107; 2nd
  Division 107, 145
Marshall, General G. 114, 118
Martin Junior, Congressman J. 161
MASH (Mobile Army Surgical
  Hospital) 140
MASH (Mobile Army Surgical
  Hospital) TV show 156, 158
'Massacre Valley' 145
massed attack strategy 101, 103
Matray, J. 9
Matthews, F. 119

Meade, E. 27
media 6, 25, 137, 138, 152; casualty
  reporting 132–4; censorship 146, 150;
  cover-up allegations 141; MacArthur's
  handling 139–40; post-intervention
  military control 145–6, *see also*
  journalists
memory of the war 3, 155–70
Menzies, Prime Minister R. 72, 86
Millett, A. 9
mobility 103, 113
Moore, C. 143
Moscow 3, 22, 40, 49–68, 50–1, 63, 65,
  118, 122
Muccio, J. 17, 42
Mueller, J. 5, 129–30
Mun, Il 55–6
Myers, Brigadier General D. 28
Myth of the Lost Cause 159

Naktong River 55–6
National Guard 145, 149
National Security Council (NSC) 115;
  NSC-48/5 document 120–1; NSC-68
  document 159–60
national security planners (US) 159, 168
NATO 5
negotiations *see* ceasefire
Nehru, Prime Minister J. 72–3, 77, 82–3,
  85–6, 87, 89; government 74
New York 77, 79, 82, 84, 88, 162
New York Herald Tribune 140, 141, 143
New York Times 23
New Zealand 72, 76, 86–7
New Zealand government 85, 89
Newfoundland 71
Nitze, P. 108
Nixon, President R.: administration 159
North Korea 16, 18, 41–3; allegiances
  49–68; invading South Korea 2, 136;
  offensive (Aug 1950) 44; UN invasion
  156
North Korean People's Army (NKPA)
  53–4, 56, 58–61, 96, 101–2, 104, 106,
  122–3, 136; advances 54–5;
  deteriorating situation 56–7
Northeast Border Defense Force 52, 57;
  strengthening 56

Office of Public Information (OPI) 137
Office of War Information (OWI):
  'horror' photographs 135
Oliver, R. 35
Operation 'Detonate' 5, 9, 105

INDEX

Operation Overwhelming 111
Ottawa 87
Ottoboni, F. 37–9

Pacific War 29, 144; veterans 30
Pak, H. 20, 60
Pak, Il-u 61
Pakistan 72–3, 88
Palestine 72
Panikkar, S. 74, 82
Panmunjom 110
Pax Americana 168
Pearson, D. 141
Pearson, L. 72, 78–9, 81–4, 86–7
Peking 88
Peng, D. 60, 64–5
Peng, Marshal T. 100–2, 105, 111
Pentagon 17, 40–1, 136–9, 141–2, 144, 149–50; Casualty Section 136–7
people's committees 26, 28
People's Liberation Army 57
People's Republic of China (PRC) *see* China
Podhoretz, N. 9
police 23, 26, 33, 164
political warfare 164
politics 19–20, 24–5, 157
poverty 31, 34
prisoners-of-war (POWs) 7, 9, 155–70; anti-communist prisoners 164; compounds 164
propaganda: POW mistreatment claims 167–8; US 140
psychological operations (psyops) 163–4
Pusan 35, 164; perimeter 44, 138
Pyongyang 50, 53, 58, 61–2, 64, 67, 105–6, 108, 110, 122, 124; Pyongyang-Wonsan line 105, 119, 122

rape charges 32, 32n
Rau, B. 74, 76, 81–4, 86–7
rearmament 115
Red Cross 144
Reeder, General W. 40n
reflexive restraint 95–6
Republic of Korea (ROK) 2–3, 18, 41–3, 45, 164, 168; Army 44; leaders 41–3; ROK government 17, 41–2; US alliance 15–47
Republican Party 140–1, 157; casualty claims 147–8, 150; national convention (7 July 1952) 158; opposition 6
revisionism 9

Rhee, President S. 16–17, 20, 24, 35, 40–1, 53, 168
Ridgway, UN Commander General M. 5, 9, 86, 95, 98, 100–2, 106–7, 109–11, 113–14, 117, 119, 121, 163
Right-wing politics 17, 19–20, 24–5, 157
Roberts, R. 33
Roh, M. 15
Roosevelt, President F. 135; administration 135
Roshchin, N. 51–3, 58–9, 61, 64
Rusk, D. 107

Saint Laurent, Prime Minister L. 72, 82–3
scandals 31, 32n, 145
Se, Hee Oh 164
Second World War *see* World War II
Selective Service Act violations 149
Seoul 2–3, 19–20, 23, 33, 37, 39, 45, 53, 59–60, 104, 156, 162
Seven-Power conference 88
Shanghai 52, 55
Shen, Z. 1, 3, 8, 49–68
Shenyang 54, 57–8, 62, 66
Sheridan, Congressman J. 35
Sherman, Admiral F. 108, 119, 122
Shtykov, T. 53–6, 59–60
Simmons, W. 33–4
Singapore Declaration (1971) 70
Sino-Soviet Treaty 118
Sino-Soviet-North Korean alliance 3–4, 49–68
Six-Power draft resolution 75, 77–8
society 130, 148
South Africa 72, 86
South African government 85
South Cholla province 27
South Korea *see* Republic of Korea (ROK)
Soviet Air Force 3, 123; 32nd Air Attack Division 62; 151st Fighter Air Division 57; Belov Air Division 62; combat deployment 65–6; deployment issues 49–68; MiG-15 Fighter Air Division 58; Stalin's commitment 50–3; Stalin's deployment refusal 62–6; training Chinese pilots 55, 57; US attack (8th Oct) 63
Soviet Army: General Staff headquarters 51
Soviet government 58–9
Soviet Union 3–4, 18–20, 22–5, 40–1, 114, 118–19, 123, 159; allegiances 49–

INDEX

68; archives 3, 8, 49–68, 96, 111–12, 119; Chinese negotiations 49–68; Council of Ministers 55; Ministry of Defense 57; North Korea occupation 16; US escalation fears 118–19, *see also* Moscow

Sparks, F. 143

Spender, P. 72, 85, 86

stalemate 163

Stalin, Joseph 3, 5, 53–62, 66–7, 95, 111–12, 119; air cover refusal 62–6; Air Force promise 50–3; conservatism 123–4

State Department (US) 17, 23, 25, 35, 41, 115, 119, 165

status quo ante bellum 97, 115

Stelle, C. 165, 167

Stevenson, A. 151

strategic opportunity and escalation risk 5, 93–128; contemporary debate (28 May 1951) 106–9; contrasting MacArthur and Van Fleet's plans 115–17; critical case misread 93–6; domestic politics 114–21; government machinery 120–1; Korean military situation (Jan-June 1951) 99–104; lost chance 99, 109–13; priorities 114–15; turbulent spring (Feb-May 1951) 96–8; Van Fleet's exploitation plans 104–14; Van Fleet's plans relevance 121–4

Stueck, W. 8, 15–47, 89; and Yi, B. 1–3, 7

Summers, H. 9

Taejon: US loss 139

Taft, R. 147, 157

Taiwan 77, 79, 82, 164

Tarawa battle 144

Third World 71

Thomas, General G. 106

Time 138, 144, 151

Tokyo 26, 36, 39, 107, 136, 141

Tongchon: amphibious landing plans 5, 93–128

Truce Tent and the Fighting Front (Hermes) 165–6

Truman, President H. 9, 77, 79–80, 82, 84, 94, 146, 156–8, 160; administration 4, 6–7, 9, 69–91, 96–7, 117, 121, 140, 147, 159, 165–6

'Truman's war' 157

Turkey 159

UN forces 64–6, 74, 81, 86, 97–8, 148, 156; 38th parallel advance 97–8; advance 110; advantages 101, 103, 162–3; air support 102–3; counterattack 103, 111–12; line 150; losses 122; Northern invasion 156; retreat 99, 162

Unified Command 78–80

United Kingdom (UK) *see* Britain

United Nations Command (UNC) 5–6, 8–9, 44, 63, 79–80, 96–7, 100–1, 104, 106, 109–10, 113–14, 116, 165–6

United Nations (UN) 4, 6, 74, 78, 116, 163; Arab-Asian proposal 78–80, 87–8; before China's intervention 70–4; Collective Measures Committee 84; General Assembly 74, 83–5, 88; influence on the US 69–91; intervention 51; POWs 160; Security Council 73–4; US hegemony 80–1, 89

United States of America (USA) 1–3, 7, 9, 15–47, 57, 72, 74, 97, 129–54, 155–70; branding China aggressors 76–7, 81; draft resolution 85–8; intervention 50–1; Korean policy 35, 40; policymakers 94, 115, 120, 124; public opinion 5–6, 9, 129–54, 166–7; UN Delegation 79, 83–4, 88; War Department 35–6, *see also* Washington

United States Army Military Government in Korea (USAMGIK) 2, 7

university students 149

US Air Force 119; bombings 53–4, 57, 59

US Congress 6, 7, 17, 35, 40, 140–1, 147

US Government 3, 9, 63, 70, 73, 75, 79, 81–2, 84–5, 136; casualty reporting 129–54; election issues 151–2; UN concessions 89

US military 28, 44, 132; amphibious landing 93–128; Army Divisions 28, 28n, 55, 98, 99–100, 102–7, 111–12, 123, 138, 143, 156, 163–4; casualty reporting 129–54; draft 149–50; early war problems 136, 138; food shortages 37–8; medical teams 139–40; morale 34–40; officer quality 38–9; official history 165; operations suspension (1951) 93–128; policies 93–128; poor troop behaviour 27–34; post-war presence 43, 45; retreat 143;

176

INDEX

staff turnover 36, *see also* US Air Force
US News (magazine) 157
US Senate 109
US war experience 129–54; casualty controversy 140–52; casualty reporting before Korea 132–5; casualty reporting theory 135–7; mass opinion 148–52, 166–7; war casualty reporting reality 137–40; war's effects 156
US-South Korean alliance 1–3, 15–47; Americans and Koreans interacting 18–43; creating and sustaining alliance 43–7; training problems 27, 29, 39; US soldiers morale 34–40; US troops arrival 20–1, 23; US troops poor behaviour 27–34

Van Fleet, General J. 5, 9, 94–5, 97–8, 101–2, 104, 121; lost chance 99; plans 115–18, 121–4; war exploitation plans 104–14
Vandercook, J. 166
Vasilevskii, Marshal A. 55, 57, 62
Vietnam War 9, 96, 124, 129, 149, 158–9
Vipperman, C. 38
Vladivostok 58
voluntary repatriation 7, 9, 155–70; cover-up rationale 166–7; stalling negotiations 165; substitute victory 161
Vyshinskii, A. 63

Walker, General W. 100
War Department (US) 132–5; casualty reporting revision 134
war intensification (Aug-Oct 1951) 146
war origins literature 7
war termination attempts (1951) 93–128
Washington 2–6, 17–18, 21–2, 26, 35, 41, 44, 75–7, 80, 82, 99, 115, 132, 141, 145, 157, 159–61, 165–6, 168; Commonwealth's influence 69–91; correspondents 144; military authorities 97; policy environment

121; POW mistreatment accusations 168; war strategy 5
Washington Post 143
Western alliance 4, 8
Westminster Statute (1931) 70–1
White Horse Mountain assault 150–1
Whitehead, D. 162
Wilson, C. 167–8
Wonsan 98, 101, 106, 108, 110, 112, 119; line 123; plan 107; Wonsan-Pyongyang 108, 110, 119, 122
World War I 163; casualty reporting 132–3
World War II 30, 71, 114, 144, 159; aftermath 16, 18; casualty reporting 133–5, 137–8; comparison 147, 149; European Theater 134
Wu, General H. 76, 79
Wyoming line 102, 107, 109, 122

X Corps 98, 102–5, 107, 138, 143, 156

Yalu River 8, 65–6, 74, 96, 99, 103, 118; border area 3
Yi, B.: and Stueck, W. 1–3, 7, 15–47
Yi, C. 59
Yo, U. 19
Yonchon-Chorwon-Kumwha line 111
Young, C. 1, 6, 7, 9, 155–70
Younger, K. 87
Yudin, P. 55

Zakharov, M. 65
Zhang, S. 8, 112, 123n
Zhou, Premier En-lai 3, 51–3, 58–9, 61–5, 80, 84–5

UNITED STATES INSTITUTE OF PEACE

1200 17th Street NW
Suite 200
Washington D.C. 20036
(202) 457-1700
Fax (202) 429-6063
www.usip.org

Online applications are available from our Web site:
www.usip.org

JENNINGS RANDOLPH FELLOWSHIP PROGRAM

The United States Institute of Peace invites applications for Senior Fellowships for up to ten months as part of the Jennings Randolph (JR) Program for International Peace.

Senior Fellowships are awarded annually to scholars, policymakers, journalists, and other professionals to write and conduct research on peace, conflict, and international security issues. Citizens of any country may apply. *Senior Fellow application deadline:* **September 8, 2010.** For more information on JR Fellowship programs, please visit our Web site.

The JR program also supports doctoral research. For more on the **Peace Scholar Dissertation Fellowships,** please visit our Web site.

www.usip.org/fellows
E-mail: jrprogram@usip.org

GRANT PROGRAM

The United States Institute of Peace (USIP) invites applications for its Grant competitions.

Annual Grant Competition considers applications that focus on preventing, managing, and resolving violent conflict and promoting post-conflict peacebuilding outside the United States. *Annual Grant application deadline:* **October 1, 2010.** *Award announcements will be made by March 31, 2011.*

Priority Grant Competition: Through Summer 2010, USIP continues to focus its grantmaking on seven countries as they relate to USIP's mandate: Afghanistan, Colombia, Iran, Iraq, Nigeria, Pakistan, and Sudan. *Applicants may apply at any time throughout the year.*

For more information about the Grant Program's priorities and eligibility requirements, please visit our Web site.

www.usip.org/grants
E-mail: grants@usip.org

Contemporary Security Policy

EDITORS:
Aaron Karp, *Old Dominion University, USA*
Regina Karp, *Old Dominion University, USA*

One of the oldest peer reviewed journals in international conflict and security, ***Contemporary Security Policy*** promotes theoretically based research on policy problems of armed violence, peace building and conflict resolution. Since it first appeared in 1980, *CSP* has established its unique place as a meeting ground for research at the nexus of theory and policy.

Spanning the gap between academic and policy approaches, *CSP* offers policy analysts a place to pursue fundamental issues, and academic writers a venue for addressing policy.

The journal emphasizes debate on:

- War and armed conflict
- Strategic culture
- Defence policy
- Weapons procurement
- Conflict resolution
- Arms control and disarmament

Contemporary Security Policy, is committed to a broad range of intellectual perspectives. Articles promote new analytical approaches, iconoclastic interpretations and previously overlooked perspectives. Its pages encourage novel contributions and outlooks, not particular methods or outlooks. Authors are encouraged to examine established issues in innovative ways and to apply traditional methods to new problems.
In addition to regular articles and book reviews, *CSP* features *special issues* and *symposia* on particular topics. Relying on solicited and unsolicited contributions, these apply academic analysis to cutting-edge debates previously beyond the purview of scholarly journals. Peer reviewed, special issues and symposia balance spontaneity and incisiveness with academic rigor.

To sign up for tables of contents, new publications and citation alerting services visit www.informaworld.com/alerting

 Register your email address at www.tandf.co.uk/journals/eupdates.asp to receive information on books, journals and other news within your areas of interest.

For further information, please contact Customer Services at either of the following:
T&F Informa UK Ltd, Sheepen Place, Colchester, Essex, CO3 3LP, UK
Tel: +44 (0) 20 7017 5544 Fax: 44 (0) 20 7017 5198
Email: subscriptions@tandf.co.uk

Taylor & Francis Inc, 325 Chestnut Street, Philadelphia, PA 19106, USA
Tel: +1 800 354 1420 (toll-free calls from within the US)
or +1 215 625 8900 (calls from overseas) Fax: +1 215 625 2940
Email: customerservice@taylorandfrancis.com

When ordering, please quote: YE04902A

View an online sample issue at:
www.tandf.co.uk/journals/fcsp

CPSIA information can be obtained
at www.ICGtesting.com
Printed in the USA
BVHW040820271018
531365BV00006B/72/P